西方经典阅读

READINGS IN WESTERN CLASSICS

修订版

总主编 杨小彬
主编 陈西军
编者 周义媛 许洲 熊紫瑞
杨格格 马泳斐

清华大学出版社
北京

内 容 简 介

《西方经典阅读》(修订版)所选篇章多样,结构灵活,习题丰富,旨在帮助非英语专业本科学生在通用英语学习的基础上,通过进一步阅读大量的西方经典作品,提高综合理解和运用英语的能力,提升英语语言素养,丰富对经典文化内涵的理解,培养其跨文化交际意识和能力。

本书为修订版,更加符合大学英语的教学实际,进一步增强文本的权威性,降低难度,增加可读性。在内容设计上既保持了大学英语基础阶段语言学习方式的连贯性,帮助学生提高英语语言技能,拓展语言知识面,又根据新的需要扩展了学生自主学习和教师自由发挥的空间,培养学生自主学习、团队合作的能力。

版权所有,侵权必究。举报:010-62782989,beiqinquan@tup.tsinghua.edu.cn。

图书在版编目(CIP)数据

西方经典阅读 / 杨小彬总主编;陈西军主编. —修订版. —北京:清华大学出版社,2020.8(2025.1重印)
大学英语拓展课程系列教材
ISBN 978-7-302-54470-8

Ⅰ. ①西… Ⅱ. ①杨… ②陈… Ⅲ. ①英语－阅读教学－高等学校－教材 Ⅳ. ① H319.37

中国版本图书馆 CIP 数据核字(2019)第 265444 号

责任编辑:曹诗悦
封面设计:子 一
责任校对:王凤芝
责任印制:丛怀宇

出版发行:清华大学出版社
网 址:https://www.tup.com.cn, https://www.wqxuetang.com
地 址:北京清华大学学研大厦 A 座　邮 编:100084
社 总 机:010-83470000　邮 购:010-62786544
投稿与读者服务:010-62776969, c-service@tup.tsinghua.edu.cn
质量反馈:010-62772015, zhiliang@tup.tsinghua.edu.cn
印 装 者:三河市铭诚印务有限公司
经 销:全国新华书店
开 本:185mm×260mm　印 张:15.75　字 数:305 千字
版 次:2017 年 6 月第 1 版　2020 年 8 月第 2 版　印 次:2025 年 1 月第 8 次印刷
定 价:69.00 元

产品编号:086419-02

FOREWORD

　　《西方经典阅读》根据教育部制定的《大学英语教学指南》编写，旨在帮助非英语专业本科学生在通用英语学习的基础上，通过进一步阅读大量的西方经典作品，提高综合理解和运用英语的能力，提升英语语言素养，开阔视野，陶冶情操。与基础阶段的大学英语课程相比，"西方经典阅读"课程着力于对所学英语知识的全面应用，增强学生的英语阅读能力，丰富学生对经典文化内涵的理解，培养他们的跨文化交际意识和能力。有鉴于此，《西方经典阅读》教材的编写遵循以下原则：

　　●经典性。作为大学英语教学的一部分，本教材以语言学习为中心，所选篇章的语言既在学生力所能及的范围之内，又都经受住了时间的考验，是当之无愧的经典。

　　●思想性。按照博雅教育的原则，同时考虑到学生不同的专业背景，所选经典篇目涉及哲学、文学、经济、政治、历史、文化等方方面面，有助于拓展学生视野，激发学习兴趣。

　　●适用性。兼具人文性和工具性，提升学生文化素养和培养其语言能力并重，帮助学生加深对西方文化的了解，并提升其用英语进行文化交流的有效性。

　　●实用性。教材所选篇章多样，结构灵活，习题丰富，读者可以根据自己的实际情况和需要灵活取舍。

　　为了实现《西方经典阅读》的编写理念，我们在每个单元的设计上既保持了大学英语基础阶段语言学习方式的连贯性，帮助学生提高英语语言技能，拓展语言知识面，又根据新的需要扩展了学生自主学习和教师自由发挥的空间，培养学生自主学习、团队合作的能力。为了帮助学生更准确地理解所选的篇章，每个单元结构如下：

　　●引言：帮助学生了解所选作品的相关信息；

　　●注义：将较难的词汇用中文标记出来，方便学生快速理解原文；

● 注释：将较难的句子、词组以及相关文化背景通过注释为学生提供讲解，帮助他们正确理解原文；

● 练习：习题的设计以理解经典文本为中心，提高学生的理解和运用能力，以及对经典文本的鉴赏能力。

本书为修订版，是在第一版的基础上，新团队合作的成果。本次修订遵循了以下原则：一、更加符合大学英语的教学实际；二、进一步增强文本的权威性；三、降低难度，增加可读性。具体为：一、重新选择了《奥德赛》《俄狄浦斯王》《理想国》的译本和版本。新版本更加符合原文原意，且难度也有所降低。二、根据实际情况，删减了 3 个章节，保留 12 个章节，更符合大学英语教学的实际。三、全面修订了各章的引言，将中文引言全部改为英文引言，并在引言部分增加了体裁的介绍，能够拓展学生的知识面，更加符合课程设置和教材编写的要求。四、对文章中的生词增加中文注解，大量增加重难点句的注解，降低文章的难度，增加背景知识的介绍，提升趣味性。五、全面修订了练习，增加了语言技能训练相关的练习，以及与文章主题相呼应的写作题。在修订的过程中，我们认真听取了参与教学实践的各位老师和同学们的反馈意见，特别是第一版的各位编者——王志茹教授、杨小彬教授和李丹副教授的意见，以及在编写过程中帮助试读的林子涵、戴玄、王俊森、唐清潇、胡洋、周洋、吴立清、毛爱姣等同学的建议，在此向他们表示衷心的感谢！

需要指出的是，本书的书名虽定为《西方经典阅读》，但并非全面介绍西方经典，而是帮助大学生在经过基础阶段学习之后，通过阅读英语原著继续提升英语水平、拓展视野，是贯彻博雅教育的一个全新尝试。由于编者水平有限，书中尚有一些瑕疵，希望广大读者提出宝贵的意见。

编者
2020 年春

CONTENTS

Unit 1 Greek Mythology: Myths 1

Unit 2 The Odyssey: An Epic 19

Unit 3 Oedipus the King: A Tragedy 45

Unit 4 Republic: A Socratic Dialogue..83

Unit 5 Hamlet: A Drama..107

Unit 6 The History of England: A History 121

Unit 7 An Inquiry into the Nature and Causes of the Wealth of
        Nations: An Essay..141

Unit 8 The Communist Manifesto: A Pamphlet 157

Unit 9 Pride and Prejudice: A Novel 179

Unit 10 The Idea of a University: A Discourse..197

Unit 11 I Wandered Lonely as a Cloud: Poems......................................213

Unit 12 A Scandal in Bohemia: A Detective Fiction 219

UNIT 1

Greek Mythology
Myths

Oral tasks

1. How many Greek gods do you know? Say something about them.
2. Do you know how the universe and human beings come into being?
3. In different cultures, there are different myths about the creation of the universe. Please tell different creation stories that you know.

Introduction

The word *myth* comes from the Greek word *mythos*, which means "story" or "speech". Myth is often used to describe a story that explains events or objects that occur in nature, such as the creation of certain flowers or animals, the location of deserts or oceans, and even the origin and cycle of the seasons. Myths may also be stories about the origins of customs or traditions.

The gods and goddesses were a major part of everyday life in ancient Greece, and each god had a particular role. Zeus, for example, the ruler of the sky and the leader of the gods, was also a protector of guests and travelers. Athena was the protectress of Athens, and she was also the goddess of wisdom and war. Poseidon was another protector of Athens, and as the ruler of the sea, he was an important god for sailors and those who traveled by boat.

Within the Pantheon, the gods often married each other, and some of them had more than one spouse or partner at a time. Sometimes the gods married their siblings, parents, or children. The god Zeus, for example, had many partners other than his wife, Hera, who was also his sister. Throughout the various mythological stories, Zeus appeared to have had more than one hundred fifteen mistresses! The gods and goddesses were often paired in different ways because the myths were always developing and being retold. As people began to believe different things about different gods, they associated the gods with one another in new ways. Zeus, as the most powerful god, often seemed to be a part of all the other gods' lives.

Greek Mythology: Myths UNIT 1

This excerpt recounts the creation of the universe, how different gods and goddesses have come into being, how they fight against each other, and how human beings come into being.

PART 3

TEXTUAL READING[1]

Creation

1 ▸ Before there was land or sea, people or gods, nothing existed, except Chaos[2]. Chaos was a space of neither order nor disorder. During Chaos' reign, there was no organization of any kind in the universe. There was no sun or moon. There were no mountains or rivers, nor any such features on earth. In fact, there was no earth at all. It was a period of vast emptiness. Even time did not exist. Eventually, Chaos divided itself into the earth, the sky, and the sea. When the division was complete, everything was peaceful and perfect.

reign: 统治

emptiness: 空无

peaceful: 和平的

2 ▸ After Chaos divided into the earth, the sky, and the sea, one goddess came into being without being born to any mother. Her name was Gaia[3], which means earth, and she took control over the earth as it took shape. Mountains became separate from the plains, and rivers and oceans were formed. Like an artist at a canvas, Gaia was busy creating a beautiful masterpiece. Soon, however, the goddess began to long for children to help populate and rule this magnificent new world.

goddess: 女神

canvas: 画布
masterpiece: 杰作
populate: 居住，生活
magnificent: 宏大的

3 ▸ Gaia's desire for children was so great that eventually she became pregnant by herself. The child she bore was named Uranus[4], and he became the ruler of the sky. In every way, Uranus was the equal of his mother, and

pregnant: 怀孕的

---

1 本篇出自：Michelle M. Houle. *Gods and Goddesses in Greek Mythology*. Berkeley Heights, N. J.: Enslow Publishers, Inc., 2001。

2 *Chaos*: 混沌。希腊神话中指天地未分时的混沌状态。

3 *Gaia*: 盖娅。希腊神话中的大地母神，从混沌状态中繁衍出来，是古老的一类神，为天神宙斯的祖母。

4 *Uranus*: 乌拉诺斯。盖娅女神的第一个孩子，掌控天空，为天神。天神与大地神盖娅生育了下一代神。

soon Gaia and Uranus had children together.

4▸ Gaia's first three children were monsters, called the Hundred-handed Ones[5]. They were giants, and each had fifty heads and a hundred hands. Although Gaia loved her children and was proud of them, Uranus was afraid that someday one of these children would overthrow him. Because of this fear, Uranus hated the children and forced them back into Gaia's womb.

5▸ After the hundred-handed monsters had been born and were pushed back into their mother's womb, Gaia gave birth to three more monstrous children. These were giants called the Cyclopes[6]. Each had but a single eye, which was positioned directly in the middle of his forehead. Although they were frightening to look at, these young gods were exceedingly strong, and they were excellent craftsmen who made thunder and lightning for their mother to use as tools and weapons. Unfortunately, Uranus was afraid of these children, too. So, in order to get rid of them, Uranus tied the Cyclopes up and threw them into a deep cavern called Tartarus[7]. Tartarus was far, far away, and Uranus felt safe in believing that he would never see these monster-children again.

6▸ Saddened by the loss of the Hundred-handed Ones and the Cyclopes, and angry at the cruel Uranus, Gaia gave birth to a third group of children. These were called the Titans[8], and there were twelve of them—six goddesses and six gods. They were very different from their older siblings. The Titans were beings with human characteristics, and they were not monsters at all. The goddesses' names were Tethys, Theia, Mnemosyne, Rhea, Themis, and Phoebe.[9] The gods' names were Oceanus, Hyperion, Iapetus, Cronus, Crius, and Coeus.[10]

monster: 怪兽
giant: 巨人

overthrow: 推翻
womb: 子宫

monstrous: 怪兽似的

frightening: 可怕的
exceedingly: 极其地
craftsman: 匠人
thunder: 雷
lightning: 闪电
cavern: 洞穴

sibling: 兄弟姐妹

---

5 *the Hundred-handed Ones*: 百臂巨人，有 50 个头和 100 只手，是乌拉诺斯与盖娅的孩子。乌拉诺斯惧怕孩子们会推翻他，又把他们塞回了盖娅的子宫。

6 *Cyclopes*: 希腊神话中的独眼巨人，能制造雷电给母亲盖娅作工具和武器。

7 *Tartarus*: 地狱底下暗无天日的深渊；地狱。乌拉诺斯惧怕独眼巨人，再次残忍对待自己的孩子，将他们扔进地狱。

8 *Titan*: 巨人，提坦神。共有 12 位提坦巨神，包括 6 位女神和 6 位男神。

9 6 位提坦女神的名字依次是：忒提斯、忒伊亚、摩涅莫辛涅、瑞亚、西弥斯、福柏。

10 6 位提坦男神的名字依次是：俄克阿诺斯、许珀里翁、伊阿珀托斯、克罗诺斯、克利俄斯、科俄斯。

7▶ Uranus was still afraid that one day one of his children would overthrow him. Because of this fear, he pushed the Titans back into Gaia's womb alongside their siblings, the Hundred-handed Ones. Gaia was **enraged** by Uranus's refusal to allow her children to live freely. She **desperately** wanted her children to live without **restraints** and to enjoy the world. Finally, she came up with a plan that would allow her children to be born into the world and remain there.

enrage: 激怒
desperately: 极度地
restraint: 限制

8▶ Gaia could speak to the children in her **cavernous** womb, and she had no trouble convincing them to help with her plan. Cronus, the youngest of the twelve Titans, was the most eager to help his mother. So, the two set out to **trick** Uranus and free the Titans and the Hundred-handed Ones from their mother's prison-like womb.

cavernous: 洞穴状的
trick: 欺骗

9▶ Cronus and Gaia waited for the perfect opportunity to **enact** their plan. Finally, one night, when Uranus came to Gaia's bed, Cronus crept out of Gaia's womb and **stabbed** his cruel father with a **sickle**, a **curved** knife used to harvest crops. As Uranus lay dying, his fears of being overthrown by one of his children having come true, Uranus leaned forward and **cursed** his son: "Cronus," he pronounced, **gasping** for breath, "it will come to pass that one of your children will do to you what you have just done to me." Then, with a final **shudder**, Uranus died, a look of anger and **betrayal** in his eyes.

enact: 实施
stab: 刺
sickle: 镰刀
curved: 弯曲的
curse: 诅咒
gasp: 喘气
shudder: 颤抖
betrayal: 背叛

10▶ After Uranus died, Gaia and her children felt free for the first time. The Titans and the Hundred-handed Ones were reborn from their mother's womb, and the Cyclopes were freed from Tartarus. All of Gaia's children decided to make Cronus their king. Cronus married his sister, the Titan named Rhea, and ruled over the universe for a long, peaceful time.

The War Between the Titans and the Olympians

11▶ After the death of Uranus, the world was at peace again. Cronus, the king of the Titans, and Rhea, his most noble sister and wife, had matters well in hand. Unfortunately, the curse of his father, Uranus, **haunted** Cronus day and night. Was it possible that one day he, too, would have a child who would overthrow him?

haunt: 萦绕

12▶ One day, Rhea announced that she was going to have a baby, but her husband was not happy. Cronus was so afraid that history would repeat itself that he did, in fact, manage to repeat history. Like his father before him,

overpower: 战胜
grab: 抓住
swallow: 吞下
horrified: 恐惧的
sadden: 使悲伤

Cronus reasoned that if he could keep his children from growing up, none could ever become strong enough to overpower him. So, when Rhea gave birth to her first child, Cronus quickly grabbed it and swallowed it whole. Rhea was both horrified and saddened at the loss of her first-born child. In a similar manner, Cronus swallowed all of the next four children that she gave birth to, and Rhea vowed to get them back, any way she could.

13 ▸ By the time Rhea discovered that she was pregnant for the sixth time, she had figured out a plan to trick her husband and save the newborn child from being swallowed whole. So, when it was nearly time for her to give birth, Rhea pretended to have her baby. She took a large stone and wrapped it in a baby's blanket. When Cronus came to gobble down the newborn child, Rhea gave him the wrapped-up stone. Quickly, Cronus swallowed the stone, just as he had swallowed the other children. In fact, Cronus' focus on swallowing the newborn god was so great that he did not even realize that he had been tricked.

wrap: 包裹
blanket: 毯子
gobble: 吞食

14 ▸ Later, when the time came for Rhea actually to have her child, she fled to the island of Crete[11]. There, away from the glaring eyes of her husband, Rhea secretly gave birth to a son, whom she named Zeus[12]. He was a beautiful and strong baby, and Rhea knew that when he grew up, he would be a truly powerful god. Rhea realized that she could not return home to her husband with the child. Cronus would only try to destroy the newborn god, as he had done with the others. Therefore, for his protection, Rhea left Zeus to grow up secretly on Crete where he was suckled by a goat and raised by minor native deities called nymphs. While Zeus was a child, Cronus never suspected that he had been tricked and that he actually had a stone resting solidly in his stomach.

glaring: 愤怒的

suckle: 哺乳
deity: 神
nymph: 仙女
suspect: 怀疑
solidly: 牢牢地

15 ▸ When he had grown into a young man, Zeus left Crete to join his mother. Rhea arranged for Zeus to become a servant to his father. Cronus did not know that his new servant was actually his son. One day, Zeus brought his father a cup of wine, which Cronus drank quickly. This cup of wine contained a special potion, which made Cronus throw up. Cronus was so violently ill

potion: 药剂
throw up: 呕吐

11　*Crete*: 希腊的克里特岛。

12　*Zeus*: 宙斯。古希腊神话中的众神之王，奥林匹斯十二主神之首，统治宇宙万物的至高无上的主神。人们常用"众神和人类的父亲""神王"来称呼他。

that he even threw up the stone wrapped in the blanket. Then he threw up all of the children he had swallowed before. The children emerged from their father's stomach as fully grown adults. Their names were Poseidon, Hades, Hera, Demeter, and Hestia.[13] These were Zeus' brothers and sisters, and they were all glad to see each other in the light of day. Although they were happy to be free, the six siblings knew they must do something immediately, or their father would swallow them all over again. Quickly, they ran away while their father continued to moan and clutch his stomach.

moan: 呻吟
clutch: 紧紧抓紧

16 ▸ This young generation of gods fled to Mount Olympus[14] to escape their irate father, and because they claimed Mount Olympus as their home, the young gods were called the Olympians. After they had fled to safety, the Olympians quickly formed a plan. At once, they declared war on Cronus and many of the other Titans. The young gods wanted to rule the world in their father's place. Yet their struggle had a dual purpose: while they were fighting for control over the earth, they were also fighting for their lives, since they knew that Cronus would swallow them again if he ever got the chance.

irate: 发怒的

dual: 双重的

17 ▸ And so a great war began. At first, it seemed likely that the Titans would be victorious and remain in control of the earth. The young Olympian gods felt outnumbered and overpowered. The tide began to turn, however, when a few Titans changed sides and fought with Zeus and his siblings. Prometheus[15], the son of the Titans Themis and Iapetus, was one who switched his allegiance. Prometheus' name means "one who thinks ahead", and with his ability to see the future he could foresee that the Titans would lose the battle against the Olympian gods. Prometheus and his brother Epimetheus[16] refused to fight against the Olympians because of this foresight.

victorious: 胜利的
outnumber: 数目上超过
switch: 改变
allegiance: 效忠
foresee: 预见

18 ▸ The Cyclopes and the Hundred-handed Ones also joined the Olympians in their fight against the Titans. They did not feel bound to the Titans, and they believed that the Olympian gods would rule with steadier hands. Zeus

steady: 稳定的

---

13 克罗诺斯将曾经吞进肚里的孩子吐了出来，他们分别是波塞冬、哈德斯、赫拉、德米忒耳、赫斯提。

14 *Mount Olympus*: 奥林匹斯山。克罗诺斯的六个孩子逃亡奥林匹斯山，并居住在那里。

15 *Prometheus*: 普罗米修斯。提坦巨神西弥斯和伊阿珀托斯之长子，具有先知先觉的能力。

16 *Epimetheus*: 厄庇墨透斯。提坦巨神西弥斯和伊阿珀托斯之次子，普罗米修斯之弟，是后知后觉者。

asked the one-eyed Cyclopes to make weapons for his army, and these skilled craftsmen made a special weapon for each of the gods. For Zeus, the leader, the Cyclopes fashioned a special thunderbolt, which could be thrown long distances with great force. For Poseidon, they created a magnificent trident, or three-pronged spear, which could defeat any enemy. Finally, knowing that resistance came in many forms, the Cyclopes made Hades a magic helmet that could make him invisible, even to the immortal eyes of Cronus and the other Titans.

thunderbolt: 霹雳

trident: 三叉戟

helmet: 头盔

19▸ The war between the Titans and the Olympians was terrible. With the help of the Hundred-handed Ones, who fought bravely without ever tiring, the Olympians soon forced the Titans to surrender. After the Titans had given up, Zeus challenged Cronus to a wrestling match. The winner would control Mount Olympus, to which the Titans were still laying claim. After beating Cronus three times, Zeus declared the Olympian gods to be the winners.

surrender: 投降

20▸ After the war, the Olympians sent most of the Titans to Tartarus to be locked up for eternity. The victors built a bronze gate over the mouth of the cavern, and the Hundred-handed Ones were placed outside as guards. Atlas[17], another child of Iapetus and Themis, who had led the Titans into battle, received a special punishment. He was forced to hold the world on his back for all eternity. This turned out to be a far more challenging task than imprisonment in Tartarus.

eternity: 永恒

bronze: 铜

imprisonment: 囚禁

21▸ Cronus, the former ruler of the universe, was not sent to Tartarus with his siblings. Though Cronus had swallowed his children whole, Zeus and the other Olympians did not want to destroy him in revenge. Instead, Cronus was sent away to live on the Island of the Dead, where he stayed forever. Although originally he had wanted to destroy the Olympian gods, Cronus, once defeated and exiled, sent dreams to his son Zeus to guide him from afar.

revenge: 复仇

22▸ After all the punishments were handed out, Zeus, Hades, and Poseidon made a bet to determine who would rule each part of the world. Hades became the lord of the dead and the Underworld, which was sometimes called Hades in his honor. Poseidon gained control of the seas and all the

---

17 *Atlas*: 阿特拉斯，是提坦巨神西弥斯和伊阿珀托斯的另一个孩子。以肩顶天的提坦巨神之一，因与提坦神一起反对奥林匹斯诸神而被宙斯惩罚用双肩在世界最西处支撑天宇，以防止天空（乌拉诺斯）和大地之母（盖娅）再度结合。

waters on earth. Zeus became the lord of the sky; and since the sky covers everything on earth, he became the king, or father, of the gods.

23 ▶ After these important decisions were made, the other Olympian gods were also given jobs. Demeter became the goddess of agriculture and of all growing things. Hestia became the goddess of the hearth, or fireplace, and the home. Hera, too, protected the home and became the goddess of marriage and childbirth after she married her brother, Zeus.[18]

hearth: 灶台

24 ▶ Once the Olympians had defeated the Titans and taken on their new roles, they, too, had children. Some of these gods were born under rather extraordinary circumstances. Athena, for example, was born out of the side of Zeus' head. She became the goddess of wisdom and the protector of Athens. Hera became pregnant on her own and gave birth to Hephaestus[19]. Hephaestus was the god of fire and became the blacksmith of the gods. Ares[20] was the child of Hera and Zeus, and he became the god of war.

25 ▶ Apollo, the god of light and music, and his twin sister, Artemis, the maiden goddess of the hunt, were the children of Leto, who was the daughter of the Titans Phoebe and Coeus. The goddess of love and beauty, Aphrodite[21], had an unusual birth: she was born out of the waves of the sea.

26 ▶ Hermes was another son of Zeus. His mother was Maia, one of the daughters of Atlas. Hermes grew very quickly, and he was swift-footed, even as a baby. Later, he became the official messenger of the gods because he was so fast. He was often depicted with wings on his hat and sandals, and because he was always moving about, he was a particular protector of travelers.

27 ▶ These gods and others lived on Mount Olympus after their victory over the Titans. From the height of this great mountain, the new rulers could look down on all of Greece and keep watch over the world, for the control of

---

18　本句与上段是奥林匹斯诸神的分职：哈德斯成为冥界和地界的主宰，是冥界的代名词；波塞冬掌管海洋和所有水域；宙斯为天神，天管万物，也是众神之父；德米忒耳成为农业和生长女神；赫斯提是灶神；赫拉，与赫斯提一样，也守卫家园，在嫁给哥哥宙斯后成为婚姻和生育女神。

19　*Hephaestus*: 赫淮斯托斯。赫拉独自怀孕所生，火神和铁匠之神。

20　*Ares*: 阿瑞斯。赫拉和宙斯的儿子，战神。

21　*Aphrodite*: 阿芙洛狄忒。爱神与美神，从海浪中生出。

which they had fought so hard.

Prometheus and Earth's First Inhabitants

28▸ After the world was created and the gods had fought their wars, the land that lay below Mount Olympus remained unpopulated, even though Gaia, the first goddess, had long yearned to make creatures to inhabit the earth. Finally, Zeus decided it was time.

yearn: 渴望

29▸ It was a good time to be created. No monsters roamed the earth, and the world was at peace. Zeus began to make creatures to populate this beautiful world. However, just as he was beginning, he was called away to settle a matter dividing his fellow Olympians. He decided to appoint Prometheus and Epimetheus, sons of Titans who had fought with the Olympians, to continue the project of creating earth's first inhabitants.

roam: 游荡

30▸ Although the brothers were Titans by birth, they had sided with the Olympians in the war against Cronus and the other Titans because, blessed with the gift of being able to see the future, Prometheus had foreseen the Olympian victory. Prometheus was the more sensible of the two brothers, and he always planned ahead. Epimetheus, on the other hand, always meant well, but he never planned ahead. Epimetheus never thought about the consequences of his actions until after he had completed them.

31▸ Zeus had chosen these brothers for the project of creating the first people and animals on earth because Prometheus was an excellent potter and sculptor. Prometheus could make just about anything, and he had a good imagination. Epimetheus was invited to work on the project because he was always eager to help his brother.

sculptor: 雕塑家

32▸ Because Zeus had only just started to make the various earth creatures, the brothers had a lot of work ahead of them. After using clay to sculpt the new creatures into their basic shapes, Prometheus went to Athena, the goddess of wisdom, for advice on how to complete the work. Epimetheus stayed behind to give the unfinished creations their final distinguishing features.

clay: 泥土
sculpt: 雕塑

33▸ Athena's advice was simple. She told Prometheus that since the creatures were already composed of earth and water, having been fashioned from clay, the only element lacking for life was air. So, Athena advised Prometheus to hold each of the newly shaped creatures up to the sky. When the wind blew

compose: 组成

into them, she promised, they would breathe and be truly alive.

34▸ Meanwhile, Epimetheus continued to work. He enjoyed showing off his creative powers and granted a wide variety of interesting physical attributes to all the different creatures. Epimetheus gave some of them fur and hair, which would protect them from the elements. He gave others teeth and claws so that they could easily collect and eat food. In addition, he gave some of the creatures strength and speed.

attribute: 特征，属性

claw: 爪子

35▸ When Prometheus returned from his talk with Athena, he found that once again, his brother had acted before thinking. Epimetheus had been so excited about designing the new animals and so generous with his creative powers that he had completely forgotten to save any special gifts for the human beings. By the time the sculptor had gotten around to the humans, he had run out of ideas. They were left weak and defenseless, and they would have remained so forever if Prometheus had not stepped in. Once he realized that his brother had created a species unable to stand on its own in the new world, Prometheus set forth to fix the mistake and make human beings strong and capable of surviving among earth's other inhabitants.

species: 物种

36▸ First, Prometheus decided to help the humans stand upright like the gods. He turned their heads upward to the sky. This adjustment gave them the power to reason. Then he raced to the heavens where he lit a torch, using the fire of the sun. He used this fire to light up the new creatures' powers of thought and speech. These special powers helped set the humans apart from the other animals.

upright: 直立的

torch: 火炬

37▸ At first, the gods approved of Prometheus' work. They were glad to see that there was a species on earth that had the ability to think and speak. But Prometheus was still not satisfied. He saw that Epimetheus' poor planning had left the new humans physically weak compared to the other inhabitants of the earth. They were hungry, sad, and scared. Finally, to help the humans, Prometheus left Mount Olympus and went to live on earth with the people, in order to teach them the skills they would need to survive in the new world.

38▸ First, Prometheus showed the humans how to build houses so they would not have to live in caves. Then he taught them how to read, and how to write numbers and letters. He helped the people learn how to tame animals and how to sail on the seas. He showed them how to heal themselves when they were sick. After he had shown the people how to foretell the future and recognize omens by looking at the way birds flew, some of the other gods became impressed by the new people. They decided to help, too. Demeter, the Olympian earth goddess, taught the new race of creatures about edible plants. With this help, the humans had better access to food, and they began to prosper and live happily for the first time.

39 ▶ Although some of the gods were excited about the development of the humans, other gods were beginning to worry that the humans were becoming too powerful. However, despite the growing concerns of his fellow gods, Prometheus was so pleased with his creations that he decided to help the humans even more. Until this time, humans were only allowed to slaughter other animals if they were performing a sacrifice to the gods. They ate only the plants that Demeter instructed them to eat. Prometheus could see that the humans would probably need to eat the meat of other animals to survive.

40 ▶ So Prometheus came up with a plan. First, he cut up an ox, as if for a sacrifice. Then, he divided the sections into two piles. In one pile, Prometheus wrapped up the bones of the ox and hid them under shiny morsels of fat. This pile looked like the more attractive offering in a sacrifice. For the other pile, Prometheus took the lean meat and other edible parts of the ox and wrapped them in hide, topping the pile with entrails to make the offering look disgusting.

41 ▶ Once this was done, Prometheus asked Zeus to choose one of the two piles and keep it as the sacrificial offering; the humans would take whichever pile Zeus rejected. Not knowing that the good meat was actually hidden beneath the hide and entrails, Zeus chose the pile shimmering with fat. Once Zeus had made his choice, he had to stick with it, even after he discovered that he had chosen a pile with no edible meat in it. From then on, people offered the fat and bones of animals to the gods, and they kept the savory parts of the animals for themselves. Zeus was outraged that Prometheus had tricked him, but he decided to save his revenge for later.

42 ▶ This was not the only trick Prometheus played on the Olympian gods for the sake of the humans. Since the new race of creatures had no fur, they were often cold, and even though they were now allowed to eat meat, they had no way to cook it. Human beings did not know about fire or how to control it because, until this point, fire belonged only to the gods. Prometheus decided to change things. He went up to heaven and secretly stole fire from the gods. Hiding the fire inside the stalk of a fennel plant, Prometheus brought it back to the people on earth. Then he taught the people how to cook grains and meat, and how to keep fire burning so that it would always be available. Prometheus also showed the humans how they could use fire to forge metal, just as Hephaestus, the god of fire and the forge, was doing on Mount Olympus.

fennel: 茴香

grain: 粮食

forge: 锻造

43▶ Prometheus did all these things to help the humans because he wanted them to survive in the world now populated by other more physically powerful creatures. Unfortunately, Prometheus' efforts angered some of the other gods. The new people were getting too powerful and too smart. Zeus thought they needed to be stopped before they believed their own powers were supreme and they no longer heeded the authority of the gods. Furthermore, Zeus was furious with Prometheus for all his tricks.

44▶ To punish Prometheus for tricking the king of the gods and for making humans so powerful, Zeus had him captured and chained to a rock on the crest of one of the Caucasus Mountains[22]. Every day, an enormous eagle came to the spot where Prometheus was tied. The eagle was fierce and relentless, and each day it swooped down and pecked away at Prometheus' liver, devouring the greater part of it. Because Prometheus was immortal, his liver grew back every night, and he never died. Despite this intense torture, he endured the punishment for thirty years until Hercules came and freed him.

capture: 抓获

relentless: 无情的
swoop: 猛扑
peck: 啄食
devour: 吞噬
torture: 折磨

45▶ Unfortunately, punishing only Prometheus did not satisfy Zeus' desire for revenge. The king of the gods had other plans that would affect the entire human race, and it was a punishment that would last forever.

---

22 *the Caucasus Mountains*: 高加索山脉。为了惩罚普罗米修斯欺骗宙斯，且使人类如此强大，宙斯将他缚在高加索山峰上。每天巨鹰啄食其肝脏，夜间肝脏又重新长出。普罗米修斯忍受折磨30年，直到后来大力神赫拉克勒斯将其救下。

Pandora[23]

46▸ Zeus was furious. Prometheus had tricked him, and the king of the gods wanted revenge. He also wanted to remind the humans that they would never be as powerful as the gods.

47▸ So far, there were only men in the human population. Women did not yet exist, although certainly there were female gods, or goddesses. Introducing women to the human race was part of Zeus' plan for revenge. First, Zeus went to the forge of Hephaestus and asked him to design a human being that would be female. Carefully, Zeus explained that she should be like the men on earth, yet somehow slightly different.

48▸ Hephaestus was happy to do Zeus a favor, and he went right to work. The god of fire and the forge was a very talented smith. Everything he made was beautiful, and his new creation was no different. When he was finished with the creature, he showed his work to Zeus, who was very pleased with the results. The new creature was named Pandora. She was human, but she was clearly a woman. She was very beautiful and looked like a goddess. She had long flowing hair, flawless skin, and bright shining eyes. She was as graceful as a soft breeze, and she had a smile precious to see. Zeus hoped that her beauty would make the male humans accept and trust her.

flawless: 无瑕疵的

49▸ After Hephaestus had put the finishing touches on the first human woman, the gods showered her with many gifts, including golden-threaded clothes, shining jewelry, and fragrant smelling flowers. Among the gifts was a box that was covered with jewels, intricate carvings, and decorations. The box was very pretty, and Pandora was certain that such a beautiful object must surely contain something of equal magnificence. However, the gods had given Pandora the beautiful box on one condition: She could look at it as much as she liked, but she was never to open it. Pandora did not understand the reasoning behind this rule, but because the box was so pretty, she agreed to follow the warning of the gods.

fragrant: 芳香的
intricate: 精美的

---

23 *Pandora*: 潘多拉。宙斯为报复普罗米修斯而惩罚人类，请火神铸造女性，火神为这位女子取名为潘多拉。潘多拉美艳无比，众神送上礼物，其中有一件是一个镶满珠宝等饰物、精雕细刻的盒子，众神告诫潘多拉只能观赏盒子而不能打开它。潘多拉最终没能禁住诱惑，打开盒子，里面的罪恶，例如悲伤、饥饿、愤怒、疾病、疯狂以及上百种可怕景象迅速散播到人类中，吓坏了的潘多拉匆忙关上盒子，慌乱中却将一样东西留在了盒子里，那就是希望。

50 ▸ Soon Pandora went to live on earth with the other humans. When she got there, she met Epimetheus who was living among the humans with his brother Prometheus. Epimetheus was overwhelmed by Pandora's dazzling beauty, and he fell in love with her instantly. Prometheus, aware of his brother's infatuation with Pandora, became suspicious that Zeus and the other Olympians were planning a trick. Prometheus warned his brother to be wary of any gift sent to earth by the Olympian gods. As usual, Epimetheus did not listen to his brother. He was very much in love with Pandora, and despite his brother's warning, he married the wonderful new creature and brought her to his home. Epimetheus never thought to ask his new bride about the beautiful box she always carried with her.

dazzling: 炫目的

infatuation: 迷恋

51 ▸ The couple lived very happily after their marriage. Every day, Pandora would lovingly admire her beautiful box, but she obeyed the order of the gods and never opened it. Soon, however, looking at the box was not enough. Her curiosity became stronger and stronger, and finally one day she could no longer resist the urge to open the box, regardless of the consequences.

52 ▸ When Pandora opened the box and discovered what was hidden inside its beautiful exterior, she knew at once that Zeus' revenge had been accomplished. Inside the magnificent box were all the evil spirits known to the gods. Now that the lid was open, they all quickly flew out. Sorrow, hunger, anger, disease, madness, and a hundred other horrible conditions filled Pandora's room and, like smoke, they escaped out into the world to plague mankind for the rest of time. As the evils swarmed around her, Pandora became frightened. As quickly as she could, she slammed shut the lid of the box, but Pandora realized that it was too late to regret not having obeyed the gods. Their revenge was final. However, Pandora noticed that one spirit still remained in her box. This was the spirit of hope.

exterior: 外表

plague: 折磨
swarm: 聚集
slam: 砰地关上

53 ▸ Soon, when they felt the effects of the various plagues and evil spirits that had flown out from Pandora's box, the people on earth understood that their time of peace had ended. The people recognized the power of the gods' revenge, and understood that forces existed that were stronger than their own modest powers. From that time on, the people vowed to do their best to keep from angering the gods any further and were comforted by the fact that hope was safe in Pandora's box. The knowledge that hope had not been destroyed gave the people faith that peace would return some day.

PART 4

EXERCISES

I. Answer the following questions according to the reading text.

1. What existed before the earth was formed?
2. What was unique about Gaia's first children, and what happened to them? Who were Gaia's second children, and what happened to them? Who were Gaia's third set of children, and what happened to them?
3. Why and how did Rhea trick her husband?
4. How did Zeus, Hades, and Poseidon divide up the control of the universe?
5. How did Prometheus help humans be capable of surviving in the new world?
6. How did Zeus punish Prometheus?
7. Who was Pandora and how was she created?
8. What happened when Pandora opened the box?

II. Paraphrase the following sentences with your own words, and then translate them into Chinese.

1. Like his father before him, Cronus reasoned that if he could keep his children from growing up, none could ever become strong enough to overpower him. So, when Rhea gave birth to her first child, Cronus quickly grabbed it and swallowed it whole. (Para. 12)
2. Yet their struggle had a dual purpose: while they were fighting for control over the earth, they were also fighting for their lives, since they knew that Cronus would swallow them again if he ever got the chance. (Para. 16)
3. After the world was created and the gods had fought their wars, the land that lay below Mount Olympus remained unpopulated, even though Gaia, the first goddess, had long yearned to make creatures to inhabit the earth. (Para. 28)
4. Although the brothers were Titans by birth, they had sided with the Olympians in the war against Cronus and the other Titans because, blessed with the gift of being able to see the future, Prometheus had foreseen the Olympian victory. (Para. 30)

5. Epimetheus had been so excited about designing the new animals and so generous with his creative powers that he had completely forgotten to save any special gifts for the human beings. (Para. 35)

6. Once he realized that his brother had created a species unable to stand on its own in the new world, Prometheus set forth to fix the mistake and make human beings strong and capable of surviving among earth's other inhabitants. (Para. 35)

7. The eagle was fierce and relentless, and each day it swooped down and pecked away at Prometheus' liver, devouring the greater part of it. Because Prometheus was immortal, his liver grew back every night, and he never died. (Para. 44)

8. Sorrow, hunger, anger, disease, madness, and a hundred other horrible conditions filled Pandora's room and, like smoke, they escaped out into the world to plague mankind for the rest of time. (Para. 52)

III. Figure out the meanings of the phrases in bold, and then make another sentence with each of the phrases.

1. As Uranus lay dying, his fears of being overthrown by one of his children having **come true**, Uranus leaned forward and cursed his son: "Cronus," he pronounced, gasping for breath, "it will come to pass that one of your children will do to you what you have just done to me." (Para. 9)

2. Cronus, the king of the Titans, and Rhea, his most noble sister and wife, **had matters well in hand**. (Para. 11)

3. By the time Rhea discovered that she was pregnant for the sixth time, she had **figured out** a plan to trick her husband and save the newborn child from being swallowed whole. (Para. 13)

4. After the Titans had **given up**, Zeus challenged Cronus to a wrestling match. (Para. 19)

5. After all the punishments were **handed out**, Zeus, Hades, and Poseidon made a bet to determine who would rule each part of the world. (Para. 22)

6. From the height of this great mountain, the new rulers could look down on all of Greece and **keep watch over** the world, for the control of which they had fought so hard. (Para. 27)

7. He enjoyed **showing off** his creative powers and granted a wide variety of interesting physical attributes to all the different creatures. (Para. 34)

8. They were left weak and defenseless, and they would have remained so forever if Prometheus had not **stepped in**. (Para. 35)

IV. Because of their long history and cultural influence in the West, some words and expressions in Greek Mythology carry on cultural meanings. Now try to find out the cultural meanings of the following words and expressions.

1. Prometheus
2. Pandora's box
3. Hercules' task
4. Titan

V. Write another story of Greek Mythology with no less than 200 words.

UNIT 2

The Odyssey
An Epic

ORAL TASKS

1. Have you ever heard of *The Odyssey*? Please talk as much as you can.
2. In your understanding, what is an epic?
3. Do you know any other epics, other than Homer's *The Odyssey* and *The Iliad*?

INTRODUCTION

An epic is traditionally a genre of poetry, known as epic poetry, which is a lengthy narrative poem, ordinarily concerning a serious subject containing details of heroic deeds and events significant to a culture or nation. It has been argued that the Homeric epics, *The Iliad* and *The Odyssey*, the earliest works of Western literature, were fundamentally oral poetic forms. *The Iliad* was set during the Trojan War, focusing on a quarrel between King Agamenon and the warrior Achilles lasting a few weeks during the last year of the war. *The Odyssey*, "the story of Odysseus", focuses on the journey home of Odysseus, king of Ithaca, after the fall of Troy, who took ten years to find his way back from Troy to his home on the island of Ithaca, off the western coast of mainland Greece.

Aristotle gave us the essence of the plot: "A certain man has been abroad many years; he is alone, and the god Poseidon keeps a hostile eye on him. At home the situation is that suitors for his wife's hand are draining his resources and plotting to kill his son. Then, after suffering storm and shipwreck, he comes home, makes himself known, attacks the suitors: he survives and they are destroyed."

Very little is known for sure about Homer the poet, his date and place of birth, but everyone believes that he was blind. It is also generally assumed that Homer was a poet using the same means of composition as his fifth-century successors—that is, writing.

The Odyssey: An Epic UNIT 2

PART 3

TEXTUAL READING[1]

Book One: Athena Inspires the Prince

Sing to me of the man, Muse[2], the man of **twists and turns**
driven time and again off course, once he had **plundered**
the **hallowed** heights of Troy[3].
Many cities of men he saw and learned their minds,
5   many pains he suffered, **heartsick** on the open sea,
fighting to save his life and bring his **comrades** home.
But he could not save them from disaster, hard as he strove—
the **recklessness** of their own ways destroyed them all,
the blind fools, they devoured the cattle of the Sun
10 and the Sungod[4] wiped from sight the day of their return.
Launch out on his story, Muse, daughter of Zeus,
start from where you will—sing for our time too.
                                    By now,
all the survivors, all who avoided **headlong** death
15 were safe at home, escaped the wars and waves.
But one man alone...

twist and turn: 曲折，蜿蜒

plunder: 夺取

hallowed: 神圣的

heartsick: 难过的

comrade: 伙伴

recklessness: 鲁莽

launch out: 开始

headlong: 轻率的

---

1 本篇出自：Homer. *The Odyssey*. Translated by Robert Fagles. New York: Penguin Books, 1996。

2 *Muse*: 缪斯。她是宙斯和记忆女神的女儿，博古通今，知晓每一件事由。缪斯也是史诗中经常提及的女神。（注：本篇部分注释内容来自陈中梅翻译的《奥德赛》，南京：译林出版社，2003。本篇译文也参考了该译文。由于本篇原文和陈中梅所翻译的原文版本不同，有些内容无法一一对应，所以在参考该译文的同时，根据本篇原文对译文进行了相应的调整。下同。）

3 *Troy*: 特洛伊城。

4 *Sungod*: 日神，也可直接使用 Sun 来表示。奥德修斯的伙伴们不知神导的命运，杀死并吃了赫利俄斯的牧牛，招致神明的惩罚。尽管在荷马看来，人间的争斗和重大事件的进展无不受到宙斯和命运的掌控，但奥德修斯的伙伴们难辞其咎，必须为自己的过错承担应负的责任。

set on: 倾心于	his heart set on his wife and his return—Calypso[5],
bewitching: 令人销魂的	the bewitching nymph, the lustrous goddess, held him back,
lustrous: 显赫的	deep in her arching caverns, craving him for a husband.
arching: 拱形的	20 But then, when the wheeling seasons brought the year around,
trial: 磨难	that year spun out by the gods when he should reach his home,
	Ithaca[6]—though not even there would he be free of trials,
	even among his loved ones—then every god took pity,
seethe: 恼怒	all except Poseidon[7]. He raged on, seething against
	25 the great Odysseus till he reached his native land.

                                                                                But now

    Poseidon had gone to visit the Ethiopians worlds away,
Ethiopians off at the farthest limits of mankind,
a people split in two, one part where the Sungod sets

	30 and part where the Sungod rises. There Poseidon went
bull: 公牛	to receive an offering, bulls and rams by the hundred—
ram: 公羊	far away at the feast the Sea-lord sat and took his pleasure.
feast: 宴席	But the other gods, at home in Olympian Zeus' halls,
assembly: 集会	met for full assembly there, and among them now
	35 the father of men and gods was first to speak,
sorely: 痛苦地	sorely troubled, remembering handsome Aegisthus[8],

---

5 *Calypso*: 卡鲁普索。希腊神话中的海之女神，是扛起天穹的巨人阿特拉斯的女儿。因冒犯父亲，卡鲁普索被自己的父亲阿特拉斯囚禁在岛上，并受到惩罚：命运女神每过一段时间就送来一个需要帮助的英雄，但这些英雄都不可能留下，卡鲁普索却偏偏陷入爱河。奥德修斯不幸在奥杰吉厄岛沉船，被卡鲁普索救起。卡鲁普索爱上了他，求他留在自己身边，说只要他愿意就给他永生。奥德修斯拒绝了，因为他一心爱自己的凡人妻子，女神没有办法，只好用魔力迷惑他，把他留在身边整整七年。

6 *Ithaca*: 伊萨卡。

7 *Poseidon*: 波塞冬。克罗诺斯与瑞亚的儿子，也是主神宙斯的兄弟。年轻时，波塞冬与兄弟们一起推翻了父亲的残暴统治。经宙斯分配，波塞冬成为海洋之神，掌管所有水域，地位仅次于宙斯。因为奥德修斯弄瞎了他的儿子，他掀起了滔天巨浪，阻止了奥德修斯的归程。

8 *Aegisthus*: 埃吉索斯。梯厄斯忒斯和他的女儿菲洛庇亚的儿子。如此乱伦的结合是争夺阿特柔斯的产物。为了争夺迈锡尼王位，埃吉索斯谋杀了阿特柔斯，但王位后来又被阿特柔斯的儿子阿伽门农夺回。阿伽门农在进行特洛伊战争期间，埃吉索斯成了阿伽门农的妻子的情人，并杀害了阿伽门农，最终成了迈锡尼的国王。后来，埃吉索斯又被阿伽门农的儿子俄瑞斯忒斯所杀。

the man Agamemnon's[9] son, renowned Orestes[10], killed.
Recalling Aegisthus, Zeus harangued the immortal powers:
"Ah how shameless—the way these mortals blame the gods.
40 From us alone, they say, come all their miseries, yes,
but they themselves, with their own reckless ways,
compound their pains beyond their proper share.
Look at Aegisthus now...
above and beyond his share he stole Atrides'[11] wife,
45 he murdered the warlord coming home from Troy
though he knew it meant his own total ruin.
Far in advance we told him so ourselves,
dispatching the guide, the giant-killer Hermes[12].
'Don't murder the man,' he said, 'don't court his wife.
50 Beware, revenge will come from Orestes, Agamemnon's son,
that day he comes of age and longs for his native land.'
So Hermes warned, with all the good will in the world,
but would Aegisthus' hardened heart give way?
Now he pays the price—all at a single stroke."
55 And sparkling-eyed Athena[13] drove the matter home:

harangue: 高谈阔论
immortal: 神的
mortal: 凡人
misery: 苦难
compound: 加深
proper: 应有的

warlord: 战神

dispatch: 派遣
court: 求爱

hardened: 冷酷的
stroke: 打击

---

9 *Agamemnon*: 阿伽门农。阿特柔斯之子，是迈锡尼王，也是斯巴达王墨奈劳斯的哥哥，是希腊最有权势的人，拥有最强大的军事力量和财富；在史诗中常被冠以"王中之王""军士的牧者"等称号。墨奈劳斯的妻子海伦被特洛伊王子帕里斯诱走后，请阿伽门农出面报复。而阿伽门农也想趁机霸占爱琴海，于是就有了特洛伊战争。在战争期间，阿伽门农的妻子与埃吉索斯通奸，因害怕奸情败露，同时也憎恨丈夫为求顺风献祭他们的女儿，于是，密谋杀害了阿伽门农。

10 *Orestes*: 俄瑞斯忒斯，阿伽门农的儿子。阿伽门农从特洛伊返回，被妻子和埃吉索斯谋杀的时候，俄瑞斯忒斯并不在迈锡尼。从雅典返回后，他杀死了埃吉索斯和自己的亲生母亲。在荷马看来，俄瑞斯忒斯是位了不起的青年英雄，因而是青年人忒勒马科斯——处于人生转折时期而又面临外出寻找父亲和为家族的耻辱雪恨——所学习的榜样。

11 *Atrides*: 阿特柔斯之子，既指阿伽门农，也指墨奈劳斯。

12 *Hermes*: 赫耳墨斯。宙斯和玛亚的儿子，也有人认为他是奥德修斯的祖先之一，能用魔杖开闭人的眼睛。他双脚长有双翼，因此行走如飞，在奥林匹斯山担任宙斯和诸神传令的使者，为诸神传送消息，并完成宙斯交给他的各种任务。

13 *Athena*: 雅典娜，宙斯的女儿。关于她的出生，有多个版本。其中之一是宙斯与智慧女神墨提斯相处，并致其怀孕。根据盖娅与乌拉诺斯的预言，他们的子女将比宙斯更具有智慧，并会推翻他。唯恐预言成真，宙斯将墨提斯吞入肚子，但为时已晚。之后，宙斯头痛不已，百般无奈，只好请诸神劈开他的头颅，雅典娜从中蹦了出来，亭亭玉立，仪态万方，并且身披铠甲。她既是智慧女神，也是艺术和军事的女神。雅典娜最喜欢的凡人是奥德修斯，在《奥德赛》中，基本上都是她帮助奥德修斯回乡，并和奥德修斯及他的儿子忒勒马科斯一起向诸求婚者报仇。

mighty: 伟大的		"Father, son of Cronus, our high and mighty king,
		surely he goes down to a death he earned in full!¹⁴
		Let them all die so, all who do such things.
		But my heart breaks for Odysseus,
seasoned: 饱经风霜的	60	that seasoned veteran cursed by fate so long—
veteran: 老兵		far from his loved ones still, he suffers torments
torment: 折磨		off on a wave-washed island rising at the center of the seas.
		A dark wooded island, and there a goddess makes her home,
wicked: 邪恶的		a daughter of Atlas, wicked Titan who sounds the deep
	65	in all its depths, whose shoulders lift on high
colossal: 巨大的		The colossal pillars thrusting earth and sky apart.
pillar: 柱子		Atlas' daughter it is who holds Odysseus captive,
thrust: 猛推；挤		luckless man—despite his tears, forever trying
captive: 俘虏		to spellbind his heart with suave, seductive words
spellbind: 魅惑	70	and wipe all thought of Ithaca from his mind.
suave: 温柔的		But he, straining for no more than a glimpse
seductive: 引诱的		Of hearth-smoke drifting up from his own land,
strain: 竭力		Odysseus longs to die...
hearth-smoke: 炊烟		Olympian Zeus,
lofty: 崇高的	75	have you no care for him in your lofty heart?
		Did he never win your favor with sacrifices
		burned beside the ships on the broad plain of Troy?
dead set: 铁了心		Why, Zeus, why so dead set against Odysseus?"
thunderhead: 雷雨云砧		"My child," Zeus who marshals the thunderheads replied,
	80	"what nonsense you let slip through your teeth. Now,
let slip: 说漏嘴		how on earth could I forget Odysseus? Great Odysseus
		who excels all men in wisdom, excels in offerings too
vaulting: 苍穹		he gives the immortal gods who rule the vaulting skies?
unappeased: 怒气未消的		No, it's the Earth-Shaker, Poseidon, unappeased,

---

14 **surely he goes down to a death he earned in full**: 该句中，he earned in full 是 death 的定语从句，限定说明 death，表示"他的死是咎由自取，罪有应得"。in full 在这里表示强调。可译为："的确，他（埃吉索斯）完全是咎由自取，死得理所当然。"

85	forever fuming against him for the Cyclops	**fume:** 怒气冲冲
	whose giant eye he blinded: godlike Polyphemus[15],	
	towering over all the Cyclops' clans in power.	**tower:** 高耸
	The nymph Thoosa bore him, daughter of Phorcys[16],	**clan:** 宗族
	lord of the barren salt sea—she met Poseidon	**barren:** 荒凉的
90	once in his vaulted caves and they made love.	**vaulted:** 拱形的
	And now for his blinded son the earthquake god—	
	though he won't quite kill Odysseus—	
	drives him far off course from native land.	
	But come, all of us here put heads together now,	
95	work out his journey home so Odysseus can return.	
	Lord Poseidon, I trust, will let his anger go.	
	How can he stand his ground against the will	
	Of all the gods at once—one god alone?"	
	Athena, her eyes flashing bright, exulted,	**flash:** 闪烁
100	"Father, son of Cronus, our high and mighty king!	**exult:** 欢欣鼓舞
	If now it really pleases the blissful gods	**blissful:** 给人幸福的
	that wise Odysseus shall return—home at last—	
	let us dispatch the guide and giant-killer Hermes	
	down to Ogygia Island[17], down to announce at once	
105	to the nymph with lovely braids our fixed decree:	**braid:** 辫子
	Odysseus journeys home—the exile must return!	**decree:** 法令
	While I myself go down to Ithaca, rouse his son	**exile:** 流放者
	to a braver pitch, inspire his heart with courage	**rouse:** 激励

---

15 *Polyphemus*: 波吕斐摩斯。希腊神话中吃人的独眼巨人，海神波塞冬和海仙女托俄萨之子。奥德修斯回家途中登陆独眼巨人聚居的西西里岛，为了寻找补给，他带领12个希腊人进入了波吕斐摩斯的巢穴。波吕斐摩斯发现后，立刻用巨石封堵了洞口，并吞食了几人。于是，奥德修斯设计把未勾兑的烈性葡萄酒给波吕斐摩斯喝，并告诉他自己的名字叫"没有人"。趁波吕斐摩斯喝酒之际，奥德修斯等人戳瞎了巨人的独眼。瞎了眼的巨人大声呼救，"没有人攻击我"，但是却被当做玩笑，无人理睬。奥德修斯和他的手下藏在羊肚子下面安全逃出。回到船上的奥德修斯大声嘲笑波吕斐摩斯，"没有人没有伤害你，伤你的是奥德修斯"。波吕斐摩斯向他的父亲波塞冬祈祷，请求他报复奥德修斯，波塞冬唤起巨浪和大风，将奥德修斯的船吹离了回家的航线，后面遭遇了更多艰险。

16 *Thoosa, daughter of Phorcys*: 托俄萨，海神福耳库斯的女儿。福耳库斯是大地之母盖娅的女儿。托俄萨与波塞冬结合，生下了波吕斐摩斯。

17 *Ogygia Island*: 俄古吉亚岛。卡鲁普索居住的岛屿，她将奥德修斯强留在这个岛上，不让他回家。

summon: 召集

suitor: 求爱者

drove: 畜群

shamble: 拖沓的

sandy: 多沙的

supple: 柔软的

boundless: 无边的

rush: 极速

gust: 猛吹

rugged: 粗犷的

massive: 巨大的

shaft: 矛杆

wield: 挥舞

sweep: 掠过

craggy: 峭壁的

peak: 山峰

threshold: 门槛

court: 庭院

      to summon the flowing-haired Achaeans[18] to full assembly,
110 speak his mind to all those suitors, slaughtering on and on
      his droves of sheep and shambling longhorn cattle.[19]
      Next I will send him off to Sparta[20] and sandy Pylos[21],
      there to learn of his dear father's journey home.
      Perhaps he will hear some news and make his name
115 throughout the mortal world."

                                                So Athena vowed

      and under her feet she fastened the supple sandals,
      ever-glowing gold, that wing her over the waves
      and boundless earth with the rush of gusting winds.
120 She seized the rugged spear tipped with a bronze point—
      weighted, heavy, the massive shaft she wields to break the lines
      of heroes the mighty Father's daughter storms against.
      And down she swept from Olypus' craggy peaks
      and lit on Ithaca, standing tall at Odysseus' gates,
125 the threshold of his court. Gripping her bronze spear,
      she looked for all the world like[22] a stranger now,
      like Mentes, lord of the Taphians.[23]

18 *Achaeans*：阿开亚人。《荷马史诗》中对希腊人的统称。

19 *If now it really pleases... his droves of sheep and shambling longhorn cattle* (Lines 101–111)：严格来说，第 101—111 行是一个完整的句子，但在第 107 行被分成了两个句子。前半部分讲的是派遣信使赫耳墨斯到俄古吉亚岛传达宙斯的法令，要求让奥德修斯回家；后半部分讲的是雅典娜到伊萨卡要做的事情，其中 rouse..., inspire..., speak... 是并列成分，列举了雅典娜要做的事情；slaughtering... 是用来修饰限定 suitors 的。可译为："倘若此事确能欢悦幸福的神祇，/ 让精于谋略的奥德修斯回到家里，那就 / 让我们派遣导者和巨人杀手赫耳墨斯，/ 前往俄古吉亚岛，以便尽快宣告 / 我们的决议，对美发的仙女：/ 让奥德修斯返程——流放者必须回家！/ 我这就动身，去往伊萨卡岛地，以便着力 / 催励他的儿子，把勇气注入他的心里，/ 召聚长发飘洒的阿开亚人集会，/ 对所有的求婚人论议，后者日复一日，宰杀 / 他步履蹒跚的弯角壮牛和羊群簇挤。"

20 *Sparta*：斯巴达。在希腊神话中，斯巴达城由宙斯的儿子建立。斯巴达国王墨奈劳斯，即阿伽门农的弟弟，因为妻子海伦被特洛伊的王子诱走，从而挑起了特洛伊战争。

21 *Pylos*：普洛斯。在《荷马史诗》中，该地位于迈锡尼王国。

22 *for all the world like*：也可以是 for all the world as if (as though)，"完全像，活像"。e.g. That sounds for all the world like a lark. 那声音听起来完全像是云雀的啼鸣。for all the world 也可以单独表示"无论如何，不管怎样（用于否定句）"。e.g. I wouldn't part with that picture for all the world. 那幅画我怎么样也不愿意割爱的。

23 *Mentes, lord of the Taphians*：门忒斯，塔菲亚人的首领，与奥德修斯是世交。

There she found the swaggering suitors, just then
amusing themselves with rolling dice before the doors,
130　lounging on hides of oxen they had killed themselves.
While heralds and brisk attendants bustled round them,
some at the mixing-bowls, mulling wine and water,
others wiping the tables down with sopping sponges,
setting them out in place, still other servants
135　jointed and carved the great sides of meat.[24]
First by far to see her was Prince Telemachus[25],
sitting among the suitors, heart obsessed with grief.
He could almost see his magnificent father, here...
in the mind's eye—if only he might drop from the clouds
140　and drive these suitors all in a rout throughout the halls
and regain his pride of place and rule his own domains!
Daydreaming so as he sat among the suitors,
he glimpsed Athena now
and straight to the porch he went, mortified
145　that a guest might still be standing at the doors.
Pausing beside her there, he clasped her right hand
and relieving her at once of her long bronze spear,
met her with winged words[26]: "Greetings, stranger!
Here in our house you'll find a royal welcome.

swaggering: 自大的

dice: 骰子

lounge: 懒散地躺

ox: 牛

herald: 使节

brisk: 活泼的

bustle: 喧闹

mull: 调制热饮

sponge: 海绵

obsessed: 受困扰的

rout: 击退

regain: 收复

domain: 领地

daydream: 做白日梦

porch: 门廊

mortified: 感到窘迫的

royal: 盛大的

24　*There she found the swaggering suitors... jointed and carved the great sides of meat* (Lines 128-135): 严格来讲，这几行是一个句子，但是，在第 131 行被划分成了两部分。在前半部分中，amusing... 和 lounging... 作为补语来说明 suitors。在后半部分中，有三个短语结构：some..., others..., still others... 分别说明在求婚者的欢宴中，奥德修斯家的仆人们忙碌的情形。可译为："她眼见那帮高傲的求婚者，正在 / 门前把玩骰块，愉悦自己的身心，/ 坐在被他们宰剥的牛皮上，/ 信使和勤勉的随从们忙碌在周围，/ 有的在兑缸里调匀酒和清水，/ 有的则用多孔的海绵将桌子擦抹干净，/ 搁置就绪，还有的 / 正切分熟肉，大份堆起。"

25　*Telemachus*: 忒勒马科斯，奥德修斯和珀涅罗珀的儿子。奥德修斯出征特洛伊的时候，忒勒马科斯还在襁褓之中。在雅典娜准备帮助奥德修斯返家的时候，忒勒马科斯已经长大成人。在雅典娜的指引下，忒勒马科斯分别拜访了普洛斯的国王奈斯托耳（特洛伊战争中希腊的贤明长老）、墨奈劳斯和他的妻子海伦，了解了他的父亲的辉煌历史。在奥德修斯出征期间，许多人向他的母亲求婚，并耗尽了他的家产。在雅典娜的帮助下，他与父亲见面，并最终杀死了所有的求婚者。

26　*with winged words*: 长了翅膀的语言。这是《荷马史诗》中程式化的表达方式，经常出现，是史诗的特征之一。

	150	Have supper first, then tell us what you need."
		He led the way and Pallas Athena followed.
lance: 长矛		Once in the high-roofed hall, he took her lance
burnished: 铮亮的		and fixed it firm in a burnished rack against
rack: 架子		a sturdy pillar, there where row on row of spears,
sturdy: 坚固的	155	embattled Odysseus' spears, stood stacked and waiting.
embattled: 严阵以待的		Then he escorted her to a high, elaborate chair of honor,
stack: 堆放		over it draped a cloth, and here he placed his guest
escort: 护送		with a stool to rest her feet. But for himself
elaborate: 精致的		he drew up a low reclining chair beside her,
drape: 覆盖	160	richly painted, clear of the press of suitors,
stool: 凳子		concerned his guest, offended by their uproar,
reclining: 倾斜的		might shrink from food in the midst of such a mob.[27]
uproar: 喧闹		He hoped, what's more, to ask her about his long-lost father.
mob: 乌合之众		A maid brought water soon in graceful golden pitcher
pitcher: 水罐	165	and over a silver basin tipped it out
tip: 倒（水）		so they might rinse their hands,
rinse: 清洗		then pulled a gleaming table to their side.
gleaming: 闪闪发光的		A staid housekeeper brought on bread to serve them,
staid: 古板的		appetizers aplenty too, lavish with her bounty.
appetizer: 开胃品	170	A carver lifted platters of meat toward them,
aplenty: 大量		meats of every sort, and set beside them golden cups
lavish: 慷慨		and time and again a page came round and poured them wine.
bounty: 丰盛		But now the suitors trooped in with all their swagger
carver: 切肉者		and took their seats on low and high-backed chairs.
platter: 大盘	175	Heralds poured water over their hands for rinsing,
page: 男伺者		serving maids brought bread heaped high in trays
troop: 成群结队		and young men brimmed the mixing-bowls with wine.
heap: 堆积		They reached out for the good things that lay at hand,
tray: 托盘		and when they'd put aside desire for food and drink
brim: 注满	180	the suitors set their minds on other pleasures,
		song and dancing all that crowns a feast.

....

27　*Then he escorted... in the midst of such a mob* (Lines 156-162): 这两句描写忒勒马科斯招待雅典娜就座的细节。可译为："忒勒马科斯引她到高贵精美的椅子上就座，/ 铺上布垫子，并给他的客人／搬来一张脚凳，给她歇脚。而他自己／在她的旁边拉过一把便椅／上面涂有各种颜色，（他们）避离求婚者，／（他）生怕来客受芜杂的喧闹的惊扰，/ 在那帮肆无忌惮的乌合之众中失去了胃口。"

A herald placed an ornate lyre in Phemius'[28] hands,
the bard who always performed among them there;
they forced the man to sing.

185   A rippling prelude—
and no sooner had he struck up his rousing song
than Telemachus, head close to Athena's sparkling eyes,
spoke low to his guest so no one else could hear:
"Dear stranger, would you be shocked by what I say?

190 Look at them over there. Not a care in the world,
just lyres and tunes! It's easy for them, all right,
they feed on another's goods and go scot-free—
a man whose white bones lie strewn in the rain somewhere,
rotting away on land or rolling down the ocean's salty swells.[29]

195 But that man—if they caught sight of him home in Ithaca,
by god, they'd all pray to be faster on their feet
than richer in bars of gold and heavy robes.[30]
But now, no use, he's died a wretched death.
No comfort's left for us... not even if

200 someone, somewhere, says he's coming home.
The day of his return will never dawn.
                                  Enough.
Tell me about yourself now, clearly, point by point.
Who are you? where are you from? your city? your parents?

205 What sort of vessel brought you? Why did the sailors
land you here in Ithaca? Who did they say they are?
I hardly think you came this way on foot!
And tell me this for a fact—I need to know—
is this your first time here? Or are you a friend of father's,

ornate: 华美的
lyre: 竖琴
bard: 吟游诗人
rippling: 起伏的；潺潺流水般声音的
prelude: 序曲
rousing: 活泼的

scot-free: 逍遥法外的
strew: 撒满
rot away: 腐烂
roll: 翻滚

wretched: 悲惨的

dawn: 出现

vessel: 船只

---

28 *Phemius*: 菲弥俄斯。在奥德修斯出征期间，专门在他家演奏的伊萨卡的诗人。奥德修斯回家后，与儿子忒勒马科斯一起杀死向珀涅罗珀求婚的人，但是，赦免了菲弥俄斯。

29 *a man whose... salty swells* (Lines 193-194): 这句中 a man 指的是奥德修斯，是忒勒马科斯描述父亲可能的状况。可译为："物主的白骨已在阴雨中霉烂，/ 不是弃置陆地，便是在奔腾的海浪里翻滚。"

30 *But that man... heavy robes* (Lines 195-197): 这句话是忒勒马科斯假设奥德修斯返回家园时可能发生的情形。可译为："倘若他们（求婚者）看到那人（奥德修斯）返回伊萨卡的家园，/ 神啊！他们的全部祈祷将是愿自己有更迅捷的双腿，/ 而不是成堆的黄金和厚重的衣袍。"

	210	a guest from the old days? Once, crowds of other men
would come to our house on visits—visitor that he was,
when he walked among the living."
glinting: 闪闪发光的		Her eyes glinting,
goddess Athena answered, "My whole story, of course,
	215	I'll tell it point by point. Wise old Anchialus[31]
was my father. My own name is Mentes,
oar: 船桨		lord of the Taphian men who love their oars.
crew: 船员		And here I've come, just now, with ship and crew,
wine-dark: 暗红的		sailing the wine-dark sea to foreign ports of call,
cargo: 货船
iron: 铁	220	to Temese[32], out for bronze—our cargo gleaming iron.
Our ship lies moored off farmlands far from town,
moor: 停泊		riding in Rithron Cove, beneath Mount Nion's woods[33].
As for the ties between your father and myself,
we've been friends forever, I'm proud to say,
	225	and he would bear me out[34]
if you went and questioned old lord Laertes[35].
venture: 冒险		He, I gather, no longer ventures into town
but lives a life of hardship, all to himself,
off on his farmstead with an aged serving-woman
	230	who tends him well, who gives him food and drink
weariness: 疲倦
withered: 枯萎的
haul: 拖拉
vineyard: 葡萄园
slope: 斜坡
thwart: 阻碍		when weariness has taken hold of his withered limbs
from hauling himself along his vineyard's steep slopes.[36]
And now I've come—and why? I heard that he was back...
your father, that is. But no, the gods thwart his passage.

---

31 *Anchialus*: 安基阿洛斯。特洛伊战争中的希腊斗士，被赫克托耳所杀。

32 *Temese*: 忒墨塞。古希腊时期的一个城邦。

33 *Rithron Cove, beneath Mount Nion*: 内昂山下，雷斯荣港湾。古希腊神话中的地名。

34 *bear... out*: 为……作证，证实。e.g. The belief that there was a Roman settlement there in ancient times was borne out by the discovery of a number of Roman coins. 古时候那儿曾经有罗马人居住的观点在人们发现大量罗马硬币之后得到了证实。

35 *Laertes*: 拉厄耳忒斯，奥德修斯的父亲。

36 *He, I gather... steep slopes* (Lines 227-232): 这一句是借雅典娜之口对奥德修斯年迈的父亲拉厄耳忒斯的描写。可译为："此君，我想，现今已不来城镇垣 / 独居一隅，经受生活的煎熬，/ 在他的土地上由一位老妇照顾 / 每当他苦作在坡地之上的葡萄园，/ 每当疲乏侵袭他的残败的身骨，/ 老妇对他无微不至，伺候水饮食餐。"（注：该译文的语序有些调整。）

235	Yet I tell you great Odysseus is not dead. He's still alive,	
	somewhere in this wide world, held captive, out at sea	
	on a wave-washed island, and hard men, savages,	**savage:** 野蛮人
	somehow hold him back against his will.	
	Wait,	
240	I'll make you a prophecy, one the immortal gods	**prophecy:** 预言
	have planted in my mind—it will come true, I think,	
	though I am hardly a seer or know the flights of birds.	**seer:** 预言家，先知
	He won't be gone long from the native land he loves,	
	not even if iron shackles bind your father down.	**shackle:** 镣铐
245	He's plotting a way to journey home at last;	**plot:** 密谋
	he's never at a loss.	
	But come, please,	
	tell me about yourself now, point by point.	
	You're truly Odysseus' son? You've sprung up so!	**spring up:** 迅速成长
250	Uncanny resemblance... the head, and the fine eyes—	**uncanny:** 难以置信的
	I see him now. How often we used to meet in the old days	**resemblance:** 相似
	before he embarked for Troy, where other Argive[37] captains,	**embark:** 乘船出发
	all the best men, sailed in the long curved ship.	
	From then to this very day	
255	I've not set eyes on Odysseus or he on me."	
	And young Telemachus cautiously replied,	**cautiously:** 谨慎地
	"I'll try, my friend, to give you a frank answer.	**frank:** 坦诚的
	Mother has always told me I'm his son, it's true,	
	but I am not so certain. Who, on his own,	
260	has ever really known who gave him life?	
	Would to god I'd been the son of a happy man	
	whom old age overtook in the midst of his possessions![38]	**overtake:** 突然降临
	Now, think of the most unlucky mortal ever born—	
	since you ask me, yes, they say I am his son."	
265	"Still," the clear-eyed goddess reassured him,	**reassure:** 使安心
	"trust me, the gods have not marked out your house	

---

37 *Argive*: 阿耳吉维人。《荷马史诗》中泛指参与特洛伊战争的希腊人。

38 *Would to god... of his possessions* (Lines 261–262): 在这个句子中，would to god 表示希望，相当于 I would to god...，我希望……。可译为："我希望自己是某个幸运者的儿男，/ 其人守着自己的财富，迈入老年。"

unsung: 未被赞扬的		for such an unsung future,
		not if Penelope³⁹ has borne a son like you.⁴⁰
spare: 省去		But tell me about all this and spare me nothing.
banquet: 欢宴	270	What's this banqueting, this crowd carousing here?
carouse: 狂饮		And what part do you play yourself? Some wedding-feast,
		some festival? Hardly a potluck supper, I would say.
obscenely: 下流地		how obscenely they lounge and swagger here, look,
gorge: 饕餮		gorging in your house. Why, any man of sense
	275	who chanced among them would be outraged,
		seeing such behavior."
		Ready Telemachus
		took her up at once: "Well, my friend,
probe: 探究		seeing you want to probe and press the question,
press: 追问	280	once this house was rich, no doubt, beyond reproach
reproach: 指责		when the man you mentioned still lived here, at home.
reverse: 翻转		Now the gods have reversed our fortunes with a vengeance—
fortune: 运气		wiped that man from the earth like no one else before.
vengeance: 报复		I would never have grieved so much about his death
grieve: 悲伤	285	if he'd gone down with comrades off in Troy
		or died in the arms of loved ones,
coil: 纷乱		once he had wound down the long coil of war.
tomb: 坟墓		Then all united Achaea would have raised his tomb
		and he'd have won his son great fame for years to come.
whirlwind: 旋风	290	But now the whirlwinds have ripped him away, no fame for him!
rip: 撕扯		He's lost and gone now—out of sight, out of mind—and I...
rack: 折磨		he's left me tears and grief. Nor do I rack my heart
		and grieve for him alone. No longer. Now the gods
		have invented other miseries to plague me.
	295	Listen.

---

39 *Penelope*: 珀涅罗珀。奥德修斯的妻子，以其对丈夫的忠贞闻名。在奥德修斯出征期间，尽管有众多的求婚者，但是她仍然忠贞于自己的丈夫。Penelope 可能源自于"penelops"，意为一种毛色斑驳的鸭子。在一些民族的传说里，鸭子象征忠贞。

40 *trust me... a son like you* (Lines 266-268): 可译为"神祇无意让你的家族消隐，/日后声名不得远扬，/既然珀涅罗珀生养了像你这样的儿郎。"

All the nobles who rule the islands round about,	
Dulichion, and Same, and wooded Zacynthus⁴¹ too,	**wooded:** 树木茂盛的
and all who lord it in rocky Ithaca as well—	
down to the last man they court my mother,	
300 they lay waste my house! And mother...	
she neither rejects a marriage she despises	**despise:** 鄙视
nor can she bear to bring the courting to an end—	
while they continue to bleed my household white.	**bleed:** 榨取
Soon—you wait—they'll grind me down as well."	**grind:** 折磨
305 "Shameful!"—	
brimming with indignation, Palla Athena broke out.	**indignation:** 义愤
"Oh how much you need Odysseus, gone so long—	
how he'd lay hands on all these brazen suitors!	**brazen:** 无耻的
If only he would appear, now,	
310 at his house's outer gates and take his stand,	
armed with his helmet, shield and pair of spears,	**shield:** 盾牌
as strong as the man I glimpsed that first time	
in our own house, drinking wine and reveling there...	**revel:** 狂欢
just come in from Ephyra, visiting Ilus, Mermerus' son.⁴²	
315 Odysseus sailed that way, you see, in his swift trim ship,	
hunting deadly poison to smear on his arrows' bronze heads.	**smear:** 涂抹
Ilus refused—he feared the wrath of the everlasting gods—	**wrath:** 愤怒
but father, so fond of him, gave him all he wanted.	**everlasting:** 永恒的
If only that Odysseus sported with these suitors,	
320 a blood wedding, a quick death would take the lot!	**sport:** 戏弄
True, but all lies in the lap of the great gods,	

---

41 *Dulichion, and Same, and wooded Zacynthus*: 杜利基昂、萨墨和林木繁茂的扎昆索斯。这些地方都与下行提到的"山石嶙峋的伊萨卡"相距不远，地理情况当与伊萨卡相似。

42 *from Ephyra, visiting Ilus, Mermerus' son*: 从厄芙拉过来，拜访伊洛斯，墨耳墨罗斯的儿郎。厄芙拉是希腊神话中的城镇。墨耳墨罗斯是伊阿宋和美狄娅的儿子，伊洛斯是墨耳墨罗斯的儿子。*Oh how much... Mermerus' son* (Lines 307-314): 这一段（305—323行）讲的都是雅典娜假设奥德修斯回家时的情形。可译为："哦，你多么需要奥德修斯啊，他已经离家太久——/（假设他在家）他会如何打击这些无耻的求婚者！/但愿他即刻现身，/出现在大门口，整装以待，/头戴钢盔，手持盾牌与双枪，/一如我初见他时那样/在我们家中，喝着酒，享受欢畅，/当他从厄芙拉过来，拜访伊洛斯，墨耳墨罗斯的儿郎。"

whether or not he'll come and pay them back[43],
here, in his own house.

But you, I urge you,
325 think how to drive these suitors from your halls.
Come now, listen closely. Take my words to heart.
At daybreak summon the island's lords to full assembly,
give your orders to all and call the gods to witness:
tell the suitors to scatter, each to his own place.
330 As for your mother, if the spirit moves her to marry,
let her go back to her father's house, a man of power.
Her kin will arrange the wedding, provide the gifts,
the array that goes with a daughter dearly loved.

For you,
335 I have some good advice, if only you will accept it.
Fit out a ship with twenty oars, the best in sight,
sail in quest of news of your long-lost father.
Someone may tell you something
or you may catch a rumor straight from Zeus,
340 rumor that carries news to men like nothing else.
First go down to Pylos, question old King Nestor[44],
then cross over to Sparta, to red-haired Menelaus[45],
of all the bronze-armored Achaeans the last man back.
Now, if you hear your father's alive and heading home,
345 hard-pressed as you are, brave out[46] one more year.
If you hear he'd dead, no longer among the living,
then back you come to the native land you love,
raise his grave-mound, build his honors high

witness: 见证
scatter: 散开

kin: 族人
array: 盛装

hard-pressed: 被紧逼的

grave-mound: 坟墓

---

43 *pay back*: 报复。e.g. We will pay them back for the trick they played on us. 我们要报复他们对我们的捉弄。

44 *Nestor*: 奈斯托耳，普洛斯的国王。因其年长，经验丰富而受到尊重。奥德修斯的儿子忒勒马科斯在寻找父亲的过程中曾向他了解父亲的情况。

45 *Menelaus*: 墨奈劳斯。斯巴达国王，阿伽门农的弟弟，海伦的丈夫。因为海伦被特洛伊王子诱骗，从而引发特洛伊战争。

46 *brave out*: 多作 brave it out，拼着干到底，勇敢地面对麻烦。e.g. I don't want to see him because I know he suspects me of disloyalty. But I suppose I'll just have to brave it out. 我不想见他，因为我知道他怀疑我对他不忠，但我想此事我非硬着头皮干下去不可。

with the full funeral rites that he deserves—
350 and give your mother to another husband.⁴⁷

                                      Then
once you've sealed those matters, seen them through,
think hard, reach down deep in your heart and soul
for a way to kill these suitors in your house,
355 by stealth or in open combat.
You must not cling to your boyhood any longer—
it's time you were a man. Haven't you heard
what glory Prince Orestes won throughout the world
when he killed that cunning, murderous Aegisthus,
360 who'd killed his famous father?⁴⁸

                                And you, my friend—
how tall and handsome I see you now—be brave, you too,
so men to come will sing your praises down the years.
But now I must go back to my swift trim ship
365 and all my shipmates, chafing there, I'm sure,
waiting for my return. It all rests with you.
Take my words to heart."

                                        "Oh stranger,"
heedful Telemachus replied, "indeed I will.
370 You've counseled me with so much kindness now,
like a father to a son. I won't forget a word.
But come, stay longer, keen as you are to sail,
so you can bathe and rest and lift your spirits,
then go back to your ship, delighted with a gift,
375 a prize of honor, something rare and fine
as a keepsake from myself. The kind of gift
a host will give a stranger, friend to friend."

rite: 仪式

stealth: 秘密行动
combat: 战斗
cling to: 坚持

cunning: 狡猾的
murderous: 凶残的

chafe: 焦躁

heedful: 有心的
counsel: 劝告

keepsake: 纪念品

---

47 *If you hear... to another husband* (Lines 346-350)：这是一个假设句，第 347—350 行讲的是假设成立之后的几个并列的结构。可译为："如果听说他已死了，不再存活世上，/ 你可动身回返亲爱的故乡，/ 堆筑坟茔，高颂他的声名，/ 举办与其声望相称的隆重葬礼，/ 然后嫁出母亲，给另一位夫家。"

48 *You must not cling to... his famous father* (Lines 356-360)：这句话中 what 引导宾语从句，when 引导时间状语从句，who 引导定语从句。可译为："别再抱住儿时的稚嫩，/ 你已长大成人。难道你不曾听闻，俄瑞斯忒斯声名在凡人中赢得的荣耀，/ 当他宰除奸诈而凶残的埃吉索斯，/ 他曾将他光荣的父亲谋杀？"

decline: 拒绝		Her eyes glinting, Pallas declined in haste:
haste: 匆忙		"Not now. Don't hold me here. I long to be on my way.
	380	As for the gift—whatever you'd give in kindness—
		save it for my return so I can take it home.
		Choose something rare and fine, and a good reward
		that gift is going to bring you."
		With that promise,
	385	off and away Athena the bright-eyed goddess flew
soaring: 翱翔的		like a bird in soaring flight
nerve: 胆量		but left his spirit filled with nerve and courage,
		charged with his father's memory more than ever now.
		He felt his senses quicken, overwhelmed with wonder—
	390	this was a god, he knew it well and made at once
		for the suitors, a man like a god himself.
		Amidst them still
		the famous bard sang on, and they sat in silence, listening
		as he performed *The Achaeans' Journey Home from Troy*:
doom: 注定	395	all the blows Athena doomed them to endure.
endure: 承受		And now,
		from high above in her room and deep in thought,
strain: 曲调		she caught his inspired strains...
wary: 机警的		Icarius'[49] daughter Penelope, wary and reserved,
reserved: 含蓄的	400	and down the steep stair from her chamber she descended,
steep: 陡峭的		not alone: two of her women followed close behind.
chamber: 卧室		That radiant woman, once she reached her suitor,
descend: 下来		drawing her glistening veil across her cheeks,
radiant: 光芒四射的		paused now where a column propped the sturdy roof,
	405	with one of her loyal handmaids stationed either side.
glistening: 闪亮的		Suddenly, dissolving in tears and bursting through
veil: 面纱		the bard's inspired voice, she cried out, "Phemius!
prop: 支撑		So many other songs you know to hold us spellbound,
handmaid: 侍女		works of the gods and men that singers celebrate.
dissolve: 情不自禁	410	Sing one of those as you sit beside them here
		and they drink their wine in silence.
burst: 爆发		But break off this song—
spellbound: 被迷住		

---

49 *Icarius*: 伊卡里俄斯，珀涅罗珀的母亲。

the unendurable song that always rends the heart inside me...
the unforgettable grief, it wounds me most of all!
415 How I long for my husband—alive in memory, always,
that great man whose fame resounds through Hellas[50]
right to the depths of Argos[51]!"
                              "Why, mother,"
poised Telemachus put in sharply, "why deny
420 our devoted bard the chance to entertain us
any way the spirit stirs him on?
Bards are not to blame—
Zeus is to blame. He deals to each and every
laborer on this earth whatever doom he pleases.
425 Why fault the bard if he sings the Argives' harsh fate?
it's always the latest song, the one that echoes last
in the listeners' ears, that people praise the most.
Courage, mother. Harden your heart, and listen.
Odysseus was scarcely the only one, you know,
430 whose journey home was blotted out at Troy.
Others, so many others, died there too.
                              So, mother,
go back to your quarters. Tend to your own tasks,
the distaff and the loom, and keep the women
435 working hard as well. As for giving orders,
men will see to that, but I most of all:
I hold the reins of power in this house."
                              Astonished,
she withdrew to her own room. She took to heart
440 the clear good sense in what her son had said.
Climbing up to the lofty chamber with her women,
she fell to weeping for Odysseus, her beloved husband,
till watchful Athena sealed her eyes with welcome sleep.
But the suitors broke into uproar through the shadowed halls,

unendurable:	无法忍受的
rend:	撕裂
resound:	回荡
devoted:	忠诚的
stir:	激起
doom:	命运
harsh:	严酷的
echo:	回响
blot out:	抹掉
distaff:	纺纱杆
loom:	织布机
rein:	控制
withdraw:	退出
lofty:	高耸的
weep:	哭泣
watchful:	警觉的

---

50 *Hellas*: 赫拉斯。在《伊利亚特》里，赫拉斯为裴琉斯的城国，位于塞萨利亚南部。在这里，该词泛指希腊北部。

51 *Argos*: 阿耳戈斯。在此泛指伯罗奔尼撒，阿伽门农、墨奈劳斯、奈斯托耳和狄俄墨得斯等将领的属地均在该岛上。

prayer: 祈祷	445	all of them lifting prayers to lie beside her, share her bed,
discreet: 审慎的		until discreet Telemachus took command: "You suitors
insolent: 无礼的		who plague my mother, you, you insolent, overweening...
overweening: 自负的		for this evening let us dine and take our pleasure,
		no more shouting now. What a fine thing it is
	450	to listen to such a bard as we have here—
		the man sings like a god.

But at first light

we all march forth to assembly, take our seats
so I can give my orders and say to you straight out:

455 You must leave my palace! See to your feasting elsewhere,
devour your own possessions, house to house by turns.

fare: 伙食

But if you decide the fare is better, richer here,
destroying one man's goods and going scot-free,

carve: 切断

all right then, carve away!

460 But I'll try out to the everlasting gods in hopes
that Zeus will pay you back with a vengeance—all of you
destroyed in my house while I go scot-free myself!"
So Telemachus declared. And they all bit their lips,

daring: 胆量

amazed the prince could speak with so much daring.

465 Eupithes' son Antinous[52] broke their silence:
"Well, Telemachus, only the gods could teach you
to sound so high and mighty! Such brave talk.
I pray that Zeus will never make you king of Ithaca,

crown: 王冠

though your father's crown is no doubt yours by birth."

counter: 反驳

470 But cool-headed Telemachus countered firmly:
"Antinous, even though my words may offend you,
I'd be happy to take the crown if Zeus presents it.

befall: 降临

You think that nothing worse could befall a man?
It's really not so bad to be a king. All at once

475 your palace grows in wealth, your honors grow as well.
But there are hosts of other Achaean princes, look—

---

52 *Eupithes' son Antinous*: 欧培塞斯之子安提努斯。安提努斯是珀涅罗珀的主要求婚者，行为残暴、品性恶劣、狂妄自大。在奥德修斯离家期间，玷污了奥德修斯的家，并且试图杀死忒勒马科斯。幸好忒勒马科斯得到了雅典娜的帮助，躲过这一劫难。在安提努斯被奥德修斯杀死之后，他的父亲欧培塞斯忘记了奥德修斯曾经对他有过救命之恩，试图反抗奥德修斯的统治，却被奥德修斯的父亲拉厄忒斯杀死。

young and old, crowds of them on our island here—	
and any one of the lot might hold the throne,	throne: 王位
now great Odysseus is dead...	
480	But I'll be lord of my own house and servants,	
all that King Odysseus won for me by force."	
And now Eurymachus, Plybus' son[53], stepped in:	
"Surely this must lie in the gods' lap, Telemachus—	
which Achaean will lord it over seagirt Ithaca.	seagirt: 环海的
485	Do hold on to your own possessions, rule your house.	
God forbid that anyone tear your holdings from your hands	forbid: 禁止
while men still live in Ithaca.	
But about your guest,	
dear boy, I have some questions. Where does he come from?	
490	where's his country, his birth, his father's old estates?	estate: 庄园
Did he bring some news of your father, his return?	
Or did he come on business of his own?	
How he leapt to his feet and off he went!	leap: 跳跃
No waiting around for proper introductions.	
495	And no mean man, not by the looks of him, I'd say."	
"Eurymachus," Telemachus answered shrewdly,	shrewdly: 机敏地
"clearly my father's journey home is lost forever.	
I no longer trust in rumors—rumors from the blue—	
nor bother with any prophecy, when mother calls	
500	some wizard into the house to ask him questions.	wizard: 巫师
As for the stranger, though,	
the man's an old family friend, from Taphos[54],	
wise Anchialus' son. He says his name is Mentes,	
lord of the Taphian men who love their oars."	

---

53 *Eurymachus, Plybus' son*: 欧鲁马科斯，波鲁波斯之子。欧鲁马科斯与安提努斯一起，是珀涅罗珀的主要求婚者之一，傲慢无礼，不尊重伊萨卡的风俗。他狡猾富有心机，声称自己是奥德修斯和忒勒马科斯的朋友，并让珀涅罗珀相信他没有恶意。但是，他在追求珀涅罗珀的同时，与珀涅罗珀的侍女关系暧昧。奥德修斯回家后，他将所有的责任推给了安提努斯，但最终还是被奥德修斯所杀。与他的儿子相比，波鲁波斯显得聪明睿智，也是珀涅罗珀的追求者。奥德修斯回家后，并没有杀波鲁波斯。但是，在雅典娜的安排下，波鲁波斯被他人所杀。

54 *Taphos*: 塔福斯，古希腊的地名。

	505	So he said

           505   So he said
but deep in his mind he knew the immortal goddess.
Now the suitors turned to dance and song,

sway: 摇摆
      to the lovely beat and sway,

dusk: 黄昏
      waiting for dusk to come upon them there...

   510 and the dark night came upon them, lost in pleasure.
Finally, to bed. Each to his own house.

                                           Telemachus,

courtyard: 庭院
    off to his bedroom built in the fine courtyard—

commanding: 居高临下的
    a commanding, lofty room set well apart—

swarm: 充满

misgiving: 疑虑
   515 retired too, his spirit swarming with misgivings.
His devoted nurse attended him, bearing a glowing torch,

glowing: 发光的
    Eurycleia the daughter of Ops, Pisenor's son.[55]
Laertes had paid a price for the woman years ago,
still in the bloom of youth. He traded twenty oxen,

   520 honored her on a par with his won loyal wife at home
but fearing the queen's anger, never shared her bed.
She was his grandson's escort now and bore a torch,
for she was the one of all the maids who loved
the prince most—she'd nursed him as a baby.

snug: 舒适的
   525 He spread the doors of his snug, well-made room,
sat down on the bed and pulled his soft shirt off,

toss: 扔
    tossed it into the old woman's conscientious hands,

conscientious: 尽责的
    and after folding it neatly, patting it smooth,

pat: 轻拍
    she hung it up on a peg beside his corded bed,

peg: 挂钩
   530 then padded from the bedroom,

pad: 放轻脚步走
    drawing the door shut with the silver hook,

hook: 钩子

---

[55] *Eurycleia the daughter of Ops, Pisenor's son*: 欧鲁克蕾娅，裴塞诺耳之子俄普斯的女儿。欧鲁克蕾娅是奥德修斯的父亲拉厄耳忒斯购买的侍女，被当做妻子对待，但并未与她同房，以表示对结发之妻安提克蕾娅的尊重。她先是奥德修斯的乳母，后来又照料了忒勒马科斯。在奥德修斯的身上具有生母安提克蕾娅和乳母欧鲁克蕾娅的双重特性。生母的高贵身份赋予了他英雄的特质，能征善战，能说会道，足智多谋，使他能够在特洛伊战争中建立不朽的功勋。乳母卑微的出身使他能够两次成功扮演乞丐：一次是装扮成乞丐，偷偷溜进特洛伊城；一次是装扮成乞丐返回伊萨卡，杀掉珀涅罗珀的求婚者。他回家时，只有欧鲁克蕾娅认出了他是假扮乞丐的奥德修斯。这样的结局暗示欧鲁克蕾娅对于奥德修斯更重要。

sliding the doorbolt home with its rawhide strap.⁵⁶
There all night long, wrapped in a sheep's warm fleece,
he weighed in his mind the course Athena charted.

doorbolt: 门闩
strap: 皮带
fleece: 羊毛
weigh: 权衡

EXERCISES

I. Answer the following questions according to the reading text.

1. What happened to Odysseus at the beginning of the story?

2. When Athena asked his father Zeus to release Odysseus, who did Zeus blame for?

3. What was happening at Odysseus' home when Athena arrived at Ithaca?

4. In his conversation with Athena, what did Telemachus think of his father? What did he want to know from the stranger, Athena?

5. What did Athena tell Telemachus to do?

6. After Athena took her leave, what happened to Telemachus?

7. What did Telemachus say that made his mother astonished?

8. What did Telemachus say that amazed those suitors?

9. After Telemachus' remarks, who questioned him? What was his response?

II. Paraphrase the following lines with your own words, and then translate them into Chinese.

1. (Lines 67–70)   Atlas' daughter it is who holds Odysseus captive,

   luckless man—despite his tears, forever trying

   to spellbind his heart with suave, seductive words

   and wipe all thought of Ithaca from his mind.

---

56 *He spreads... with its rawhide strap* (Lines 525-532): 这个长句是描写忒勒马科斯就寝以及欧鲁克蕾娅服侍他就寝的细节。525—527 行是忒勒马科斯的动作，后面是欧鲁克蕾娅的动作。可译为："他打开门扇，走进舒适、坚固的睡房，/ 坐在床边，脱下松软的衣衫，/ 扔到尽责的老妇手中，/ 后者叠起衣衫，抚弄平整，/ 伸手到衣钉，在绳线穿绑的床边挂好。/ 然后，她轻步走出卧室，/ 手握银环，将房门关上，/ 攥动生皮带，将门栓插牢。"

2. (Lines 178–181)　　They reached out for the good things that lay at hand,

　　　　　　　　　　　and when they'd put aside desire for food and drink

　　　　　　　　　　　the suitors set their minds on other pleasures,

　　　　　　　　　　　song and dancing all that crowns a feast.

3. (Lines 239–242)　　　　　　　　　　　　　　　　Wait,

　　　　　　　　　　　I'll make you a prophecy, one the immortal gods

　　　　　　　　　　　have planted in my mind — it will come true, I think,

　　　　　　　　　　　though I am hardly a seer or know the flights of birds.

4. (Lines 384–388)　　　　　　　　　　　　　With that promise,

　　　　　　　　　　　off and away Athena the bright-eyed goddess flew

　　　　　　　　　　　like a bird in soaring flight

　　　　　　　　　　　but left his spirit filled with nerve and courage,

　　　　　　　　　　　charged with his father's memory more than ever now.

5. (Lines 512–515)　　　　　　　　　　　　　　　Telemachus,

　　　　　　　　　　　off to his bedroom built in the fine courtyard—

　　　　　　　　　　　a commanding, lofty room set well apart—

　　　　　　　　　　　retired too, his spirit swarming with misgivings.

III. Figure out the meanings of the phrases in bold, and then make another sentence with each of the phrases.

1. (Lines 1–3)　　Sing to me of the man, Muse, the man of twists and turns

　　　　　　　　driven time and again **off course**, once he had plundered

　　　　　　　　the hallowed heights of Troy.

2. (Line 55)　　　And sparkling-eyed Athena **drove the matter home**.

3. (Line 291)　　He's lost and gone now—**out of sight, out of mind**.

4. (Lines 292–293)　Nor do I **rack my heart**

　　　　　　　　　and grieve for him alone.

5. (Lines 305–306)　"Shameful!"—

　　　　　　　　　brimming **with indignation**, Palla Athena **broke out**.

6. (Lines 307–308)   Oh how much you need Odysseus, gone so long—
how he'd lay hands on all these brazen suitors!

7. (Lines 336–337)   **Fit out** a ship with twenty oars, the best in sight,
sail **in quest of** news of your long-lost father.

8. (Lines 429–430)   Odysseus was scarcely the only one, you know,
whose journey home was **blotted out** at Troy.

IV. Because of their long history and cultural influence in the West, some words and expressions in *The Odyssey* carry on cultural meanings. Now try to find out the cultural meanings of the following words and expressions.

1. Odyssey
2. Ithaca
3. Telemachus
4. Penelope
5. Penelope's web
6. Nestor's advice

V. Epic, as a particular genre, has its own way of expression. Read the following two excerpts from two famous epics and try to imitate them. Create an epic of your own, and then write down a short piece of beginning of your epic with no less than 200 words.

Of Man's first disobedience, and the fruit
Of that forbidden tree whose mortal taste
Brought death into the World, and all our woe,
With loss of Eden, till one greater Man
Restore us, and regain the blissful seat,
Sing, Heavenly Muse, ...

... I thence
Invoke thy aid to my adventurous song,
That with no middle flight intends to soar
Above th' Aonian mount, while it pursues
Things unattempted yet in prose or rhyme.

... what in me is dark

说起人啊，他的第一次违忤和禁树之果，他那致命的一尝之祸，给世界带来死亡，给我们带来无穷无尽的悲痛，从此丧失伊甸园，直到一位比凡人更加伟大的人使我们失去的一切失而复得，赢回幸福生活的世界。歌唱吧，天上的缪斯女神，

……我祈求你帮助我完成我这一鸣惊人的诗篇，让我的神思酣畅淋漓，一鼓作气，意在要高高飞越爱奥尼之巅，追求诗歌或散文迄今为止尚未尝试过的题材。

……光明才驱散

Illumine, what is low raise and support;
That, to the height of this great argument,
I may assert Eternal Providence,
And justify the ways of God to men.

    John Milton: *Paradise Lost*

我心中的黑暗，才使我从平庸平步高雅，
从而激励我要攀登这一伟大主题的巅峰，
但愿我能够坚决维护永恒的天道，证明
上帝之道对人之正当。

    ——弥尔顿：《失乐园》

What dire offence from am'rous causes springs,
What mighty contests rise from trivial things,
I sing—This verse to Caryll, Muse! is due:
This, ev'n Belinda may vouchsafe to view:
Slight is the subject, but not so the praise,
If She inspire, and He approve my lays.

严重的冒犯起自爱慕的心思，
剧烈的争斗源自细小的琐事——
我这诗就为缪斯卡里勒而吟，
甚至贝琳达也可能屈尊承认：
这题目虽小，只要她给我灵感，
卡里勒满意，这诗将大受称赞。

Say what strange motive, Goddess! could compel
A well-bred Lord t' assault a gentle Belle?
Oh say what stranger cause, yet unexplor'd,
Cou'd make a gentle Belle reject a Lord?
In tasks so bold, can little men engage,
And in soft bosoms dwells such mighty Rage?

 —Alexander Pope: *The Rape of the Lock*

女神哪你说，是什么奇怪动机
使谦谦公子对贤淑佳人无礼？
是什么未经探究的古怪理由
叫贤淑佳人拒绝公子的请求？
小小男子怎承担这重大任务，
柔肠里怎有如此强烈的愤怒？

 ——蒲伯：《秀发遭劫记》（《夺发记》）

UNIT 3

Oedipus the King
A Tragedy

Oral Tasks

1. How do you understand tragedy?
2. Have you ever heard of Oedipus Complex? Do you know where it comes from?
3. Have you ever heard of the Riddle of Sphinx? What is it?

Introduction

Tragedy is a form of drama based on human suffering that evokes an accompanying catharsis or pleasure in audiences.

Oedipus the King is an Athenian tragedy by Sophocles that was first performed around 429 BC. Oedipus has become the king of Thebes while unwittingly fulfilling a prophecy that he would kill his father, Laius (the previous king), and marry his mother, Iocasta (whom Oedipus took as his queen after solving the riddle of the Sphinx). The play concerns Oedipus' search for the murderer of Laius in order to end a plague ravaging Thebes, unaware that the killer he is looking for is none other than himself. At the end of the play, after the truth finally comes to light, Iocasta hangs herself while Oedipus, horrified at his patricide and incest, proceeds to gouge out his own eyes in despair.

Sophocles is one of the three ancient Greek tragedians whose plays have survived. His first plays were written later than those of Aeschylus, and earlier than or contemporary with those of Euripides. He is famous for his Theban plays, which deal with the story of Oedipus, *Oedipus the King* was the second to be written. However, in terms of the chronology of events that the plays describe, it comes first, followed by *Oedipus at Colonus* and then *Antigone.*

PART 3

TEXTUAL READING[1]

SCENE 1

Oedipus enters from the palace doors. Children and young people, accompanied by an old priest, come on from the "city" side, and sit around the altar in front of the palace, holding leafy branches *with woolen wreaths tied round them.*

branch: 树枝

Oedipus: My children, youngest generation
from this ancient land the Thebes[2],
why have you hurried here with suppliant branches[3]?
why is the city thick with incense smoke,
5 and chants of Paean[4] mixed with cries of pain?
I though it would be wrong
to find this out through other sources,
so I've come to hear you for myself—
I, Oedipus, whose fame is known to all the world.
10 It's proper you, old man, should act as spokesman for them:
is it fear that brings you here like this? Or need?
It is my wish to offer every help I can—

suppliant: 祈求的
incense: 敬香
chant: 曲调

---

1 本篇出自: Sophocles. *Four Tragedies.* Translated by Olirer Taplin. Oxford: Oxford Universiey Press, 2015。

2 *ancient land of Thebes*: 底比斯城，也称忒拜城。在悲剧中，也被称为卡德摩斯城（the city of Cadmus）。传说该城是由四代之前的卡德摩斯所建。卡德摩斯是腓尼基国王阿格诺耳的儿子。宙斯化成一头牛，把他的姐姐欧罗巴拐走以后，他父亲便叫他去寻找，找不到不许回家。卡德摩斯遍寻不遇，便去向阿波罗求问，阿波罗告诉他去尾追一头母牛，在牛累死的地方建一座城。他因此建立了卡德墨亚，即后来的忒拜城的卫城。

3 *suppliant branches*: 祈求的树枝。一种仪式，乞援人在祈求某人或者某神怜悯的时候，往往在带有树叶的树枝上缠上羊毛。乞援人举着这种橄榄枝，如果请求不成功，就把橄榄枝留在祭坛上；如果成功，便把树枝带走。

4 *Paean*: 赞歌。有些赞歌是专门用来赞美阿波罗的，因此，Paean 有时也专指阿波罗的赞歌。

impervious: 无动于衷的			I'd have to be impervious not to melt
melt: 心软			with pity seeing such a gathering.
altar: 祭坛	15	**Priest:**	Great Oedipus, commander of our land,
			you see us here, all ages, on your altar steps:
			some still too little to fly far;
			some bowed with age, like me, the priest of Zeus;
			and these here chosen form among the young.
assemble: 集合	20		Yet others are assembled with their garlands
garland: 花环			in the centre of the town before the double temple[5]
mantic: 预言的			of Athena and the mantic altar of Apollo.
			You see this for yourself:
founder: 衰败			our city's foundering, and can no longer
surf: 波涛	25		keep its head above the bloody surf of death.
bud: 幼苗			The buds that should bear fruit become disease,
grazing: 放牧的			our grazing cattle-flocks become disease;
still-birth: 死胎			our women's labour-pains produce still-births.
detest: 可恶			Detested Plague, the god who lights the fever-fires,
pounce: 猛扑	30		has pounced upon our town,
drain: 耗尽			and drains the homes of Thebes to empty husks.
husk: 空壳			Dark Hades is enriched, a profiteer in groans and tears.
profiteer: 谋取暴利的人			We, old and young, are suppliants here,
			because we value you, not as the equal of the gods,
groan: 呻吟	35		but as a man outstanding in the tos and fros[6] of human life,
			and in exchanges with the higher powers.
			You once arrived in Thebes, and freed us
due: 税捐			from the dues exacted by that cruel singing lynx[7].
			Despite no clues from us, without instruction,

---

5 *double temple*: 双庙。一个是俄格卡庙，在西门俄格卡附近；另一个是卡德墨亚庙，又叫伊斯墨诺斯庙。

6 *to and fro*: 来回地，往返地。

7 *that cruel singing lynx*: 残酷的歌女。"歌女"指狮身人面的妖兽，即斯芬克斯。这种妖兽在埃及人的想象中没有翅膀。在希腊，它是经悲剧家描写成有翼的妖兽以后才被加上翅膀的。这种妖兽在埃及为男性，在希腊为女性。他曾经吃掉许多忒拜城的人，向他们征收供命税。本剧多次暗示到斯芬克斯，但极少直接提及，因为直呼其名会带来厄运。

40　　　　　　but, it is believed, with backing from a god,
　　　　　　　you set us straight upon our feet.
　　　　　　　So now, all-powerful Oedipus, we all
　　　　　　　submit ourselves into your hands as suppliants;
　　　　　　　we beg of you to find some safety-shield for us.　　　　**safety-shield:**
45　　　　　　Perhaps you've heard some message from a god,　　　　安全屏障
　　　　　　　or man? (Those people with experience
　　　　　　　I find most skilled at gathering advice.)
　　　　　　　Do something, best of men, raise up our land once more;
　　　　　　　do something, but be careful too.
50　　　　　　This country calls you "saviour" now,　　　　　　　　**saviour:** 救主
　　　　　　　because you showed effectiveness back then:
　　　　　　　don't make our record of your rule a time
　　　　　　　when we were lifted up, but only to collapse once more.[8]
　　　　　　　No, plant our country firm to stand unshakably.　　　　**unshakably:**
55　　　　　　You brought good luck with you before:　　　　　　　　坚定不移地
　　　　　　　now be that man again.
　　　　　　　If you are going to go on ruling in this land, as now,
　　　　　　　it's preferable to have that power with people
　　　　　　　round about than with an emptiness.
60　　　　　　[A city's like a ship: if it's unmanned, no crew to people it,　**unmanned:**
　　　　　　　then it is nothing but a hulk.]　　　　　　　　　　　　　　无人驾驶的
　　　Oedipus:　My pitiable children, yes,　　　　　　　　　　　　　　　**hulk:** 废船
　　　　　　　I know full well what longing has impelled you here;　　　**impel:** 驱使
　　　　　　　I know how you're all sick at heart.
65　　　　　　And yet not one of you knows sickness
　　　　　　　that can equal mine—for each of you is suffering singly　　**singly:** 逐一地，
　　　　　　　for himself alone, whereas my heart aches　　　　　　　　一个接一个地
　　　　　　　for our land as well as you and me.
　　　　　　　So you are not awakening me from idle sleep:　　　　　　**idle:** 懒散的
70　　　　　　I've wept so many tears;

8　*This country... once more* (Lines 50-53)：这个句子的难点在于涉及的时间关系交错，在讲现在的情况的同时提到了以前的情况，在讲未来的情况时，又提及了过去和现在的状况。可译为："现在这个国度称你为"救星"，/因为你先前显示出了效力：/不要让我们对您的统治留下这样的记忆，/我们曾被救起，结果再次衰落。"[注：本篇译文来自《罗念生全集》（第二卷：埃斯库罗斯悲剧三种；索福克勒斯悲剧四种），上海：上海人民出版社，2007，343-397。下同。]

and I've explored the many tracks
my thoughts have taken me along.
And after all my searching I have found
once single remedy—and that I've set in action:
75　　　I've sent off Creon, brother of my wife, to Delphi[9]
to inquire from great Apollo's oracle
what I should do or speak to make this city safe.
But when I calculate the days, I'm worried
that he has been gone for longer than the usual time.
80　　　But when he does return, I would be in the wrong
if I do not enact whatever is directed by the god.

remedy: 补救

oracle: 神谕

SCENE 2

Creon is seen approaching from the "abroad" side.

Priest: And timely fitting with your words, these people signal here
that Creon is approaching now.

Oedipus: Apollo, may he bring with him reviving fortune,
85　　　light that's like a gleaming eye.

Priest: His news is surely good, since otherwise
his head would not be garlanded with laurel-leaves.

Oedipus: Now he's in earshot and we soon shall know.
My kinsman, Creon, say:
90　　　what message do you bring us form the god?

Creon: It's good—for even our ordeals
may prove a benefit, I say, if all ends well[10].

Oedipus: The message, though? From what you say,
I cannot tell if I should be encouraged or alarmed.

95　**Creon:** If you would like to hear before this crowd,
then I'm prepared to speak... or shall we go inside?

Oedipus: Speak out in front of everyone:

revive: 复活

laurel: 月桂冠
earshot: 听得见的地方
kinsman: 亲戚
ordeal: 考验

9　*Creon, brother of my wife, to Delphi*: 克瑞翁和俄狄浦斯的妻子都是卡德摩斯的后裔。德尔菲是古希腊太阳神阿波罗的神庙，忒拜城离德尔菲不远。

10　*if all ends well*: 这可以看作是 all is well that ends well 的变体，意思是"只要结局好，什么都好"。e.g. I'm sorry you had such difficulty in finding us, but all's well that ends well and now we can enjoy ourselves. 很抱歉，让你好不容易才找着我们，但找着了就算是好事，而今我们可以尽兴地玩啦。

	I feel more grief for these poor people than for my own life.	grief: 悲伤
Creon:	Then I declare that this is what I gathered from the god:	
100	Apollo tells us clearly that there is miasma here,	miasma: 瘴气
	pollution inbred in this very land;	inbred: 天生的
	and that we have to drive it out,	
	not to let it thrive incurable.	thrive: 繁盛
Oedipus:	What kind of cleansing? What is it that's occurred?	incurable: 无可救药的
105 Creon:	It's blood which blasts this land:	cleanse: 净化
	and so we must eject the guilt,	blast: 摧毁
	or else repay the death by further death.	eject: 驱逐
Oedipus:	Who is the man whose fate the oracle proclaims?	repay: 偿还
Creon:	The ruler of this land, my lord, was Laius[11],	proclaim: 声明
110	before you came and took the reins in hand.	
Oedipus:	I know of him by hearing—but never saw him face to face.	
Creon:	He met with violent death—	
	and now the oracle speaks clear:	
	we must exact revenge upon his murderers.	murderer: 谋杀者
115 Oedipus:	But where on earth might they be now?	
	Where can we find the faded tracks	fade: 消逝
	left from a crime committed long ago?	
Creon:	Here in this land, it said.	
	There is a chance of catching what is looked for:	
120	while what is disregarded will escape.	disregard: 不注意
Oedipus:	Was Laius at home, or in the countryside,	
	or in another land, when he was murdered?[12]	
Creon:	He said that he was going on a pilgrimage,	pilgrimage: 朝觐
	but never came back home again.	
125 Oedipus:	And was there no report of what occurred?	
	no fellow-traveller with evidence that might give help?	fellow-traveller: 同行的人
Creon:	No, all of them were killed—except for one.	
	He ran away in fright, and said he only saw	fright: 恐惧
	one thing for sure, and nothing more.	

---

11 *Laius*: 拉伊俄斯，忒拜城的前国王。从悲剧的结局看，他是俄狄浦斯的亲生父亲。

12 *Was Laius at home... he was murdered* (Lines 121–122): 著名学者罗念生曾指出，这是剧情的一个弱点。俄狄浦斯只知道拉伊俄斯死了，却不知道他的故事。俄狄浦斯做国王的时候，前一位国王拉伊俄斯才死不久，况且俄狄浦斯又做了许多年的国王，怎么会不知道拉伊俄斯被杀的事情呢？

	130 **Oedipus:**	And what was that?
		One clue might lead to many more,
slender: 微弱的		if we could get a slender prompt from which to start.
prompt: 提示	**Creon:**	He said that bandits came on them;
bandit: 强盗		and that the king was killed not by one man
	135	but by the violence of many hands[13].
bold: 大胆的	**Oedipus:**	But how could any bandit have been bold enough,
incite: 唆使		unless incited by some payment made from here?[14]
	Creon:	Yes, we thought that. But after Laius was dead,
		no one was there to help us in those troubled times.
	140 **Oedipus:**	But when your king had met his end so violently,
		what could have held you back from finding out?
	Creon:	That riddle-singing Sphinx made us
obscure: 模糊的		abandon what remained obscure,
		and concentrate on what lay in our path[15],[16]
	145 **Oedipus:**	(making an announcement)
beam a light: 阐明		Back from the first beginnings I shall beam a light once more.
		For rightly has Apollo turned attention
		to this matter of the murdered man—and you as well.
		So you shall see me justly join in fighting hard
	150	to win full vengeance for this land and for the god.
		I'll act as best I can, not as for some remote
acquaintance: 相识		acquaintance, but for my own self,
banish: 驱逐		to banish this miasma from our air.
		His unknown killer might well want
	155	to make a similar attack on me,
		and so I'm acting for myself as well as him.
		Now quickly, children, stand up from these steps,

....

13 *by the violence of many hands*: 从之后的发展来看，这位见证者是拉伊俄斯的一位老奴。他对参与杀害拉伊俄斯的人数的错误回忆，导致了剧情中重构现场的重重困难。

14 *But how could... payment made from here* (Lines 136–137): 在古希腊，拦路抢劫非常罕见，因此，俄狄浦斯听到这件事的第一反应是政治谋杀。

15 *lie in one's path*: 在某人的路上；眼前的事物。e.g. A blue truck had missed a turn on the road and had rolled down, and lay in our path. 一辆蓝色的卡车冲出了弯道，侧翻下来，挡住了我们的去路。

16 *The riddle-singing... lay in our path* (Lines 142–144): 可译为"那唱着谜语的斯芬克斯迫使我们／放下依旧模糊不清的案子，／而专注眼前的事情。"

	and take your suppliant **boughs**.	**bough:** 树枝
	And someone call a meeting of the Theban people here,	
160	to make it known that I shall leave no stone unturned[17].	
	An attendant goes off towards the city.	
	We'll either shine as fortunate, thanks to the god—	
	or else we sink.	
Priest:	Let us be going, children, for this man's proclamation	
	is the thing we came here for.	
165	And may Apollo, sender of this oracle,	
	come to our rescue[18], and bring ending to this plague.	
	...[19]	

SCENE 4

Tiresias[20] approaches slowly, led by a young slave.

Oedipus:	Tiresias, you who **encompass** all things with your mind,	**encompass:** 包括
	those suitable for teaching and things **mystic**,	**mystic:** 神秘的
	both **heavenly** and **earthbound** worlds,	**heavenly:** 天国的
170	although your eyes can't see,	**earthbound:** 世俗的
	you know the way this city is **afflicted**.	**afflict:** 折磨
	You are the only **shield** and rescue we can find, my lord.	**shield:** 保护
	In case you have not heard this news,	
	Apollo has replied to us when we enquired,	
175	that there is only one solution for this plague:	
	we must **unmask** the murderers of Laius for sure,	**unmask:** 揭示

---

17 *leave no stone unturned*: 千方百计，不遗余力。e.g. In his search for his mother, he left no stone unturned, and even after 20 years he refused to believe that she was dead. 他想方设法寻找自己的母亲，即便是在 20 年后他也不愿相信她已经死了。

18 *come to our rescue*: 帮助，救援。e.g. It's always best to be wary of those eager to come to our rescue, because even the smallest of favors carries a price tag. 对那些急切想帮助我们的人最好要带着一颗机警的心，因为哪怕是最小的恩都是有价格的。

19 限于篇幅，在此省略了歌队（chorus）的演唱、第三场俄狄浦斯的独白以及俄狄浦斯与歌队长的对话。俄狄浦斯的独白主要讲述他将誓死找出凶手，无论凶手是陌生人还是亲戚。在与歌队长对话中，俄狄浦斯得知有另外一位预言者忒瑞西阿斯，他了解拉伊俄斯被谋杀的事情。俄狄浦斯要求忒瑞西阿斯来见他。

20 *Tiresias*: 忒瑞西阿斯。一位与阿波罗有密切关系的盲眼先知，是几个祭拜神话中的重要角色。在这里，俄狄浦斯急于知道忒瑞西阿斯的回复，在忒瑞西阿斯刚一到来，没有一般的问候，就直接询问情况。在他们两人接下来的对话中，俄狄浦斯一直使用的是官方语气，代表城邦在说话，而忒瑞西阿斯一直是在私人的、精神的层面交谈。

sentence: 宣判		and either sentence them to death,
expel: 驱逐		or else expel them exiled from this land.
exile: 放逐		So please do not withhold what means you have,
withhold: 隐瞒	180	a message from your birds[21], or any other route of prophecy,
		to clear yourself, our city, me as well—
		to clear away the whole miasma from the murdered man[22].
		We are in your hands,
		and it's the finest kind of service
	185	for a man to use his powers as best he can.
	Tiresias:	Ah, ah... It can be terrible to know
		what brings no benefit to him who knows it—
		I was well aware of this but had forgotten,[23]
		for otherwise I never would have ventured here.
	190 **Oedipus**:	What's this? You're so reluctant in approaching.
	Tiresias:	Send me back home again.
		Take my advice—you'll find it's easiest
		for you to bear your burden, and for me to carry mine.[24]
	Oedipus:	Your words are not acceptable, and, by refusing to respond,
disloyal: 不忠的	195	you are disloyal to Thebes, the land that bred you.
breed: 养育	**Tiresias**:	Because I see your questing thought is off the mark[25];
		I would avoid the same mistake...

....

21 *your birds*: 先知能借鸟声卜吉凶。

22 *the murdered man*: 指忒拜城的前国王拉伊俄斯。

23 *I was well aware of this but had forgotten*: 忒瑞西阿斯两次被召请，勉强前来。倘若他时常记住这是件可怕的事情，他就不会来的。这时候，他当着俄狄浦斯的面，才真正感觉到他所保守的秘密是件极其可怕的事。这里忒瑞西阿斯所说的话可译为："哎呀，当无法从所知道的事情中获得好处的时候，/ 知道事情的真相真是可怕呀！/ 这道理我明白，可是忘记了；/ 要不然，我就不会来。"

24 *Take my advice... carry mine* (Lines 192-193): 忒瑞西阿斯知道事情的真相，即俄狄浦斯杀父娶母，但不愿说出来，因为说出来将会导致更大的灾难。相比较之下，俄狄浦斯和忒拜城眼前的灾难不是那么大。因此，他建议俄狄浦斯到此为止，不要再追究，也不要问他这件事情。忒瑞西阿斯知道事情的真相，说话吞吞吐吐，一直欲言又止，而俄狄浦斯执着于向忒瑞西阿斯寻找真相。二人说话之间的差异是理解两人对话的关键。可译为："你答应我，你容易 / 对付过去，我也容易对付过去。"

25 *off the mark*: 离题；没有打中目标。e.g. His speech was off the mark. 他的发言离题了。

	Oedipus: If you have knowledge, do not turn your back[26]—	
	we all of us as suppliants beg of you.	
200	**Tiresias:** Because you all are ignorant.	
	I shall not open up my troubles, not to speak of yours.	
	Oedipus: You're saying that, though knowing, you'll not speak?	
	You mean to leave us all betrayed? Destroy your city too?	**betray:** 背叛
	Tiresias: I shall not further hurt myself nor you.	
205	You question me for nothing, since you shall not learn from me.	
	Oedipus: Despicable! You'd stir bad temper in a lump of stone.[27]	**despicable:** 卑鄙的
	Are you refusing to tell anything?	
	you mean to stand beyond our reach[28], intransigent?	**intransigent:** 固执的
	Tiresias: You criticize my temperament,	
210	yet fail to see your own, which shares your life with you;	**temperament:** 品性
	and you find fault with me instead.	
	Oedipus: Yes, who would not be moved to angry temper	
	hearing words like these, an insult to your city?	
	Tiresias: Events will turn out[29] as they will,	
215	no matter if I cover them with silence.	
	Oedipus: What will turn out...	
	that's surely what you should be telling me?	
	Tiresias: I shall explain no more.	
	Feel free to rage at that as fiercely as you like.	**rage:** 愤怒
220	**Oedipus:** All right! You've angered me so deeply	**fiercely:** 狂暴地
	that I'll not suppress what I suspect.	**suppress:** 压抑
	It's my belief you helped to hatch the plot,	**hatch:** 谋划
	and did the deed—except for actual killing with your hands.	
	Had you the power of sight, I would have said	
225	that you alone had done this thing.	

---

26 *turn one's back*: 背弃，拒绝。e.g. Whenever you turn your back on truth, love, or power, you distance yourself from experiencing wisdom, joy, and strength. 无论何时，只要你与真理、爱和权力背道而驰，你将会离智慧、喜悦和力量越来越远。

27 *You'd stir bad temper in a lump of stone*: 可译为"你都快搅起了石头的糟糕脾气。"也就是说，俄狄浦斯非常生气，就连一块石头都会对忒瑞西阿斯的行为感到生气。

28 *stand beyond our reach*: 置身事外。

29 *turn out*: 证明是，发展为，结果是。e.g. You said we shouldn't trust him, and you were right, as it turns out. 你说过我们不应该相信他，结果表明你是对的。

	Tiresias: Is that the truth? Then I tell you:
	stand by your own decree that you proclaimed,
	and from this day do not address these men, nor me—
foul: 污秽的	because you are the foul pollutant in this land.³⁰
pollutant: 污染源 230	Oedipus: You have the gall to stir this slander?
gall: 胆量	You can't believe you'll get away with³¹ this!
slander: 诽谤	Tiresias: I have escaped already.
sustain: 维持	I sustain the truth to be my strength.
strength: 力量	Oedipus: Who did you learn this from? Not from your craft, I think.
craft: 手腕 235	Tiresias: I learned from you:
	you pressed words out from me against my will.
	Oedipus: What words? Repeat them to make sure I understand.
	Tiresias: Did you not understand before? Is this a test?
	Oedipus: Not so I fully understood. Repeat again.
240	Tiresias: I say you are his murderer—the one you seek.
	Oedipus: Redoubled insults! You shall regret these words.
	Tiresias: Then shall I tell you something to enrage you even more?
	Oedipus: Say anything you want—it will be wasted breath.
	Tiresias: I say that, unaware of it, you're living
245	in a state of shame with those you hold most close;
fathom: 洞察	and you can't fathom how the place you're at is bad.
	Oedipus: You shall not get away with saying things like this.
	Tiresias: I shall, if there is strength in truth.
	Oedipus: There is, with one exception: you.
250	You have no part in this
	because your ears and brain are just as blind as are your eyes.
cast: 投掷	Tiresias: Poor fool, you cast all this abuse at me,
abuse: 辱骂	and yet that same abuse will soon
	be aimed at you by every person here.

---

30 *Is that the truth?... in this land* (Lines 226-229): 忒瑞西阿斯在这里（以及在接下来的对话中）一气之下说出了事情的真相，但是，俄狄浦斯执迷不悟，将他的话听成了政治阴谋，因此更加生气。执迷不悟也是俄狄浦斯的悲剧原因之一。可译为："真的吗？我叫你 / 遵守自己宣布的命令，/ 从此不许再跟这些长老说话，也不许跟我说话，/ 因为你就是这地方恶臭的污染源。"

31 *get away with*: 侥幸做成……而未被发觉（未受责备、惩罚）。e.g. The child ought to be punished. You shouldn't let him get away with telling lies. 要处罚这孩子。你不应该让他撒谎而不受惩罚。

255	**Oedipus:**	Your life is passed in one long night;
		and so you have no power to damage me,
		or anyone with eyes that see the light.
	Tiresias:	It is your fate to fall, but not by any power of mine.
		Apollo is enough, and shall accomplish what he will.
260	**Oedipus:**	Creon! Are these inventions his idea, or yours?
	Tiresias:	Creon presents no threat to you: you do yourself.
	Oedipus:	So: wealth and kingship and ambitious plans
		for ever-higher steps in life's ascent,
		see how resentment gets stored up for you!
265		To take control over this rule of mine—
		a gift unsought, donated by the city—
		it's for this that trusty Creon, friend right from the start,
		has been devising moves behind my back³²
		and hungering to throw me out.
270		For this he has deployed this old trick-spinning conjuror,
		this door-to-door spell-casting quack,
		who has his eye on profit only,
		while at his proper craft he's blind.
		How can you claim to have clear powers of prophecy?
275		Back when the singing-spinner bitch was here,
		how come you had no key to free these citizens?
		It's true the riddle wasn't just for anybody's guess,
		it needed some prophetic skill.
		But you displayed no special wisdom
280		from the birds or from the gods.
		But then along I come, know-nothing Oedipus:
		I put a stop to her and got the answer
		using just my wits, not learning from the birds.
		And I'm the man you're trying to eject,
285		imagining that you yourself will stand beside the throne
		as Creon's right-hand man.
		But you and your conspirator will both regret

kingship: 王位
ambitious: 野心的
ascent: 上升
resentment: 怨恨
unsought: 不经意的
donate: 赠送
trusty: 可靠的
devise: 策划
deploy: 利用
conjuror: 巫师
quack: 骗子

prophetic: 预言的
wisdom: 智慧

wit: 才智

---

32 *behind one's back*: 背着某人，暗中地。e.g. I think we should wait till he arrives; I don't like criticizing people behind their backs. 我认为我们应该等他来，我不爱背后批评人。

scapegoat: 找替罪羊		attempting to scapegoat like this.
		If you did not appear so old,
harbour: 藏匿	290	you would pay dear for harbouring such thoughts.
		...
	Tiresias:	You may be king,
		but I still have an equal right to make reply.
		I also have this power because I am no slave
		to serve your beck and call[33]: I am Apollo's.
	295	So do not write me down in Creon's list.[34]
		And since you have insulted me as blind, now listen:
		you have your sight, yet do not see the truth
		of how the place you're at is bad, or where you live,
		or who they are you share your home with.
	300	Do you know what people you are from?
kin: 亲属		You little realize you're an enemy to your own kin
		below the earth and there above.
		One day the fearful-footed curse
		from mother and from father shall
spike: 钉子	305	with double spike expel you from this land.[35]
		You see things focused now, but then you shall see dark.

33　*beck and call*: 惟命是从，召之即来。e.g. I knew he was trying to wheedle me into being at his beck and call. 我知道这是他拉拢我，好让我俯首贴耳地为他效劳。

34　*So do not write me down in Creon's list*: 此句的背景是，在古希腊，居住在雅典的外国人须请一位公民作保护人，若遇诉讼的事情，本人不能自行答辩，必须由保护人代替。忒瑞西阿斯被俄狄浦斯告发是克瑞翁的党羽，他既不是外国人（他是阿波罗的人），自然有自行答辩的权利。诗人在此处把他自己时代的法律习惯运用到了英雄时代。

35　*you have your sight... from this land* (Lines 297-305): 忒瑞西阿斯话里有话。从故事的结局俄狄浦斯挖瞎自己的眼睛来看，这句话具有预言的性质。这里的 *fearful-footed curse* (Line 303) 与俄狄浦斯这个名字有关。Oedipus 这个名字中，oid- 的意思是 swelling "肿胀"，pous 的意思是 foot，就是指婴儿双脚残损。俄狄浦斯刚一生下来就被亲生父母将双脚钉在一起。正是因为俄狄浦斯的脚有问题，行动不便，导致他在三岔路口遇到拉伊俄斯的车队的时候，回避比较缓慢，从而产生冲突，杀害了拉伊俄斯。这两个带有预言性质的含沙射影表明忒瑞西阿斯知道俄狄浦斯过去和将来的一切。从该故事的主题来看，俄狄浦斯不依不饶地追寻事情的真相这一点也反映在他的名字中。Oedipus 这个名字中，oid- 还有 know 的意思，pous 还有 where 的意思，即俄狄浦斯致力于找出自己从何而来。可译为："你虽然有眼，但是你却看不见真相，/ 看不见你所在的地方有多么糟糕，或者你生活的地方，/ 或者和什么人同居。/ 你知道你是从什么根里长出来的吗？/ 你不知道，你是你的 / 已死的和活着的亲属的仇人；/ 你父母的诅咒左右鞭打着你，可怕的向你追来，/ 把你赶出这地方。"

		There is no anchorage,	anchorage: 抛锚
		no hollow of Cithaeron's[36] mountainside,	hollow: 洞穴
		that shall not resonate in echo to your cry,	resonate: 共鸣
310		once you have learned about your marriage-song,	
		and what a treacherous harbour-home	treacherous: 危险的
		you entered in full sail, thinking your voyage fair.	
		And there's a further crowd of horrors, which you'll find	horror: 恐怖
		enough to crush you, and your children too.	crush: 压碎
315		Now, after that, go spread your smears	smear: 诽谤
		all over Creon and my words.	
		There is no human who shall be	
		more harshly ground to dust than you.	
	Oedipus:	I cannot bear to listen any more to this man's raving.	raving: 胡言乱语
320		to hell with you—best turn back round,	
		and hurry far off from this house.	
	Tiresias:	I never would have come, not I, had you not called for me.	
	Oedipus:	And if I'd known you'd talk such lunacy,	lunacy: 愚蠢，疯狂（的话或行为）
		I never would have brought you near my home.	
325	Tiresias:	That's how I seem to you, a ranting lunatic:	rant: 咆哮
		your parents, though, who gave you life,	lunatic: 疯子
		they thought me sane enough.	sane: 神志清醒的
	Oedipus:	What parent? Stop! Who were the ones who gave me life?	
	Tiresias:	This very day shall give you life,	
330		and shall unmake you too.	unmake: 使毁灭
	Oedipus:	Your words are all enigmas, too obscure.	enigma: 谜团
	Tiresias:	Aren't you the best enigma-solver here?	
	Oedipus:	Yes, mock at me, but that is where you'll find me great.	mock: 嘲弄
	Tiresias:	It was that very stroke of fortune that undid you.	undo: 摧毁
335	Oedipus:	I was the saving of this city—that's enough for me.	
	Tiresias:	I'm going, then... My boy, take me away from here.	
	Oedipus:	Yes, have him take you.	
		You're nothing but a nuisance here.	nuisance: 讨厌的人
		Once you've moved on, you'll give us no more grief.	
340	Tiresias:	I'll go then once I've had my say.	
		I do not fear to face your frown,	frown: 皱眉；不悦

---

36 *Cithaeron*: 喀泰戎山脉。

since there's no way that you can blot me out.
I tell you then:
this man you have been searching for
345 with curses and decrees, the murderer of Laius,
he is right here.
Though said to be an *immigrant*,
he shall be shown to be a *true-born* Theban—
yet he'll take no pleasure in that *turnabout*.
350 From someone who has sight he shall turn blind,
from someone rich become a beggar,
and then he'll make his way towards an *alien* land
by probing for his footsteps with a stick.
And he shall be revealed
355 as brother and as father
to the children that he has at home;
as son and husband
to the woman who once gave him birth;
as fellow-*sower* and as killer
360 to the father who *begot* him.
Now go inside and work that out.[37]
And if you can then prove me false,
feel free to say there is no *insight*
in my power of prophesy.

Tiresias is led off towards the city; Oedipus goes indoors without speaking.

SCENE 5

Enter Creon from the city direction… Enter Oedipus.

365 **Oedipus:** Well, well, it's you! What are you doing here?
How dare you come before my palace doors
with such *barefaced effrontery*,

---

[37] *I tell you then… work that out* (Lines 343-361): 在这段话中，忒瑞西阿斯不仅暗示（几乎就是明说了）杀人的真凶（即俄狄浦斯），以及他的来历，而且预言了俄狄浦斯的下场，即挖掉自己的眼睛，逃离忒拜城，到荒野流浪。受篇幅所限，本篇节选只讲到了俄狄浦斯得知事情的真相，没有涉及后来的发展。可译为："告诉你吧：／你刚才大声威胁、通令捉拿的，杀害拉伊俄斯的凶手／就在这里；／表面看来，他是个侨民，／一转眼就会发现他是个土生的忒拜人，／再也不能享受他的好运了。他将从明眼人变成瞎子，／从富翁变成乞丐，／到外邦去，用手杖探着路前进。／他将成为／和他同住儿女的父亲和兄弟，／他生母的儿子和丈夫，／他父亲的凶手和共同的播种人。"

		when you're so clearly out to murder me,	
		so blatantly to steal my throne?³⁸	**blatantly:** 公然地
370		Good god, just answer this:	
		did you regard me as a coward or fool	**coward:** 懦夫
		when you embarked upon this scheme?	**scheme:** 阴谋
		Or else perhaps you thought that if you sidled up on me	**sidle:** 偷偷行动
		by stealth, then I would blithely notice nothing,	**stealth:** 暗中行动
375		and would not defend myself.	**blithely:** 轻率地
		It is a foolish undertaking to attempt to seize	**undertaking:** 任务
		a throne without a good supply of gold and friends—	**seize:** 攫取
		you'd need a mass of troops and funds for that.	**mass:** 大量
	Creon:	I tell you this: you should now listen	
380		to my counter-speech, and only then make up your mind.	**counter-speech:** 回话
	Oedipus:	You're skilled at speaking,	
		but I'm bad at listening... to you at least,	
		because I've found in you my deadly enemy.	**deadly:** 致命的
	Creon:	Now first you should hear what I say to that.	
385	**Oedipus:**	Don't tell me that you're not corrupt.	**corrupt:** 堕落的
	Creon:	If you consider mindless stubbornness	**mindless:** 欠考虑的
		a thing of value, you're not thinking straight.	
	Oedipus:	If you consider you can harm your kin,	**stubbornness:** 固执
		and go scot-free, then you're not sensible.	
390	**Creon:**	I grant you that the sentiment is just;	**straight:** 有条理的
		but tell me how you think I've done you wrong.	**sentiment:** 态度
	Oedipus:	Was it your advice, or was it not,	
		that I should send off for that sanctimonious seer?	**sanctimonious:** 伪善的
	Creon:	It was, and I still stand by that advice.	
395	**Oedipus:**	How long a time has passed since Laius...	**stand by:** 坚持
	Creon:	Since he did what? I cannot follow you.	
	Oedipus:	... has been gone, vanished, fatally struck down.	**vanish:** 消失
	Creon:	It would amount to many, many years.	**fatally:** 致命地
	Oedipus:	Was this man active as a prophet in those days?	**strike down:** 使丧命
400	**Creon:**	He was: a wise one, honoured then no less than now.	

---

38 *How dare you... steal my throne* (Lines 366-369): 在前面与忒瑞西阿斯的谈话中，由于忒瑞西阿斯谈话吞吞吐吐，含沙射影，俄狄浦斯已经在怀疑克瑞翁是否与忒瑞西阿斯沆瀣一气，串通起来攫取他的王位。所以，在见到克瑞翁的时候，俄狄浦斯用了很重的语气。

		Oedipus:	Did he refer to me at all back at that time?
		Creon:	No—not at least when I was standing near.
mount: 发起		**Oedipus:**	Did you not mount a search to find the murderer?
		Creon:	We did, of course—but not a thing emerged.
sage: 贤人	405	**Oedipus:**	How come, then, that this sage did not speak out?
		Creon:	I've no idea. And when I do not know, I hold my tongue[39].
		Oedipus:	Yet this you know, and could admit, were you my friend…
		Creon:	What's that? For if I know it, then I'll not refuse.
conspire: 密谋		**Oedipus:**	… that had he not conspired with you, he never
	410		would have talked of me as murderer of Laius,
		Creon:	Well, you're the one to know if that is what he said.
			But now it's fair for me to question you, as you have me.
		Oedipus:	Go on then, question: I shall not be proved a murderer.
		Creon:	Well then: you're married to my sister, yes?
	415	**Oedipus:**	Yes, there is no denying that.
		Creon:	And do you give her equal power as ruler here?
		Oedipus:	Whatever she may ask from me she gets.
		Creon:	And am I not a third, and equal to the two of you?
		Oedipus:	And that is why you've proved a treacherous friend.
	420	**Creon:**	Not if you see things as I do: so just consider this.
			Do you think anyone would rather be a ruler
			dogged by fear than sleep secure,
wield: 行使			if they could still wield no less power?
			Well, I for one have no desire to be a king
	425		in preference to living like a king;
			no, nor would anyone with any sense.
			…
plotter: 阴谋者		**Oedipus:**	But when a secret plotter's making rapid moves,
countermove: 反制行动			I must be quick to countermove in turn.
			If I just sit and wait here patiently,
	430		then he'll achieve his aims
			while mine are lost and gone.
		Creon:	So what is it you want? To send me into exile?
		Oedipus:	No, no, it is your death, not just exile.

---

39 *hold one's tongue*: 保持沉默，不说话。e.g. Do not speak when you should hold your tongue. 该保持沉默的时候不要作声。

	Creon:	Now you have shown how deep resentment goes.	
435		You won't relent, or trust in me at all?	relent: 缓和；宽容
	Oedipus:	I know a traitor when I see one.	traitor: 叛徒
	Creon:	Because you are not thinking for the best.	
	Oedipus:	What's best for me, I am.	
	Creon:	But you should think of me no less.	
440	Oedipus:	But you're corrupt.	
	Creon:	Suppose you're wrong?	
	Oedipus:	Rule has to be maintained.	maintain: 维持
	Creon:	But not by someone who misrules.	misrule: 不当统治
	Oedipus:	Thebes, hear him, Thebes!	
445	Creon:	My city too, not only yours.	

Enter Iocasta from the house.

	Iocasta:	Stop! Why have you embarked	
		upon this war of words, you foolish men?	
		Have you no shame, that, though our land is sick like this,	
		you start upon some private feud?	feud: 争斗
450		(*to Oedipus*) You go inside.	
		And, Creon, go to your own home as well.	
		Don't make a mighty storm out of some petty pain.	petty: 微小的
	Creon:	Sister, your husband Oedipus is making	
		fearsome threats against me:	fearsome: 可怕的
455		to thrust me into banishment, or else put me to death.	thrust: 强加
	Oedipus:	That's true: because, dear wife, I've caught him	
		scheming ways to do me vicious harm.	vicious: 恶毒的
	Creon:	(*solemnly*)	
		May I live damned and die accursed,	damn: 谴责
		if I have done these things you charge me with.	accursed: 被诅咒的
460	Iocasta:	I beg you, by the gods, believe him, Oedipus.	
		Above all else respect the oath he swears upon the gods,	oath: 誓言
		then me and these men present here.	
		...	

SCENE 6

	Iocasta:	Please let me know as well, my lord,	
		what matter has provoked so fierce a fury in your heart.	provoke: 挑起
			fury: 愤怒
465	Oedipus:	I shall tell, seeing that I hold you, wife,	

	more highly than these men.
	It's Creon; he has laid such plots against my life.
Iocasta:	As clearly as you can, explain just how
	this quarrel was provoked.
470 Oedipus:	He says I was the murderer of Laius.
Iocasta:	He claims to know this?
	Or taking it from someone else?
Oedipus:	He sent along a crooked prophet-man to speak for him,
	so that he keeps his own mouth free from[40] blame.
475 Iocasta:	Then you can free yourself from those concerns.
	Just listen as I shall convince you there is no one human
	knows the science of prophecy.
	And here's my pithy proof of this.
	One day an oracle was brought to Laius—
480	I don't say from Apollo, but his ministers—[41]
	which said it was his fate to be killed
	by a son who would be given birth by me and him.[42]
	Yet he, as is reported, was cut down by foreign bandits
	where three wagon-tracks converge.
485	As for the child, when it was less than three days old,
	he fixed its ankle-joints,
	and put it into someone else's hands
	to cast out on a trackless mountainside.
	And so Apollo never brought those things to pass:
490	that boy was not his father's murderer,
	and Laius did not incur that dreadful fate
	at his son's hand, as he so feared.

crooked: 阴险的

concern: 忧虑

pithy: 精辟的

minister: 祭司

wagon-track: 马车道
converge: 交汇
ankle-joint: 踝关节
trackless: 无人迹的

incur: 招致
dreadful: 可怕的

---

40 *free from*: 不受……影响，免受……的。e.g. Keep the table free from dirt by putting a cover over it. 铺上一块桌布以免弄脏桌子。

41 伊俄卡斯忒本来是敬神的，但是因为神示牺牲了自己的孩子，还救不了她的丈夫。这件事使她相信只有天神才能知道未来，凡人是没有预知的本领的。所以她现在说，那种神示并不是阿波罗亲自说出来的，而是祭祀假造的。

42 神示这样说："拉布达科斯的儿子拉伊俄斯啊，我答应你的请求，给你一个儿子。但是你要小心，你命中注定会死在你儿子手中！这命运是宙斯注定的；因为他听了珀罗普斯的诅咒，珀罗普斯抱怨你杀死他的儿子，想要复仇，才祈求宙斯给你这样的命运。"拉伊俄斯曾拐带珀罗普斯的儿子克律西波斯，这孩子一离家就自杀了。这是拉伊俄斯一家人灾难的根源。

	Yet that is what the fortune-telling prophecies	
	had mapped out[43] in advance.	
495	So you should pay them no attention, none.	
	For when a god requires some course,	
	then he will easily reveal it for himself.	
Oedipus:	Something you said just now	
	has set my mind in turmoil, wife,	**turmoil:** 骚动
500	and sent it on a wandering way.	**wander:** 漫游
Iocasta:	What worry is it makes you flinch and speak like this?	**flinch:** 畏惧
Oedipus:	Did I not hear you say that Laius was murdered	
	when three wagon-tracks converge?	
Iocasta:	That's how it was reported, and is still the word.	
505 Oedipu:	What is the region where this deed took place?	
Iocasta:	The country is called Phocis:	
	there the track from Thebes divides,	
	one way to Delphi, while the other comes from Daulia.[44]	
Oedipus:	And how much time has passed since this event?	
510 Iocasta:	It was announced in Thebes not long before the time	
	when you emerged as ruler her.	
Oedipus:	Oh Zeus, what are set on[45] doing with my life?	
Iocasta:	What is this, Oedipus, so pressing on your mind?	
Oedipus:	Don't ask me. First describe what Laius looked like;	
515	what stage of life he'd reached.	
Iocasta:	Well, he was tall; his hair was newly sprinkled grey;	**sprinkle:** 点缀

---

43 *map out*: 制定（计划），筹划，安排。e.g. Each Monday we map out the week's work. 每个星期一我们把这一周的工作安排好。

44 *Phocis, Delphi, Daulia*: 这三个地名分别是：福喀斯、得尔福和道利亚。福喀斯在希腊中部，得尔福和道利亚同是这个区域里的两座古城。从忒拜城到得尔福要经过这个三岔口，现在还叫三岔口。从道利亚沿着帕耳那索斯东麓下行，一个半小时可以走到。哲布在他的《现代希腊》第 79 页这样说："从得尔福和从道利亚前来的道路会合处有一个灰色的小荒丘，还有一条道路向南支去。我们可以从那地方望见俄狄浦斯由得尔福前来的道路。我们沿着那被他杀死的人所走过的道路走去，前路很荒凉，右边是帕耳那索斯山，左边是赫利孔山北麓。那南方现出一个峡谷，上接赫利孔山，峡谷里的荒石间点缀着稀疏的青翠，那景象真是雄壮与苍凉。"得尔福在距雅典 150 公里的帕耳那索斯深山里，是世界闻名的古迹。主要由阿波罗太阳神庙、雅典女神庙、剧场、体育训练场和运动场组成，其中最著名的是古代希腊象征光明和青春并且主管音乐、诗歌及医药、畜牧的太阳神阿波罗的神庙。古希腊人认为，得尔福是地球的中心，是"地球的肚脐"。

45 *be set on (upon)*: 决心要，一心想，专心于。e.g. My daughter is set on becoming an airline pilot. 我女儿一心要当飞机驾驶员。

		and not dissimilar to you in build.
	Oedipus:	O this is terrible! I think I've put myself, all unaware,
		beneath a dreadful curse.
520	Iocasta:	What do you mean, my lord? I feel afraid to look at you.
	Oedipus:	I have a creeping fear the prophet can see clear.
		You would make things firmer with one answer more.
	Iocasta:	I'm frightened, but I'll answer anything you ask.
	Oedipus:	Did he go in a simple style,
525		or like a head of state with lots of bodyguards?
	Iocasta:	The group was five in all, with one a herald;
		and there was just a single wagon carrying Laius.
	Oedipus:	O god, this is too clear!
		But who reported all these details at the time?
530	Iocasta:	A slave, the one man to survive and come back home.
	Oedipus:	Is he by chance inside the house right now?
	Iocasta:	I know he's not, since after he returned,
		and saw you in control, upon the death of Laius,
		he grasped my hand and begged to be sent off[46]
535		to where the sheep-flocks have their grazing grounds,
		so he might be as far away from any sight
		of Thebes as he could be.[47]
		And I agreed to send him there: he was deserving,
		for a slave, of even greater gratitude than this.
540	Oedipus:	Could he be quickly fetched back here?
	Iocasta:	It's possible. But what make you ask?
	Oedipus:	I am afraid I may have said too much aloud,
		and that is why I want to see him now.
	Iocasta:	Then he shall come.
545		But surely I as well should rightly know, my lord,
		what weighs so anxiously upon your mind.
	Oedipus:	I shall not keep you in the dark,
		not now that my forebodings have advanced so far,

deserve: 应得
gratitude: 感激
foreboding: 预感

---

46 *send off*: 发送，寄出。e.g. Please see that these parcels are sent off at once. 请留意把这些包裹立即发送出去。

47 这人本是一个牧人，后来才做拉伊俄斯的侍从。他求离去的原因，一方面是害怕王宫里的污染，一方面是自觉惭愧，因为他们好几个人竟被一个路人打败了。

	for there is no one with more right than you	
550	to know what trials I'm going through.	
	My father's name was Polybus, the lord of Corinth,	
	my mother Dorian Merope.⁴⁸	
	I grew up honoured there as first among the citizens,	
	until a quirk of fortune struck—something surprising,	**quirk:** 急转
555	yet not worth all the trouble spent on it.	
	There was this man at dinner who had drunk too much,	
	and flushed with wine he called out	**flush:** 脸红
	that I was not my father's true-born son.	
	Although provoked, I just restrained myself that day,	
560	but on the next I went and put the issue	
	to my father and my mother: they were furious	**furious:** 愤怒的
	against the man who had let slip the insult.	
	I was glad of their assurances—and yet...	**assurance:** 保证
	this kept on needling me, and spreading.	
565	So without my father and my mother knowing,	
	I sailed secretly to Delphi.	
	Apollo sent me off dissatisfied	
	upon the matter that I went there for:	
	instead he uttered loud and clear	
570	foul and unbearable prediction.	**unbearable:** 无法忍受的
	He said that I was bound to make love	
	with my mother, and exhibit progeny	**progeny:** 子孙
	that people could not bear to look upon;	
	and I would be the killer	
575	of the father who begot me.	
	On hearing this, I turned my back upon⁴⁹	
	the land of Corinth; and I used the stars	
	to steer well clear of that direction, somewhere	**steer:** 引导
	where I could be sure I'd never see	
580	the shameful horrors of my evil oracle fulfilled.	**fulfil:** 实现

---

48 *My father's name... Dorian Merope*: 该句专有名词较多，可译为："我父亲名叫波吕波斯，是科林斯的国王，我母亲是多里斯人，名叫墨洛珀。"

49 *turn one's back on* (*upon*): 回避，不能面对（对付）。e.g. Why do you always turn your back on difficulties? 你为什么总是回避困难呢？

	And as I journeyed on, my path came to the region
	where you say this king of yours was killed.
	Now, wife, I'll tell you all the truth.
	As I approached this three-road place,
585	a herald came towards me with a man
cart: 马车	upon a horse-drawn cart, as you described.
	The man in front, with the old man's encouragement,
brute: 粗野的	began to use brute force to shove me off the road.[50]
shove: 猛推	I aimed a blow in anger at the one who hustled me.
hustle: 猛推 590	And then the old man kept a watch
	as I was passing by the cart,
goad: 刺棒	and brought the double spike-ends of this goad[51]
	right down upon my head.
	He more than paid for that.
595	I struck him sharply with my stick;
	and knocked down by this hand of mine,
topple: 倒下	he toppled headlong from the wagon.
headlong: 头朝下倒栽葱地	I killed them, every man.
	But if that stranger there was linked with Laius at all,
600	then who can be more wretched
	than this man before you here?
	What human more detested by the gods?
	No citizen's permitted do receive me in their house,
	no one can speak a word of greeting,
605	but must drive me from their homes.
	What's more, this curse was laid upon me
	by none other than myself.
	And I pollute the dead man's marriage-bed
embrace: 拥抱	by my embracing of his wife

---

50 那领路的人是传令官，俄狄浦斯从那条窄路下来的时候，遇见他在车前领路。那人携带着一根小杖，很容易辨认他是传令官。他很凶地叫俄狄浦斯让开，拉伊俄斯也从车上命令他让路。于是那马前的司车把俄狄浦斯推搡到一边，俄狄浦斯不能打击那神圣的传令官，便向司车打去。俄狄浦斯经过车旁的时候，被拉伊俄斯用刺棍打了一下，他便朝车上冲去，传令官赶快回头来救。俄狄浦斯竟打死了拉伊俄斯、传令官、司车和一个侍从，另一个侍从逃跑了。

51 *the double spike-ends of this goad*: 这刺棍的一端有两个尖头，是用来刺马的。司车下来带马往上走的时候，把刺棍留在了车上。

610	with these same hands as he was murdered by.	
	Am I not evil, utterly unholy?	**unholy:** 不神圣的
	I who must be exiled from this land,	
	and yet in exile never see my family,	
	nor take one step upon my fatherland—	
615	since otherwise I'm bound to go to bed	
	with my own mother, and to kill old Polybus,	
	the father who begot and raised me up.	
	Someone who reckoned this would be cruel treatment	**reckon:** 认为
	by a god would have it right.	**cruel:** 残酷的
620	By the great inviolate powers, I pray	**inviolate:** 神圣不可侵犯的
	I never, never look upon⁵² that day.	
	May I be blotted out from humankind,	
	before I see so foul a stigma branded on my life.	**stigma:** 污点
	...	**brand:** 烙印
	Iocasta: And when he has appeared, what is it that you want of him?	
625	**Oedipus:** I'll tell you what: if he turns out to say the same as you,	
	I shall have then escaped disaster's grip.	**grip:** 掌握
	Iocasta: What was it that you heard me say especially?	
	Oedipus: You said he witnessed that it was a band of robbers	**band:** 群
	killed him: if he sticks by that number—robbers—	
630	I was not the murderer.	
	There is no way that one can ever equal many.	
	If, on the other hand, he says it was a solitary men,	
	the balance of this action clearly tips me down.	**tip:** 倾覆
	Iocasta: Well, that is certainly the story as it was reported then;	
635	and he can not retract that back.	**retract:** 收回
	since all the city heard, not me alone.	
	And even if he does diverge from what he said before,	**diverge:** 偏离
	it's still impossible for him to make	
	the death of Laius confirm the oracle.	**confirm:** 证实
640	Apollo said that he was bound to meet his death	
	killed by my son: yet that poor infant	
	never murdered him, but it died first.	

---

52 *look upon*: 看待，看作。e.g. He had managed to pull himself together, and continued to look upon life as a positive experience. 他努力使自己振作起来，并一如既往地积极面对人生。

peer: 细看

                                  So as for prophecies, I never more shall **peer**
this way or that because of them.

645 **Oedipus:** You speak good sense. Yet all the same
send someone off to fetch that labourer without fail[53].

Iocasta: I'll have him fetched at once.
But now let's go indoors—I want to do whatever is your wish.

Oedipus and Iocasta go inside. ... Enter the Old Corinthian from the "abroad" direction.

prosper: 繁盛

Old Corinthian: May his lady-wife, then, **prosper** happy[54],
650   and with happy ones around her.

Iocasta: And I wish you the same for these kind words, old stranger.
But go on: what is it that you want,
and what is it you have to tell us?

Old Corinthian: Happy news, my lady, for your household and your husband.

655 **Iocasta:** What may that be? And who have you come from?

Old Corinthian: I'm from Corinth, and the news I'm bringing
will be pleasing—that's for certain—

sorrow: 悲伤

yet you may feel **sorrow** also.

Iocasta: What's this? How can it have this double power?

660 **Old Corinthian:** First, the people there intend to make him ruler
of the land of Corinth—that is what they're saying.

Iocasta: How come? Does ancient Polybus no longer rule?

bury: 埋葬

Old Corinthian: No because he'd dead and **buried**.

Iocasta: What's this you say, old man? That Polybus is dead?

665 **Old Corinthian:** Death deserves me if it's not the truth I tell you.

Iocasta: *(to servant)*
Quick, go and tell this to your master.
So, you oracles sent by the gods, see where you stand!
For ages Oedipus has steered clear of that man,
for fear that he would kill him:

---

53 *without fail*: 务必, 必定。e.g. You must be here by 10 o'clock without fail, or the coach will leave without you. 你务必于10点前到这儿来, 否则车就开了, 不等你。

54 *prosper happy*: 在这里指"全福", 即伊俄卡斯忒是有儿有女的, 与下一行中的 *with happy ones around her* 是一致的。

670		and yet now he's died by random chance,	random: 偶然的
		not by his hand at all.	

Enter Oedipus from the palace.

	Oedipus:	Well, dearest wife Iocasta, why have you	
		called me here outside the house?	
	Iocasta:	First hear the news from this old man. Then ask	
675		where all those solemn god-sent oracles have gone.	
	Oedipus:	Who is this man, and what has he to say to me?	
	Iocasta:	He's come from Corinth to report your father	
		is no longer: Polybus... he's dead.	
	Oedipus:	What is this, stranger? Give your news yourself.	
680	**Old Corinthian:**	If you want to hear my message plainly,	**plainly:** 清楚明了地
		then be certain he is dead, departed.	**departed:** 过世的
	Oedipus:	Was this by treachery? Or did some illness take him?	**treachery:** 阴谋
	Old Corinthian:	Just a little shift of balance	
		sends old bodies to their rest.	
685	**Oedipus:**	It was from illness, then, he died, poor man.	
	Old Corinthian:	Yes, and all the many years he'd measured in his life-	
		time⁵⁵.	
	Oedipus:	Well, well, dear wife!	
		So why should any man consult the mantic Pythian shrine,	**consult:** 询问
		or hearken to the birds which screech above our heads?	**shrine:** 圣殿
690		On their authority I was supposed to kill my father;	**hearken:** 倾听
		yet he's dead and laid beneath the earth,	**screech:** 尖叫
		while I stayed here, my blade at home untouched—	**blade:** 刀锋
		unless perhaps he gave up life from missing me:	
		that way he would have died because of me.⁵⁶	
695		In any case, old Polybus is resting down in Hades' realm,	**realm:** 领地
		and he has swept away these oracles of ours	
		along with him, completely valueless.	
	Iocasta:	And is that not what I've been telling you?	

---

55 *all the many years he'd measured in his lifetime*: 正常语序应该是 he'd measured all the many years in his lifetime。可译为：“他已经衡量（走完）他生命中所有这些年限”，也就是说他年高寿尽。

56 *unless perhaps... because of me* (Lines 693–694): 俄狄浦斯的意思是说，我没有用刀枪杀害我的父亲，如果他是因为思念我而死的，那么还可以说他是因我而死的。可译为：“除非说他是因为思念我而死的，／那么倒是我害死了他。”

astray: 迷失	**Oedipus:**	You have; but I've been led astray by fear.
700	**Iocasta:**	Well then, stop treating things like this so seriously.
	Oedipus:	But I must surely live in fear of making love...
		in my own mother's bed.
	Iocasta:	Why should we humans live in fear
		when fortune has control of us,
705		and there's no knowing anything
foresight: 先见		with certain foresight? It is best to live
		and let things be, so far as we are able to.
		That's why you should not be afraid about
		this union with your mother.
710		Just think how many men have gone to bed
		together with their mothers in their dreams.
		The man who wastes no time on matters such as these
weather: 经受住		can weather life most easily.
	Oedipus:	All your advice would be quite right,
715		were not my mother still alive.
		While she draws breath, I'm bound,
dread: 恐惧		however sensible your words, to live in dread.
	Iocasta:	At least your father's death shines as an eye of comfort.
	Oedipus:	A great one, yes: but I am still in dread of her who lives.
	Old Corinthian:	(*breaking in*)
720		May I ask who is this woman you are so afraid about?
	Oedipus:	It's Merope, old stranger, wife of Polybus.
	Old Corinthian:	What about her makes you fearful?
	Oedipus:	There was a dreadful, god-directed prophecy.
	Old Corinthian:	May another person hear it—or is it forbidden?
725	**Oedipus:**	You may of course: Apollo told me once
		that I was bound to sleep with my own mother,
		and to shed my father's blood with my own hands.
		And that is why I have been keeping
		Corinth at a distance for so long.
730		Meanwhile I've prospered: yet...
		how sweet it is to look into one's parents' eyes.
	Old Corinthian:	And it is in fear of that you've stayed away from there?
	Oedipus:	Yes, that, and not to be my father's murderer.
	Old Corinthian:	Since I've come in goodwill, I should surely

735		free your lordship from this terror?	lordship: 阁下
	Oedipus:	If you could, I would reward you handsomely.	terror: 恐惧
	Old Corinthian:	That is chiefly why I came here:	
		so that once you're home I might be well rewarded.	
	Oedipus:	But all the same I'll never ever venture near my parents.	
740	Old Corinthian:	Son, it's clear you have no notion what you're doing.	
	Oedipus:	Why? Tell me what you mean, old man.	
	Old Corinthian:	It's because of them you're steering clear of home?	
	Oedipus:	That's right: for fear Apollo turns out to be true.	
	Old Corinthian:	Meaning you would take pollution from your parents?	
745	Oedipus:	Precisely, old man. That's my constant dread.	constant: 持久的
	Old Corinthian:	Don't you realize that your fears are based on nothing?	
	Oedipus:	How can that be, as long as I'm the offspring of those parents?	offspring: 子孙
	Old Corinthian:	Because Polybus was nor your blood-kin.	blood-kin: 亲骨肉
	Oedipus:	What did you say? Polybus was not my parent?	
750	Old Corinthian:	Not a fraction more than I am—equally indeed.	fraction: 小部分
	Oedipus:	How can my father be the equal of a nobody?	
	Old Corinthian:	Since that man did not beget you, nor me neither.	
	Oedipus:	What was the reason, then, he called me "son"?	
	Old Corinthian:	You were once a present to him,	
755		taken from these hands of mine.	
	Oedipus:	If he'd received me from another's hands,	
		how could he then have cherished me so much?	cherish: 珍爱
	Old Corinthian:	He had long been childless, and that moved him.	
	Oedipus:	And when you gave, had you bought me?	
760		or just come upon⁵⁷ me?	
	Old Corinthian:	It was in the forest glens of Mount Cithaeron that I found you.	glen: 山谷
	Oedipus:	Why were you travelling in those parts?	
	Old Corinthian:	I was looking after flocks for summer pasture.	pasture: 草场
	Oedipus:	You mean you were a vagrant shepherd hired for pay?	vagrant: 流浪
765	Old Corinthian:	True, my son, and yet you—you I rescued at that crisis.	shepherd: 牧羊人

---

57 *come upon* (*on*): 偶然遇见，偶然发现。e.g. Any strange-looking object that is come upon by ramblers should be immediately reported to the police. 行人但凡发现任何可疑事物，应立即向警方报告。

affliction: 不幸的事

clamp: 夹子

pin: 钉住

humiliation: 蒙羞

Oedipus:	Why? What was wrong when first you took me up?
Old Corinthian:	Well, your ankle-joints could tell that story.
Oedipus:	Ah, why bring up that old affliction?
Old Corinthian:	I released you from the clamps that pinned your feet together.
770 Oedipus:	Humiliation I've derived from infancy.
Old Corinthian:	Yes, you take your name from that misfortune.
Oedipus:	For god's sake, did my mother or my father do this thing to me? Speak out.
Old Corinthian:	I've no notion. But the man who gave you must know better.
775 Oedipus:	You mean you took me from another, and you didn't come on me by chance?
Old Corinthian:	No, it was another shepherd passed you to me.
Oedipus:	Who was he? Can you say precisely who?
Old Corinthian:	I believe that he was called the slave of Laius.
780 Oedipus:	The man who used to be the ruler of this country here?
Old Corinthian:	That's it—he was shepherd to that very man.
Oedipus:	And is he still alive for me to see him?
	...
Oedipus:	Does anyone among you people present know the shepherd that he means?
785	you may have seen him working in the fields or here in town? Declare it, since the moment's come for all these things to be revealed.
	...
Oedipus:	(*turns to Iocasta*) Dear wife, you know that man we summoned recently: is he the one this man is speaking of?
790 Iocasta:	It doesn't matter who he means. Pay no attention to it. Disregard his words as empty air, don't give these things a second thought.
Oedipus:	That is impossible:

clue: 线索

795	when I have got such clues as these, I must reveal my origins.
Iocasta:	No, by the gods, if you have any care for your own life,

pry: 探查

do not pry into this.

		My suffering's enough.	suffering: 苦痛
800	Oedipus:	Take heart. For even if my mother is revealed	
		to be a slave, three generations slave,	
		you'll never be exposed as lowly born.	expose: 暴露
	Iocasta:	Please listen to me, all the same...	
		I beg of you, do not do this.	
805	Oedipus:	There is no way that you'll dissuade me:	dissuade: 劝阻
		I have got to find these matters out for sure.	
	Iocasta:	I'm only thinking of your good with this advice.	
	Oedipus:	This thinking of my good has been annoying me.	annoy: 惹恼
	Iocasta:	Poor man, I only hope	
810		you never find out who you are.	
	Oedipus:	Go, fetch that shepherd for me, someone.	
		Leave her to glory in her high-class pedigree.	glory: 荣耀
	Iocasta:	Ah sorrow, man of sorrow!	pedigree: 血统
		That's the only title I can give to you.	
815		And nothing other ever.	

Iocasta rashes off into the palace...

SCENE 8

The Old Slave of Laius slowly approaches from the "away" direction.

	Oedipus:	I would conjecture, gentlemen,
		although I've never had to do with him,
		that this must be the shepherd we've been seeking for.
		For, look, he matches this man here in length of years;
820		also I know these servants bringing him are men of mine.
		But you can tell this better than I can,
		because you've seen the man before.
		...
	Oedipus:	Stranger from Corinth, I shall ask you first:
		is this the man in question?
825	Old Corinthian:	There he stands before your eyes, sir.
	Oedipus:	*(to the old Theban)*
		Hey you, old man, here, look me in the face
		and answer everything I ask you.
		Did you once belong to Laius?

	Old slave of Laius:	That's right. I was his slave—not purchased,
830		born and bred within the household.
	Oedipus:	What kind of work? How did you use your time?
	Old slave of Laius:	Most of my life I've spent in tending flocks.
	Oedipus:	And in what regions have you mostly herded them?
	Old slave of Laius:	There was Cithaeron and the highlands thereabouts.
835	**Oedipus:**	And did you ever know this man from there?
	Old slave of Laius:	Know doing what? What man d'you mean?
	Oedipus:	This man who's standing here.
		Have you encountered him?
	Old slave of Laius:	Not such that I could say from memory.
840	**Old Corinthian:**	That is not surprising, master.
		But it should be easy to remind him clearly.
		Surely he'll remember how we, up around Cithaeron,
		used to pass the time together,
		three years in succession, six months spring to autumn,
845		him with double flock, and me with single.
		Then with winter coming, I would drive
		my creatures to their home-pens;
		and he would drive his to the folds of Laius.[58]
		(*to the old slave*) Did it used to be just as I say, or not?
850	**Old slave of Laius:**	Yes, that's all true—although it was long, long ago.
	Old Corinthian:	Tell me, then, do you remember giving me
		a little boy to foster and bring up as mine?
	Old slave of Laius:	What's that? What makes you ask me that?
	Old Corinthian:	(*indicating Oedipus*)
		This is him, my old friend:
855		he is the man who was that little babe.
	Old slave of Laius:	(*fiercely*)
		To hell with you! I tell you, hold your tongue
	Oedipus:	No, no don't threaten him, old man:
		it's your words call for threats far more than his.
	Old slave of Laius:	Why, mighty lord? What have I done that's wrong?
860	**Oedipus:**	Not answering the question

58　*Surely he'll remember... to the folds of Laius* (Lines 842-848)：波吕波斯的牧人于 3 月间从科林斯赶羊上喀泰戎山，在那里遇见拉伊俄斯的牧人，后者是从忒拜平原来的。他们在山上住了 6 个月，直到 9 月中晨星出现时，他们才各自赶着羊回家。

	this man asked about the child.
Old slave of Laius:	Because he does not realize what he's saying...
	he's **interfering** over nothing⁵⁹.
Oedipus:	If you won't speak **obligingly**:
	you'll speak when you're in pain all right.
Old slave of Laius:	No, by the gods, don't hurt me, an old man.
Oedipus:	(*to his attendants*)
	Quick, one of you tie back his arms.
Old slave of Laius:	Why, why? What is it that you want to know?
Oedipus:	First, did you give this man the child he asked about?
Old slave of Laius:	I did give him—if only I had died that day?
Oedipus:	You will die now, if you don't tell the honest truth.
Old slave of Laius:	Far worse than that, if I *do* speak.
Oedipus:	(*threatening punishment*)
	It would appear the man is trying to delay.
Old slave of Laius:	No, no, I'm not. I've said I handed him the child.
Oedipus:	Where did you get it from?
	From your own home, or someone else's?
Old slave of Laius:	No, not my own: I had the child from someone.
Oedipus:	I citizen? Which one? Out of which house?
Old slave of Laius:	No, by the gods, good master, no, don't ask me more.
Oedipus:	It's death for you, if I am made to question you again.
Old slave of Laius:	All right: the child came from the house of Laius.
Oedipus:	Was it a slave, or was it one from his own kin?
Old slave of Laius:	Ay me, I'm on the **verge** of speaking the obscene truth...
Oedipus:	And I of hearing it: yet hear it out I must.
Old slave of Laius:	The boy was called his own.
	But she inside could **hest**
	tell you the facts, your wife...
Oedipus:	Was she the one who gave it you?
Old slave of Laius:	Her, yes, my lord.
Oedipus:	What was her reason?
Old slave of Laius:	So that I would do away with it.
Oedipus:	Her own child?

interfere: 介入

obligingly: 亲切地

verge: 边缘

hest: 命令

59　*over nothing*: 无事生非，杞人忧天。e.g. There is a huge difference! I can't believe that you wasted a weekend worrying over nothing. 区别很大！我无法相信你浪费了一个周末来杞人忧天。

	Old slave of Laius:	She was afraid of deadly prophesies.
	Oedipus:	What?
895	**Old slave of Laius:**	That he would shed his parents' blood.
	Oedipus:	Then why, why hand it on to this old man?
	Old slave of Laius:	I did it out of pity, master.

I supposed that he would take the child
off to another land, to where he came from.

preserve: 保存 900 But he preserved it for the very worst:
because if you are who he says,
then you were surely born to sorrow.

Oedipus: (*with a terrible cry*)
It all has come out clear.
Now, light of day, may this be my last sight of you.⁶⁰

905 I am the man who's been exposed
as born from those I should not,

couple: 结合 coupled with those I should not,
killing those I never should have killed.

PART 4

EXERCISES

I. Answer the following questions according to the reading text.

1. At the beginning of the play, why did the old priest in Thebes come to Oedipus for help? What was Oedipus' attitude towards that?

2. What message did Creon bring back from Delphi?

3. What did Oedipus want Tiresias to tell? Did Tiresias want to tell the whole truth? Why?

4. What was Oedipus' response to Tiresias' words? Did Oedipus understand Tiresias' remarks and good intention?

5. Why did Oedipus quarrel with Creon?

6. When Iocasta knew that her husband and her brother were quarrelling, what was her attitude? Did she believe her husband's accusation?

---

60 *Now, light of day, may this be my last sight of you*: 这不仅暗示他要弄瞎眼睛，还暗示他要自杀。

7. When Iocasta knew that her husband was provoked by prophecy, what was her response? Did she believe in those prophecies? Why?

8. When did Oedipus become aware that he was closely related to the murder of Laius?

9. Why did Oedipus keep away from Corinth? What was his response when he first heard from the old Corinthian that his parents died in Corinth?

10. When the old Corinthian told Oedipus and Iocasta that Oedipus was not a true-born son of Corinthian king Polybus, what were their responses respectively?

11. Why was the old slave of Laius reluctant and angry to answer Oedipus and the old Corinthian's question?

12. Was Apollo's oracle fulfilled in Oedipus?

II. Paraphrase the following lines with your own words, and then translate them into Chinese.

1. (Lines 24–31)   Our city's foundering, and can no longer

keep its head above the bloody surf of death.

The buds that should bear fruit become disease,

our grazing cattle-flocks become disease;

our women's labour-pains produce still-births.

Detested Plague, the god who lights the fever-fires,

has pounced upon our town,

and drains the homes of Thebes to empty husks.

2. (Lines 146–153)   Back from the first beginnings I shall beam a light once more.

For rightly has Apollo turned attention

to this matter of the murdered man—and you as well.

So you shall see me justly join in fighting hard

to win full vengeance for this land and for the god.

I'll act as best I can, not as for some remote

acquaintance, but for my own self,

to banish this miasma from our air.

3. (Lines 244–246)   I say that, unaware of it, you're living

in a state of shame with those you hold most close;

and you can't fathom how the place you're at is bad.

4. (Lines 319–321) I cannot bear to listen any more to this man's raving.

to hell with you—best turn back round,

and hurry far off from this house.

5. (Lines 381–383) You're skilled at speaking,

but I'm bad at listening... to you at least,

because I've found in you my deadly enemy.

6. (Lines 420–426) Not if you see things as I do: so just consider this.

Do you think anyone would rather be a ruler

dogged by fear than sleep secure,

if they could still wield no less power?

Well, I for one have no desire to be a king

in preference to living like a king;

no, nor would anyone with any sense.

7. (Lines 485–488) As for the child, when it was less than three days old,

he fixed its ankle-joints,

and put it into someone else's hands

to cast out on a trackless mountainside.

8. (Lines 612–617) I who must be exiled from this land,

and yet in exile never see my family,

nor take one step upon my fatherland—

since otherwise I'm bound to go to bed

with my own mother, and to kill old Polybus,

the father who begot and raised me up.

9. (Lines 703–713) Why should we humans live in fear

when fortune has control of us,

and there's no knowing anything

with certain foresight? It is best to live

and let things be, so far as we are able to.

That's why you should not be afraid about

this union with your mother.

Just think how many men have gone to bed

together with their mothers in their dreams.

The man who wastes no time on matters such as these

can weather life most easily.

10. (Lines 790–793) It doesn't matter who he means.

Pay no attention to it.

Disregard his words as empty air,

don't give these things a second thought.

11. (Lines 903–908) It all has come out clear.

Now, light of day, may this be my last sight of you.

I am the man who's been exposed

as born from those I should not,

coupled with those I should not,

killing those I never should have killed.

III. Figure out the meanings of the phrases in bold, and then make another sentence with each of the phrases.

1. (Lines 73–74)   And after all my searching I have found

 once single remedy—and that I've **set in action**.

2. (Lines 140–141)   But when your king had met his end so violently,

 what could have **held you back** from finding out?

3. (Lines 173–175)   **In case** you have not heard this news,

 Apollo has replied to us when we enquired,

 that there is only one solution for this plague.

4. (Lines 218–219)   I shall explain no more.

 Feel free to rage at that as fiercely as you like.

5. (Line 394)   It was, and I still **stand by** that advice.

6. (Lines 498–499)   Something you said just now

 has **set my mind in turmoil**, wife.

7. (Lines 547–548) I shall not **keep you in the dark**,

   not now that my forebodings have advanced so far.

8. (Lines 606–607) What's more, this curse was **laid upon me**

   by none other than myself.

9. (Lines 728–729) And that is why I have been **keeping**

   Corinth **at a distance** for so long.

10. (Lines 797–802) Iocasta: No, by the gods, if you have any care for your own life,

    do not **pry into** this.

    My suffering's enough.

    Oedipus: **Take heart**. For even if my mother is revealed

    to be a slave, three generations slave,

    you'll never be exposed as lowly born.

IV. Because of their long history and cultural influence in the West, some words and expressions in *Oedipus the King* carry on cultural meanings. Try to find out the cultural meanings of the following words and expressions.

1. Oedipus Complex
2. Sphinx's riddle
3. Omphalos of Delphi or navel of the earth

V. Summarize the whole story in your own words and write them down with no less than 200 words.

UNIT 4

Republic
A Socratic Dialogue

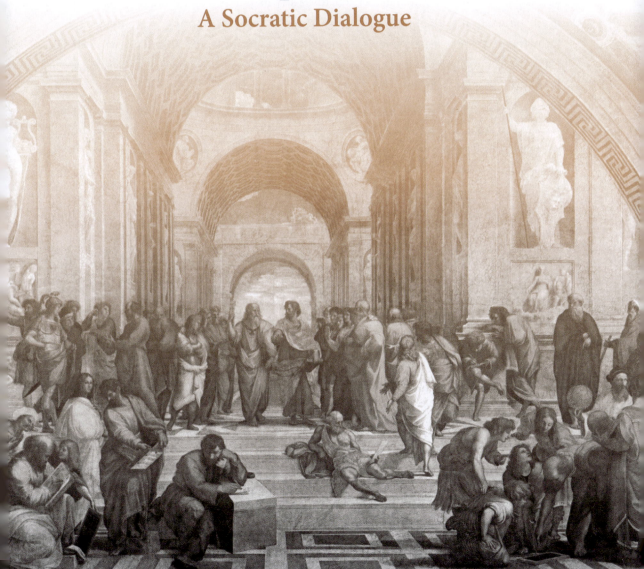

Oral tasks

1. What is morality in your understanding?
2. Have you ever heard of Plato or his *Republic*? Say something about them.

Introduction

Socratic dialogue is a literary genre developed in Greece at the turn of the fourth century BCE. The dialogues are either dramatic or narrative and Socrates is often the main participant. It mainly discusses moral and philosophical issues, such as knowledge, values, reasons, justice, morality, etc. Because Socratic dialogue is closely related to Plato's works, the subsequent philosophers also refer the literary genre as Platonic dialogue.

Plato is one of the world's best known and most widely read and studied philosophers. He was the student of Socrates and the teacher of Aristotle, and he wrote in the middle of the fourth century BCE in ancient Greece. Though influenced primarily by Socrates, to the extent that Socrates is usually the main character in many of Plato's writings, he was also influenced by Heraclitus, Parmenides, and Pythagoras.

Republic is Plato's best-known work, and has proven to be one of the world's most influential works of philosophy and political theory, both intellectually and historically. The ambitious project of the book is to demonstrate that morality is beneficial to its possessor—that, in fact, an individual gains in happiness by being moral whether or not any external advantages accrue to him. Plato gets down to the task of demonstrating that morality is the major cause of happiness in an individual's life by trying to define morality, or its psychological parameters, and then by proving that anyone with this psychological state is better off than anyone without it.

PART 3

TEXTUAL READING[1]

Chapter 2 The Challenge to Socrates: Morality vs. Immorality

Glaucon[2] and Adeimantus[3] (Plato's brothers) now become Socrates' **interlocutors** for the rest of the book. Socrates has claimed that morality enables us to proper; they demand a full **justification** of this claim. Instead of the more usual views that morality is (a) not good, but a lesser evil (Glaucon), and (b) valued only for its external rewards (Adeimantus), they challenge Socrates to prove that morality is **intrinsically** good and rewarding, and that it contributes towards a moral person's happiness.[4]

interlocutor: 对话者

justification: 辩护

intrinsically: 内在地

1 ▶ At this point, I thought I'd be **exempt** from further talking but apparently that was only the **preamble**. You see, it's not in Glaucon's nature to cut and run from anything, and on this occasion he refused to accept Thrasymachus'[5] **capitulation**, but said, "Socrates, do you want us really to be **convinced** that in all **circumstances** morality is better than immorality or merely to pretend to be?"[6]

exempt: 免除

preamble: 开场白

capitulation: 要点

convince: 信服

circumstance: 情况

---

1 本篇出自：Plato. *Republic*. Translated with introduction and notes by Robin Waterfield. Oxford: Oxford University Press, 1993。在第一章中，苏格拉底认为道德就是帮助朋友，绝不伤害任何人。色拉叙马霍斯则认为"道德对强者有利，不道德则仅对自身有利。"苏格拉底认为这个定义不清晰，逐步提出质疑，最终使得色拉叙马霍斯无言以对。本章标题中的"Morality vs. Immorality"为编者所加。与之前的大多数译本不同，本译本采用的是"morality"，而不是"justice"。

2 *Glaucon*: 格劳孔。

3 *Adeimantus*: 阿得曼托斯。

4 本段是译者对这一章的简要概括，并不是《理想国》中的内容。

5 *Thrasymachus*: 色拉叙马霍斯。

6 *Socrates... to pretend to be*: 这个句子有两个并列关系的句子，即（do you want us really）to be convinced 与（do you want us）merely to pretend to be。可译为："苏格拉底，在任何情况下道德都比不道德好，你是希望我们真心实意地接受这一点，还是希望我们假装接受？"（注：本篇译文参考了郭斌和张竹明翻译的《理想国》，北京：商务印书馆，1986。下同。）

conviction: 判断
genuine: 真诚的

2 ▸ "If it were up to me," I replied, "I'd prefer your conviction to be genuine."

3 ▸ "Well," he remarked, "your behaviour is at odds with[7] your wishes, then. I mean, here's a question for you. Don't you describe as good something which is welcomed for its own sake[8], rather than because its consequences are desired? Enjoyment, for instance, and all those pleasures which are harmless and whose future consequences are only enjoyable?"[9]

4 ▸ "Yes," I agreed, "'good' seems to me the right description for that situation."

5 ▸ "And what about things which are welcome not just for their own sakes, but also for their consequences? Intelligence, sight, and health, for instance, are evidently welcomed for both reasons."

6 ▸ "Yes," I said.

moneymaking: 赚钱的

7 ▸ "And isn't there, in your experience," he asked, "a third category[10] of good things—the category in which we find exercise, medical treatment, and any moneymaking job like being a doctor? All these things are regarded as nuisances, but beneficial, and are not welcomed for their own sakes, but

---

7 *at odds (with)*: 争吵，不一致，不和。e.g. The two brothers were often at odds. 这两兄弟经常争吵。

8 *for one's own sake*: 为自己打算，只是为了……本身。e.g. For my own sake as well as for yours, I will do my best. 出于对我自己和对你的考虑，我一定尽力而为。

9 *Enjoyment... are only enjoyable*: 这里并不是一个完整的句子，说话者只是在这里列举了两种情况，即 enjoyment 和 all those pleasures，后面的两个定语从句是用来限定这两种情况的。可译为："例如，欢乐，以及所有那些无害的快乐，它们未来的后果仅仅只是欢乐而已。"也就是没有后果。前面一句说，人们渴望某些善是因为它的后果，而不是善本身。本例是想证明人们可以不因为后果而喜欢这些善，比如欢乐等。

10 在英文版中，这里是 category，但在《理想国》的原文中这里第一次出现著名词语 eidos。它给予所谓的"思想或形式的理论"一个名称，是柏拉图首要的或最基本的存在学说。这个学说的意义一直存在争议。从词源上讲，eidos 是从动词"to see"（看）派生出来的，表示"一个事物的外表"——它是什么样子，它区分于其他一切事物的可视特征。在这段对话中，它表示"某种事物"，一个"类"；这个意义与前面的意义之间的联系非常明显。（本注释来自谢祖均翻译的《理想国》，北京：中央编译出版社，2013。以下简称"谢祖均译本"。）

for their financial rewards and other consequences."[11]

8▶ "Yes," I agreed, "there is this third category as well. What of it?"

9▶ "To which category do you think morality belongs?" he asked.

10▶ "In my opinion," I replied, "it belongs in the best category—the category which anyone who expects to be happy should welcome both for its own sake and for its consequences[12]."

11▶ "That's not the usual view," he said, "which consigns morality to the nuisance category of things which have to be done for the sake of financial reward and for the prospect of making a good impression, but which, taken in isolation, are so trying that one should avoid them."

consign: 交付

prospect: 前景
isolation: 孤立
trying: 难受的

12▶ "I'm aware of this view," I said, "and it's the reason why Thrasymachus has been running morality down all this time, and praising immorality. But I'm slow on the uptake[13], apparently."

run down: 贬低

13▶ "All right, then," he said, "listen to what I have to say too, and see if you agree with me. The point is that Thrasymachus gave up too soon, in my opinion: you charmed him into docility as if he were a snake. The arguments that have been offered about both morality and immorality leave me unsatisfied, however, in the sense that I still want to hear a definition of them both, and to be told what the effect is of the occurrence of each of them in the mind—each of them in isolation, without taking into consideration financial reward

charm: 施魔法
docility: 顺从

---

11 *All these things... other consequences*: 这个句子中的几个片段都拥有同一个主语 all these things，完整的句子应为 All these things are regarded as nuisances, but (all these things are) beneficial, and (all these things) are not welcomed for their own sakes, but for their financial rewards and other consequences。可译为："所有这些事物都被认为是让人讨厌的，但又都是有利可图的，它们受欢迎并不是由于他们自身的原因，而是因为它们的经济回报和其他的后果。"

12 *both for its own sake and for its consequences*: 事实上，柏拉图只用了很少的篇幅来谈论道德的后果。书中接下来主要谈论道德是"因其自身的原因"（for its own sake），即非外部的、内在的、相伴相生的，如快乐与幸福。柏拉图认为，正确理解的道德能够体现其本性，因此能够带来真正的快乐和幸福。

13 *slow (quick) on the uptake*: 理解力差（强），领会得慢（快）。e.g. Mary's always been a bit slow on the uptake. You have to say something a few times before she understands what you're talking about. 玛丽一向理解力差一点。你必须把话说上好几遍，她才听得懂你说的是什么。

or any other consequence they might have."[14]

revive: 重申

14 ▸ "So if it's all right with you, what I'll do is revive Thrasymachus' position. First, I'll explain the usual view of the nature and origin of morality; second, I'll claim that it is only ever practiced reluctantly, as something necessary, but not good; third, I'll claim that this behaviour is reasonable, because people are right to think that an immoral person's life is much better than a moral person's life."

countless: 无数的

hymn: 赞歌

virtue: 美德

possess: 具有

rejoinder: 反驳

commend: 赞美，称颂

15 ▸ "Now, I don't agree with any of this, Socrates, but I don't know what to think. My ears are ringing from listening to Thrasymachus and countless others, but I've never yet heard the kind of support for morality, as being preferable to immorality, that I'd like to hear, which is a hymn to the virtues it possesses in and of itself[15].[16] If I can get this from anyone, it'll be the immoral life; by doing so, I'll be showing you the kind of rejoinder I want you to develop when you criticize immorality and commend morality.[17] What do you think of this plan?"

---

14 *The arguments... they might have*: 在这个句子中，the arguments... unsatisfied 是一部分，指的是格劳孔对他们的探讨不满意；其余的部分讲的是格劳孔为什么不满意。这又分为两个方面：一是想弄清楚两者（指道德和不道德）的定义；二是想弄清楚两者分别会产生什么效果，而且这些都是在孤立的情况下考虑的。可译为："但是你所提出的关于道德与不道德的论证无法让我满意，无论如何，我还是想听听你对两者的定义，并告诉我两者在心灵中出现时所产生的效果——是在彼此孤立的情况下，不考虑它们的经济回报，或者其他可能产生的后果。"

15 *in and of itself*: 固有的，就其本身而言。e.g. Some, however, argue that the use of microblogs in and of itself does not make for better government. 然而，有些人却认为使用微博及其微博本身，并不能促使一个好政府的形成。

16 *My ears... in and of itself*: 这个句子中，as being preferable to immorality 用来说明前面的 morality，接下来的 that 和 which 引导两个定语从句用来限定 the kind of support for morality。可译为："我满耳朵听到的都是色拉叙马霍斯和无数其他人的议论，却从来没有听到过这种对道德的支持，即道德比不道德更可取。那是我想听到的，那是对其（道德）本身具有的美德的赞美。"

17 *If I can... morality*: 格劳孔在上一句中抱怨没有人赞美道德本身，承接上一句，格劳孔想通过与苏格拉底的辩论听到对道德本身的赞美。因此，他将在与苏格拉底的辩论中站在不道德的一方，将他不知道该如何辩驳的观点都提出来，让苏格拉底来阐述，从而得知对道德本身的赞美。这就是为什么他说"If I can get this（指的是对道德本身的赞美）from anyone, it'll be the immoral life"; it 指的是 anyone，意思是只有通过不道德的生活，我们才能听到对道德本身的赞美。可译为："如果我想听到对道德本身的赞美，那就只能是从不道德的生活那里得到。采用这种方法，我将各种反驳意见告诉你，我希望你在评判不道德和赞美道德的时候详细论述。"

16 ▶ "I thoroughly approve," I replied. "I mean, I can't think of another topic which any thinking person would more gladly see cropping up[18] again and again in his conversations."

17 ▶ "That's wonderful," he said. "Well, I promised I'd talk first about the nature and origin of morality, so here goes. The idea is that although it's a fact of nature that doing wrong is good and having wrong done to one is bad, nevertheless the disadvantages of having it done to one outweigh the benefits of doing it.[19] Consequently, once people have experienced both committing wrong and being at the receiving end of it, they see that the disadvantages are unavoidable and the benefits are unattainable; so they decide that the most profitable course is for them to enter into a contract with one another, guaranteeing that no wrong will be committed or received.[20] They then set about making laws and decrees, and from then on they use the terms 'legal' and 'right' to describe anything which is enjoined by their code. So that's the origin and nature of morality, on this view: it is a compromise between the ideal of doing wrong without having to pay for it, and the worst situation, which is having wrong done to one while lacking the means of exacting compensation. Since morality is a compromise, it is endorsed because, while it may not be good, it does gain value by preventing people from doing wrong. The point is that any real man with the ability to do wrong would never enter into a contract to avoid both wronging and being wronged: he wouldn't be so crazy. Anyway, Socrates, that is what this view has to say about the nature and origin of morality and so on."[21]

outweigh: 超过；大于

end: 结果

unattainable: 不可获得的

course: 方式

contract: 契约

guarantee: 保证

set about: 着手

right: 正义的

enjoin: 强令

code: 法规

compromise: 妥协

ideal: 理想状态

exact: 要求

compensation: 补偿

endorse: 认可

---

18 *crop up*: 被提到。e.g. The pills must be good because the name was always cropping up in the Seattle papers. 那些药片一定很不错，因为药片名经常在西雅图报纸上被提到。

19 *The idea... of doing it*: doing wrong is good 的意思是"做坏事（不道德的事情）是（对做的人）有利的"，having wrong done to one is bad 的意思是"坏事做到某人身上是不好的"。两句话一起说的是：人做坏事对自己是有利的，而当坏事发生在自己身上的时候，就是不利的。可译为："这种想法是，尽管人的本性的事实是做坏事有利，遭受坏事是不利的，但是遭受坏事所得到的不利超过了做坏事的好处。"

20 *Consequently, ... or received*: 这句反复强调的就是如何处理"对人犯错而获利"与"自己遭罪而遭殃"的关系。句子结构上，层层递进。可译为："因此，人们一旦体验犯错和遭罪之后，他们就会发现不利的一面（指遭殃）是不可避免的，而获利却并不可获得。因此，他们认为最好的方式就是彼此达成契约，保证既不犯错也不遭殃。"

21 格劳孔陈述在5世纪时期本性与惯例之间的区别。这种区别与诡辩运动尤其相关，更倾向于自然法中不同价值的竞争，而不是惯例法中不同价值的合作。服从法律是自然的，而不是因为我们选择形成和维护社会的结果——这种观点在现代社会是常见的。

scope: 能力范围

red-handed: 当场被抓的

superiority: 优越

destination: 目的

convention: 习俗

deviate: 偏离

crack: （使）破裂

chasm: 裂口

pasture: 放牧

fascinate: 着迷

artefact: 工艺品

hollow: 空的

stoop: 弯腰

corpse: 尸体

naked: 裸体的

protagonist: 主人公

18 ▸ "As for the fact that morality is only ever practiced reluctantly, by people who lack the ability to do wrong—this would become particularly obvious if we performed the following thought-experiment. Suppose we grant both types of people—moral and immoral—the scope to do whatever they want, and we then keep an eye on[22] them to see where their wishes lead them. We'll catch our moral person red-handed: his desire for superiority will point him in the same direction as the immoral person, towards a destination which every creature naturally regards as good and aims for, except that people are compelled by convention to deviate from this path and respect equality.[23]

19 ▸ They'd have the scope I'm talking about especially if they acquired the kind of power which, we hear, an ancestor of Gyges of Lydia once acquired. He was a shepherd in the service of the Lydian ruler of the time, when a heavy rainstorm occurred and an earthquake cracked open the land to a certain extent,[24] and a chasm appeared in the region where he was pasturing his flocks.[25] He was fascinated by the sight, and went down into the chasm and saw there, as the story goes, among other artefacts, a bronze horse, which was hollow and had windows set in it; he stooped and looked in through the windows and saw a corpse inside, which seemed to be that of a giant. The corpse was naked, but had a golden ring on one finger; he took the ring off the finger and left. Now, the shepherds used to meet once a month to keep the king informed about his flocks, and our protagonist came to the meeting wearing the ring. He was sitting down among the

---

22 *keep an eye on*: 密切注意，对……留心。e.g. The police have been keeping an eye on the thief ever since he came out of prison. 自从那个小偷出狱后，警方一直在密切地监视着他。

23 *We'll catch... respect equality*: 该句是为了说明前面的两句话而举的例子，即有道德的人也会与不道德的人一样做出同样的事情。可译为：“我们当场就能发现，有道德的人渴求优越感的欲望会驱使他到不道德的人同一个方向（即干相同的事情），驱使他到每一个生灵都自然而然地认为好的而且想到达的目的地，除非在习俗（惯例）的迫使下，偏离这条道路，尊重平等。”

24 *when a heavy rainstorm... a certain extent*: 在柏拉图时代，大雨被认为是造成地震的原因。另外，这一点也与希腊神话有关，波塞冬既是掌管水的神，也是掌管地震的神。

25 *He was a shepherd... his flocks*: 这个句子比较长，但结构并不复杂，整个句子的意思是由几个小句组合而成的。可译为：“他是一位牧羊人，当时为吕底亚人的统治者服务。一天出现了一阵狂风暴雨，地震劈裂了大地，在他放牧的地区出现了一个裂口。”

others, and happened to twist the ring's bezel in the direction of his body, towards the inner part of his hand. When he did this, he became invisible to his neighbours, and to his astonishment they talked about him as if he'd left. While he was fiddling about with the ring again, he turned the bezel outwards, and became visible. He thought about this and experimented to see if it was the ring which had this power; in this way he eventually found that turning the bezel inwards made him invisible and turning it outwards made him visible. As soon as he realized this, he arranged to be one of the delegates to the king; once he was inside the palace, he seduced the king's wife and with her help assaulted and killed the king, and so took possession of the throne."

20▸ "Suppose there were two such rings, then—one worn by our moral person, the other by the immoral person. There is no one, on this view, who is iron-willed enough to maintain his morality and find the strength of purpose to keep his hands off what doesn't belong to him, when he is able to take whatever he wants from the market-stalls without fear of being discovered, to enter houses and sleep with whomever he chooses, to kill and to release from prison anyone he wants, and generally to act like a god among men. His behaviour would be identical to that of the other person: both of them would be heading in the same direction.

21▸ Now this is substantial evidence, it would be claimed, that morality is never freely chosen. People do wrong whenever they think they can, so they act morally only if they're forced to, because they regard morality as something which isn't good for one personally. The point is that everyone thinks the rewards of immorality far outweigh those of morality—and they're right, according to the proponent of this view. The sight of someone with that kind of scope refusing all those opportunities for wrongdoing and never laying a finger on²⁶ things that didn't belong to him would lead people to think that he was in an extremely bad way, and was a first-class fool as well—even though their fear of being wronged might make them attempt to mislead

---

26 *lay a finger (hand) on*: 触动，触犯，对……动一根毫毛。e.g. It was always their mother who had to scold the children because their father wouldn't lay a finger on them. 倒是孩子们的母亲不得不经常责骂他们几句，因为父亲碰都不会碰他们一下。

others by singing his praises to them in public.²⁷

22 ▸ That's all I have to say on this. As for actually assessing the lives of the people we're talking about, we'll be able to do that correctly if we make the gap between a moral person and an immoral person as wide as possible. That's the only way to make a proper assessment. And we should set them apart from each other by leaving their respective immorality and morality absolutely intact, so that we make each of them a consummate professional. In other words, our immoral person must be a true expert. A top-notch ship's captain, for instance, or doctor, recognizes the limits of his branch of expertise and undertakes what is possible while ignoring what is impossible; moreover, if he makes a mistake, he has the competence to correct it. Equally, our immoral person must get away with any crimes he undertakes in the proper fashion, if he is to be outstandingly immoral; getting caught must be taken to be a sign of incompetence, since the acme of immorality is to give an impression of morality while actually being immoral. So we must attribute consummate immorality to our consummate criminal, and if we are to leave it intact, we should have him equipped with a colossal reputation for morality even though he is a colossal criminal.²⁸ He should be capable of correcting any mistakes he makes. He must have the ability to argue plausibly, in case²⁹ any of his crimes are ever found out, and to use force wherever necessary, by making use of his courage and strength and by drawing on his fund of friends and his financial resources.

---

assess: 评价
respective: 各自的
absolutely: 绝对地
intact: 原封不动的
consummate: 技艺高超的；完美的
professional: 专业人士
top-notch: 拔尖的
captain: 船长
expertise: 专长
fashion: 方式
outstandingly: 极其，非常
incompetence: 能力不足
acme: 极致
attribute: 归因于
criminal: 罪犯
reputation: 声望
plausibly: 貌似有理地

27　*The sight... in public*: 该句较长，主体结构是 The sight... would lead people to think... even though...。of someone... belong to him 都是作 sight 的定语，refusing all those... 与 never laying a finger on... 是并列结构，用来说明 someone with that kind of scope。可译为："某人具备了那种能力，拒绝所有做坏事的机会，绝不染指任何不属于他的东西。看到这样的人让人们以为他行为极其恶劣，而且还是头等傻瓜。尽管人们会因担心遭殃，而试图在公共场合对其他人高唱他的赞歌，来误导他们。"

28　*So we... a colossal criminal*: 因为前面一句已经说了将不道德的人做坏事看作是一个行业，因此，不道德到了极致其实就是一个极致的罪犯。这个极致的罪犯干了极致的坏事，但是，没有被抓住（如果被抓住了，那么他就算不上一个极致的罪犯了）。这样一来，我们就要赋予他巨大的声望，称他是一个非常有道德的人（因为从来就没有被抓住做坏事），尽管他是一个巨大的罪犯。可译为："因此我们必须将极致的不道德看作是极致的罪犯，而且如果我们不改变这种现状，那么我们就要赋予他巨大的道德声望，尽管他是一个巨大的罪犯。"

29　*in case*: 假使，如果，万一，以防。e.g. In case he arrives before I get back, please ask him to wait. 万一他在我回来之前到了，请叫他等一等。

23 ▸ Now that we've come up with this sketch of an immoral person, we must conceive of a moral person to stand beside him—someone who is straightforward and principled, and who, as Aeschylus says, wants genuine goodness rather than merely an aura of goodness. So we must deprive him of any such aura, since if others think him moral, this reputation will gain him privileges and rewards, and it will become unclear whether it is morality or the rewards and privileges which might be motivating him to be what he is. We should strip him of everything except morality, then, and our portrait should be of someone in the opposite situation to the one we imagined before. I mean, even though he does no wrong at all, he must have a colossal reputation for immorality, so that his morality can be tested by seeing whether or not he is impervious to a bad reputation and its consequences; he must unswervingly follow his path until he dies—a saint with a lifelong reputation as a sinner.[30] When they can both go no further in morality and immorality respectively, we can decide which of them is the happier."

24 ▸ "My dear Glaucon," I said, "I'm very impressed at how industriously you're ridding each of them of defects and getting them ready for assessment. It's as if you were working on statues."

25 ▸ "I'm doing the best I can," he replied. "And now that we've established what the two of them are like, I'm sure we won't find it difficult to specify what sort of life is in store for either of them. That's what I must do, then— and if my words are rather coarse, Socrates, please remember that the argument is not mine, but stems from those who prefer immorality to morality."

26 ▸ "Here's what they'll say: for a moral person in the situation I've described, the future holds flogging, torture on the rack[31], imprisonment in chains, having his eyes burnt out, and every ordeal in the book, up to and including

conceive: 设想
straightforward: 耿直的
principled: 原则性强的
aura: 光环
deprive: 剥夺
privilege: 特权
motivate: 驱动
strip of: 剥离
portrait: 描述
unswervingly: 坚定不移地
sinner: 罪人

industriously: 勤勉地
defect: 缺陷
statue: 雕像

coarse: 粗俗的
stem from: 源自

flog: 鞭挞
chain: 镣铐

---

30 *I mean, ... as a sinner*: 该句讲的是一个假设的情况，即一个有德的人却背负着无德的名声，看他是否能够无动于衷，依然坚定不移地坚守并且热爱做这样的有德人。如果依然热爱，那么就说明他真爱道德；如果不是，就说明他不过是热爱道德的声誉而已。这里的 he 是指有德之人。可译为："我是说，即使他根本没有做任何坏事，他也必须背负巨大的无德的名声，看他是否对（无德）坏名声及其后果无动于衷，这样一来就可以测试他的道德（他对道德的态度）；他必至死不渝地坚持他的道路——终其一生做一位背负着罪人名声的圣人。"

31 *on the rack*: 处于非常焦虑不安的状态；受到难以忍受的折磨（痛苦）。e.g. Let me know the result as soon as you can. I shall be on the rack till I get your wire. 尽早地让我知道结果吧。不收到你的电报，我将会非常焦虑不安。

impale: 钉住，刺穿	being impaled on a stake. Then at last he'll realize that one's goal should be not actual morality, but the appearance of morality. In fact, that phrase of Aeschylus' has far more relevance for an immoral person, in the sense that, as they will claim, it is really an immoral person who wants genuine
stake: 火刑柱	
occupation: 职业	immorality rather than merely an aura of immorality, because his occupation takes account of the way things are and his life is not concerned with appearances.³² He is the one who 'reaps the harvest of wise plans which
furrow: 沟	grow in his mind's deep furrow' ³³—and what he plans is first to use his reputation for morality to gain control over his country, and then to marry a woman from any family he wants, to have his children marry a woman from any family deal and do business with whomever he wants, and, over and
secure: 获得	above all this, to secure his own benefit by ensuring that his lack of distaste for
distaste: 厌恶	crime makes him a financial profit³⁴. If he's challenged privately or publicly, he wins the day and comes off better than his enemies; because he gains the upper hand³⁵, he gets rich; he therefore does good to his friends and harm to his enemies, and the religious rites he performs and the offerings he makes
adequate: 适当的	to the gods are not just adequate but magnificent; his service to the gods and to the men he favours is far better than a moral person's; and consequently
appropriate: 合适的	it is more appropriate for the gods to smile on him rather than on a moral person, and more likely that they will. And this, Socrates, is why both gods and men provide a better life for an immoral person than for a moral person, according to this view."

32 *In fact, ... with appearances*: 该句中 in the sense that 以及后面的成分是用来解释埃斯库罗斯的话，as they will claim 是插入语。该句主要是说只有无德的人才是真正的无德，有德的人并不是真正的有德，而只是有有德的名声而已。之所以如此，是因为无德的人没有必要考虑表面文章（只需要谋利），只考虑事物的本来面目即可。可译为："事实上，埃斯库罗斯所说的话与无德之人极其相关，即，正如他们所声称的那样，的确只有无德之人才想要真正的无德，而不是无德的光环，因为他所从事的职业只需要考虑事物的本来面目，他的生活并不关注表面文章。"

33 '*reaps the harvest... deep furrow*': 该句出自埃斯库罗斯的悲剧《七攻忒拜城》，其中定语从句 grow in his mind's deep furrow 指的是深谋远虑。可译为："拥有深谋远虑的明智计划，就能够获得丰收。"

34 *over and above... a financial profit*: 该表述中的 lack of distaste for crime 可借助译文来理解，即"并且在所有这些事情中，捞取种种好处，因为他没有怕人家说他不正义的顾忌。"

35 *the upper hand*: 优势，上风；支配地位。e.g. After a fierce struggle, he won the upper hand of his opponent. 经过一番激烈争斗，他占了对手的上风。

27 ▸ After Glaucon's speech, I was intending to make some reply to what he'd been saying, but his brother Adeimantus asked, "Surely you don't consider that an adequate treatment of the issue, do you, Socrates?"

28 ▸ "Why shouldn't I?" I said.

29 ▸ "It's precisely the most important point which has been omitted," he said.

30 ▸ "Well," I said, "as the saying goes, a man and his brother should stick together. So if Glaucon here has left anything out, you should back him up. As far as I'm concerned, however, even what he's already said is enough to floor me and make me a totally ineffective ally of morality."

back up: 援助

ally: 拥护者

31 ▸ "Rubbish," he said. "But don't let that stop you listening to what I have to say as well. In order to clarify Glaucon's meaning, we also have to go into the arguments for the opposite of his point—the arguments in favour of morality and against immorality. As you know, fathers point out to their sons the importance of morality and impress it upon them (as every guardian impresses it upon his ward) by singing the praises not of morality itself but of the good reputation it brings. The inducement they offer is that power, good marriage, and all the things Glaucon mentioned a moment ago come to someone who is thought to be moral as a result of this reputation: if a moral person gets them, it is because he is well thought of."

impress: 使牢记

inducement: 诱因

32 ▸ "They have more to say about the consequence of reputation. They adduce being well thought of by the gods, and then they have benefits galore to talk of, all the ones the gods are said to award to just people. There are, for instance, the statements of noble Hesiod[36] and of Homer. Hesiod says that the gods make 'oaks bear acorns on their outsides and bees in their centres'[37] for moral people; and he says that 'their woolly sheep are weighed

adduce: 引证
galore: 丰富的
noble: 高贵的
oak: 橡树
acorn: 橡树果子
woolly: 羊毛的;毛茸茸的

---

36 *Hesiod*: 赫西俄德，可能生活在公元前8世纪，比荷马生活的年代更久远。他以长诗《工作与农时》和《神谱》闻名于世。《工作与农时》包含许多忠告和理智的内容，它鼓励人们忠诚地工作、生活，反对休闲和不公正。《神谱》描写的是宇宙和神的诞生，是讲述希腊神话中各个神之间关系的作品。

37 '*oaks... in their centres*': 这句话中的橡树是用来比喻拥有声望的（所谓的）有德之人。果子（指好的东西）长在外面，而（有刺的）蜜蜂（指坏的东西）藏在里面。也就是说，那些所谓的有德之人不过是外表好看、内心邪恶的人。

claim: 声明；理由
righteous: 正义的
uphold: 维护
wheat: 小麦
barley: 大麦
yield: 产出
account: 描述
chaplet: 花冠
assumption: 假设
perpetual: 永久的
intoxication: 陶醉
legacy: 遗产

mud: 烂泥
sieve: 筛子

down by their fleeces'[38], and that they gain many other advantages. Homer makes very similar claims: 'As of some righteous king,' he says, 'who pleases the gods by upholding justice, and the dark earth bears wheat and barley, the trees hang heavy with fruit, the sheep steadily give birth, and the sea-waters yield fish.'"

33 ▶ "Musaeus[39] and his son claim that the gods give moral people even more exciting advantages. Once they've transported them, in their account, to Hades and got them reclining on couches for the party they've laid on[40] for just people, they next have them spending eternity wearing chaplets on their heads and drinking, on the assumption that the best possible reward for goodness is perpetual intoxication.[41] Others have the gods' rewards for morality lasting even longer: they say that the legacy left behind by a person who is just and keeps his promises is that his children's children are better people."

34 ▶ "These, and others like them, are the glowing terms in which they speak of morality. As for unjust and immoral people, they bury them in Hades in a kind of mud and force them to carry water in sieves[42], and they make sure that while they remain alive they are thought badly of; and they claim that all the punishments which Glaucon specified for people who, despite being

---

38 *'their woolly... their fleeces'*: 该引用与上面的引用一样。（作为外在的）羊毛比（作为内在的）羊本身还有价值，也就是说，外表比内在重要。

39 *Musaeus*: 墨塞俄斯，一个半神的歌手和预言家。据说他的诗都是以宇宙论为主题，柏拉图在这里不过是意指神秘的人物。

40 *lay on*: 组织，安排。e.g. A monumental feast has been laid on for the benefit of myself and of another Scottish friend. 大家为我和另外一位苏格兰朋友安排了盛大的宴会。

41 *Once they've... perpetual intoxication*: 该句的主体结构是 Once..., they next have...，其中主句是 they next have...，once 引导的是一个条件状语从句，条件状语从句中含定语从句 they've laid on for just people 来限定 the party（那一帮人）。on the assumption 后面接了一个同位语，用来说明 assumption，而 on the assumption 本身又是用来解释说明 drinking 的。可译为："按照他们的描述，他们将有德之人引导到冥界，就让诸神认为是正义的那帮人斜倚在卧榻之上享受，接下来诸神就让有德之人在永恒中头戴花冠，饮酒作乐，认为对善可能有的最好的回报就是永久的陶醉。"

42 *water in sieves*: 这是希腊神话中常见的一种惩罚措施，让受罚者重复做劳而无功的事情。

moral, are thought to be immoral are destined for immoral people.⁴³ They have no novel punishments to add to this list, however."

35 ▸ "Anyway, that's how morality is commended and immorality condemned. But there's also another point for you to take into consideration, Socrates. It's the sort of thing ordinary people say to one another about morality and immorality, but it occurs in the poets as well. They all unanimously go on and on about how self-discipline and morality may be commendable, but are also difficult and troublesome, whereas self-indulgence and immorality are enjoyable and easily gained, and it's only in people's minds and in convention that they are contemptible. They also say that, on the whole, immorality is more rewarding than morality; and whereas they're perfectly ready to admire bad men, if they're affluent and powerful in other aspects as well, and to award them political office and personal prestige, they have disrespect and look down on people who are in any way powerless or are poor, even while admitting their moral superiority to the others."

36 ▸ "The most astonishing thing of all, however, is what gets said about the gods and goodness—that the gods often assign misfortune and a terrible life to good people, and the opposite to the other type of person. Beggar-priests and soothsayers knock on the doors of wealthy households and try to persuade the owners that (as long as there's no difficulty in choosing vice in abundance: the road is smooth and it's hardly any distance to where it lives. But the gods have put sweat in the way of goodness involved⁴⁴) the gods have granted them the power to use rituals and spells to expiate any sin committed by a person or by any of his ancestors, and that if anyone has an enemy he'd like to hurt, then it'll cost hardly anything to injure him—and it makes no difference whether the target is a moral or an immoral person—by means of certain incantations and formulae, since they can persuade the gods, they say, to do

destined: 注定
novel: 新奇的

condemn: 谴责

unanimously: 一致地
self-discipline: 自律
self-indulgence: 自我放纵
contemptible: 可耻的
affluent: 富裕的
prestige: 声望

astonishing: 令人吃惊的
assign: 分配
soothsayer: 占卜者
vice: 恶
abundance: 大量
sweat: 汗
grant: 赋予
spell: 咒语
expiate: 赎（罪）
incantation: 咒语
formula: 咒文

---

43 *and they claim... for immoral people*: 该句中 that 引导宾语从句，其中含两个定语从句，which 引导的定语从句限定 punishment，who 引导的定语从句限定 people，despite 引导的是一个插入成分。句子的主体是 and they claim that all the punishments... are destined for immoral people。可译为："他们声称，对于那些尽管是有道德，但被认为是无道德的人所应该受到格劳孔所列举的所有惩罚，也注定适用于那些不道德的人。"

44 *as long as... of goodness involved*: vice in abundance 的意思是 "恶是大量存在的"，it 指 vice。可译为："只要从大量存在的恶中选择一个没有多大的困难，那么（选择和到达恶的）道路是平坦的，到达恶所在的地方也不遥远。然而，诸神却令通往善良的道路充满艰辛的汗水。"

their bidding."[45]

concede: 承认
arduous: 费力的

cite: 援引

entreaty: 乞求
appeal: 恳请
libation: 祭酒

diversion: 消遣
initiation: 入会仪式
ghastly: 可怕的

37 ▸ "The poets are called on to support all these claims. Some people concede that vice involves nothing arduous, on the grounds that 'There's no difficulty in choosing vice in abundance: the road is smooth and it's hardly any distance to where it lives. But the gods have put sweat in the way of goodness,' and a long, rough, steep road. Others cite Homer in support of the idea that humans can influence the gods, pointing out that he too said, 'Even the gods themselves can be moved by entreaty: men appeal to them by means of rites and softly spoken prayers, libations and sacrifices, and influence them, when a crime has been committed and a wrong has been done.' They come up with a noisy mob of books written by Musaeus and Orpheus[46] (who are descended from the Moon and the muses, they say), which are source-books for their rituals; and they convince whole countries as well as individuals that there are in fact ways to be free and cleansed of sin.[47] While we remain on earth, this involves ritual and enjoyable diversions, which also work for us after we have died and which they call initiations. These initiations, they say, free us from all the terrors of the other world, but ghastly things await anyone who didn't take part in the rituals."

38 ▸ "This, my dear Socrates," he went on, "is the kind of thing that gets said—and at this kind of length—about how highly gods and men regard virtue and vice. Can we tell what the effect of being exposed to all this is on

---

45 *Beggar-priests and soothsayers... to do their bidding*: 该句较长，但结构明晰。Beggar-priests and soothsayers knock... and try to persuade the owners that... and that... 是该句的主体结构，persuade 后面接了两个由 that 引导的是宾语从句。在第二个 that 引导的宾语从句中，除去一个 if 引导的条件状语从句和一个 since 引导的原因状语从句，以及一个插入成分 and it makes no... 之外，主句是 it'll cost hardly anything to injure him... by means of certain incantations and formulae。另外，该句括号中的内容也是插入成分，在理解该句的过程中，可以单独处理。可译为："乞丐祭司和占卜者造访有钱人家，极力劝说，诸神已经赋予了他们用仪式和咒语消除人及其先人犯下的罪孽的能力，并且说，如果一个人要去伤害一个敌人，只需念念咒语，写写咒文，几乎不需要花多少钱就可以伤害他，不管这个被伤害的目标是有德还是无德之人，因为他们（指乞丐祭司和占卜者）说能够劝说诸神按照他们的召唤行事。"

46 *Orpheus*: 俄耳甫斯。

47 *They come up with... free and cleansed of sin*: 这里的 they 是指包括荷马在内的诗人；括号中的内容作为插入成分，限定说明 Musaeus 和 Orpheus；which 引导的是一个非限定性定语从句，限定 books。可译为："他们列出墨塞俄斯和俄耳甫斯（他们说，这两位是月神和缪斯的后裔）写的一些乌七八糟的书，当作指导用书；而且他们还说服整个国家以及个人，宣称事实上有免去和清除罪的方法。"

a young mind which is naturally gifted and is capable of working out, as a result of flitting (so to speak) from one idea to another and dipping into them all, what type of person he has to be and what road he has to take to have as good a life as possible?⁴⁸ He would probably follow Pindar⁴⁹ and ask himself, 'Is it honesty or crooked deceit that enables me to scale the higher wall' and so live my life surrounded by secure defences? What I hear is people telling me that, unless I also gain a reputation for morality, my actually being moral will do me no good, but will be a source of private troubles and public punishments. On the other hand, an immoral person who has managed to get a reputation for morality is said to have a wonderful life. Therefore, since the experts tell me that 'Appearance overpowers reality' and is responsible for happiness, I must wholeheartedly devote myself to appearance. I must surround myself with an illusion of goodness. This must be my front, what people see of me, but behind me I must have on a leash⁵⁰ that cunning, subtle fox of which Archilochus⁵¹, the greatest of all experts, speaks. Someone might object, 'But it's not easy to cloak one's badness for ever.' That's because no important project is easy, we shall reply; nevertheless, everything we hear marks this as the road to take if we are to be happy. To help us with our disguise, we shall form clubs and pressure-groups⁵², and we can acquire skill at political and forensic speaking from teachers of the art of persuasion.

flit: 飞快掠过

deceit: 欺诈
surround: 围绕

illusion: 幻觉

subtle: 敏锐的

cloak: 掩饰

disguise: 伪装
forensic: 法庭的

48　*Can we tell... as good a life as possible*: 该句的主句是 Can we tell... 其余部分都是 tell 的宾语从句，其主体结构是 what the effect... is on a young mind which is... working out... what type of... what road...，其中包含一个由 which 引导的定语从句，限定 a young mind，和两个由 what 引导的宾语从句，作为 working out 的宾语。As a result of... 作为一个插入成分，表示原因。可译为："我们能够说出，对于一位有天赋、有能力的年轻人，在接触到所有这些之后，会产生什么影响呢？他一会儿听到这个观点，一会儿听到那个观点（也就是说，从一个观点飞快掠过到另外一个观点），对这些观点都是浅尝辄止，他会推理出，要过上尽可能好的生活，该做一个什么样的人，走什么样的路吗？"

49　*Pindar*: 品达，古希腊著名的抒情诗人。他的诗风格庄重，辞藻华丽，形式优美。品达的合唱歌对后世欧洲文学有很大影响，在 17 世纪古典主义时期被认为是"崇高的颂歌"的典范，被誉为"品达体"。相对于其他抒情诗人，品达的诗传世较多，共 45 首 3428 行，主要是赞美奥林匹亚等竞技胜利者的颂歌。

50　*on a leash*: 用绳子拴住，控制。e.g. In public areas, the owner must keep the dog on a leash. 在公共场合，养狗人必须用绳子拴住狗。

51　*Archilochus*: 阿尔赫洛霍斯，生活在公元前 18 世纪末和 17 世纪初。他是一位抒情诗人，文字风格以挖苦出名。他的作品现在留下的只有一些片段，显然在他的作品中，狐狸集中体现了狡猾和欺诈。

52　*clubs and pressure-groups*: 这是公元前 5 世纪雅典政治的一个特征。派系政治仅限于有钱人，且大多是为维护统治集团的利益，政府的安排也是如此。

dominate: 支配

Consequently, by a combination of persuasion and brute force, we shall dominate others without being punished for it."

slight: 微小的

39 ▸ "'But you can't hide from the gods, or overpower them.' 'Well, suppose there are no gods, or suppose they aren't bothered in the slightest about human affairs: then why should we in our turn bother about hiding from them? On the other hand, if the gods do exist, and do care for us, then our only sources of knowledge and information about them are tradition[53] and the poets who have described their lineage. And these are precisely the people who are telling us that the gods can be persuaded and influenced by 'rites and softly spoken prayers' and offerings. Their credibility in one respect stands or falls with their credibility in the other respect. So if we listen to them, our course is to do wrong and then make offerings to the gods from the proceeds of our crimes. The point is that if we behave morally, then the most that we'll avoid is being punished by the gods, but we'll also pass up[54] the opportunity for making a profit from our immorality; if we are immoral, however, we'll not only get rich, we'll win the gods over with our entreaties and get off scot-free, for all the crimes we commit and wrong we do.'"[55]

lineage: 世系

credibility: 可信度

proceed: 收益

exoneration: 免罪

40 ▸ "'But we'll pay in Hades for the crimes we've committed here on earth—or if we don't ourselves, then our children's children will.' He'll think about it and then reply, 'No, my friend, we won't. Initiations are very effective and the gods whose domain is exoneration have a great deal of power: that is the message we are given by very important countries and by the offspring of the gods, who have become poets and the gods' interpreters, and who reveal that is so.'"

41 ▸ "Is there any argument left, then, which might persuade us not to choose out-and-out immorality, but to prefer morality? I mean, if we combine

---

53 *tradition*: 阿得曼托斯扼要地概括了这个论据，并且肯定是城邦的传统（而不是法律）和诗人用神的愤怒告诉了我们判决。如果城邦讲述了什么东西，那是根据他们的传统。

54 *pass up*: 放弃，拒绝。e.g. He passed up the offer of a good job in America to come here. 他放弃了一个美国的不错的工作邀请，来到了这里。

55 *The point is... wrong we do*: 该句较长，但结构简单，层层递进，总的意思由各个小的分句组成。可译为："问题是如果我们行为有德，那么我们将避免绝大多数会被诸神惩罚的情况，但是，我们也拒绝了从我们无德行为中获利的机遇。如果我们是无德之人，那么，我们将不仅能够发财致富，而且还能够用我们的祈求赢得诸神，从而能够从我们犯下的各种罪行和错误中免遭责罚。"

immorality with a fraudulent, but specious, façade, then we can do as we please in this world and in the next, in the presence of both gods and men. This is what both ordinary people and outstanding people are telling us. So after all these arguments, Socrates, is there any strategy to enable someone with potential—whether it is due to mental attributes or wealth or physique or lineage—to be prepared to rate morality highly, rather than laugh when he hears it being praised?"[56]

fraudulent: 欺诈的

specious: 似是而非的

façade: 外表

potential: 潜能

physique: 体格

42 ▶ "I tell you, if there's anyone who can not only refute the arguments I've been stating, but is also secure in his knowledge that morality is best, then what he feels for immoral people is not anger but a large measure of forgiveness. He knows that people abstain from wrong either because, by divine dispensation, they instinctively find it distasteful, or because of some realization they've come to, and that otherwise no one chooses to be moral, although people find fault with immorality when cowardice or old age or some other form of weakness prevents them from doing wrong.[57] This is obviously the case: the first of these people to gain power is the first to behave immorally—and as immorally as he possibly can."

refute: 辩驳

abstain: 避免

dispensation: 天命

cowardice: 怯懦

43 ▶ "One thing is responsible for all this, and it is the same thing which constituted the starting-point of this whole discussion. Both Glaucon and I, Socrates, are saying to you, 'My friend, we can start with those original heroes[58] whose writings are extant and end with our contemporaries, but we find

extant: 尚存的

contemporary: 同代人

---

56 *So after all... being praised*: 该句的主体结构是一个一般疑问句，即 is there any...，后面接了一个 rather than... 引导的从属结构，whether it is... 为插入句。可译为："那么，苏格拉底，在探讨了这些之后，有没有某种策略使一位具有潜能的人——无论这种潜能是源自脑力特征（即聪明才智），还是财富、体格，抑或是家族世系——准备去高度评价道德，而不是在听人们赞扬它的时候嘲笑一番？"

57 *He knows... from doing wrong*: 该句中 knows 后面接有两个 that 引导的宾语从句，该句的主体结构是 He knows that people abstain...，and that otherwise no one chooses...。第一个宾语从句中有一个 either... or... 结构，表示两个原因。在第二个宾语从句中有一个 although 引导的让步状语从句，其中还有一个 when 引导的时间状语从句来说明人们什么时候 find fault with immorality。可译为："他知道，人们避免作恶要么是因为受到了神圣的天命，他们本能地发现作恶令人反感，要么是因为他们获得了某种惩恶扬善的领悟，否则，尽管人们由于怯懦、年老以及其他形式的弱点使他们无法作恶，并因此而批评无德的行为，但是没有人会选择做有德之人。"

58 *heroes*: 英雄在最初的年代是伟大的作战首领。他们被视作是神圣的，因为他们是直接从神下降来的，履行着超人的职责。其中有些被认为是一些伟大城邦的创造者或创造者的祖先。市民们因而是那些连接城邦和神的那些英雄的后裔。（见谢祖均译本）

that not a single one of you self-styled supporters of morality has ever found fault with immorality or commended morality except in terms of the reputation, status, and rewards which follow from them. What each of them does on its own, however, and what the effect is of its occurrence in someone's mind, where it is hidden from the eyes of both gods and men, has never been adequately explained either in poetry or in everyday conversation; nor has it ever been proven that the worst possible thing that can occur in the mind is immorality, and that morality is the best.[59] If this is how all of you had approached the matter from the outset, and if you had started trying to convince us when we were young, then we wouldn't now be defending ourselves against one another's wrongdoing, but everyone would be his own best defender, since he'd be afraid that if he did wrong he'd be opening his doors to the worst of all possible residents.'"[60]

44 ▸ "That, Socrates, is what Thrasymachus—though he's not the only one, of course—might say on the subject of morality and immorality, and he'd probably have even more to add. Now, I think he's crudely misrepresenting their functions, but the reason I've taken his argument as far as I can is, to be perfectly candid, because I want to hear you making the opposite claims. It's not enough just to demonstrate that morality is better than immorality. Why does one of them, in and of itself, make anyone who possesses it bad, while the other one, in and of itself, makes him good? And, as Glaucon suggested, don't bring reputation into it. You see, if you leave them with reputations which genuinely reflect their natures, and don't attribute to each of them reputations which fail to do justice to them, then we'll accuse you of praising a reputation for morality rather than morality itself, and of criticizing a

---

outset: 开始

resident: 居住者

crudely: 粗鲁地
misrepresent: 误解
function: 功用
candid: 坦诚的
demonstrate: 证明

do justice: 公平对待

---

59 *What each of them... morality is the best*: 该句主体分成两个部分，第一个部分是由 what、what 和 where 引导的三个主语从句构成的，第二个部分中 proven 后面是两个由 that 引导的并列的宾语从句。可译为："它们（指有德和无德）每个自身能做什么？而且，它的出现对人的心灵产生什么影响？它在什么地方避开了神与人的眼睛？这些问题无论是在诗歌还是在日常谈话中都没有人做出过恰当的解释，也从来没有人证明过出现在人心灵中最坏的事是无德、最好的事是有德。"

60 *If this is... possible residents*: 该句的主句是 we wouldn't now...，其余的都是从句，即两个 if 引导的条件状语从句，和 since 引导的原因状语从句。since 引导的从句中还有一个 that 引导的宾语从句，该从句中还有一个 if 引导的条件状语从句。可译为："如果你们所有人从一开始就这样探讨这个问题，如果在我们还年轻的时候你们就已经开始试图说服我们，那么，我们现在就不用彼此提防别人作恶了，每个人都是自己最好的捍卫者了，因为他害怕他一旦作恶，他就为最坏的居住者（作恶者）打开了大门。"

reputation for immorality rather than immorality itself;⁶¹ and we'll claim that what you're recommending is being immoral and getting away with it, and that you actually agree with Thrasymachus that morality is good for someone else—that it is the advantage of the stronger party—while it is immorality that is to one's own advantage and profit, but is disadvantageous to the weaker party."⁶²

45▸ "So, since it is your expressed opinion that morality is one of those **paramount** good things which are worth having not just for their consequences, but also and especially for themselves (like sight, hearing, intelligence—health, of course—and any other good things which are not just thought to be worthwhile, but are **inherently** so), then this is the aspect of morality which you should pay tribute to⁶³. You should show how morality is worth while in and of itself for anyone who possesses it and how immorality harms him, and leave others to praise rewards and reputations. I mean, I can accept the fact that others praise morality and criticize immorality in these terms, by **eulogizing** or abusing their reputations and rewards, but I won't put up with⁶⁴ that from you (unless you insist), because this and this alone is what you've spent your whole life investigating. So it's not enough just to demonstrate that morality is better than immorality: show us why one of them, in and of itself, makes anyone who possesses it good, whether or not it is hidden from the eyes of gods and men, while the other one, in and of itself, and whether or not it is hidden from the eyes of gods and men, makes him bad."

paramount: 首要的

inherently: 内在地

eulogize: 颂扬

---

61 *You see, if you... immorality itself*: 该句的主体结构是 if you leave..., and (if you) don't attribute..., then we'll accuse you of..., and (accuse you) of...,其中两个 that 引导的定语从句限定 reputations。可译为:"你看,如果你赋予它们(指有德与无德)名副其实的声誉,不将那些名不符实的声誉赋予它们,那么,我们就会说你称颂的不是道德本身,而是道德的名声,你批评的不是无德,而是无德的名声。"

62 *and we'll claim... to the weaker party*: 该句的主体结构是 we'll claim that what you're... and that you actually agree...,claim 有两个宾语从句,其中第二个宾语从句中的 agree 后面还有一个宾语从句,即 that morality is good... while...。可译为:"而我们就会声称,你所推荐的不过是行无德的事且能够侥幸逃脱,你实际上同意色拉叙马霍斯的想法,即道德对他人是好事——是强者的优势——而无德则对本人是优势且有利可图,但是对于弱者则是不利的。"

63 *pay (a) tribute to*: 称赞,歌颂,致敬。e.g. We must pay tribute to his great courage. 我们一定要赞扬他巨大的勇气。

64 *put up with*: 忍受,容忍。e.g. If I were you I wouldn't put up with his behaviour any longer. 如果我是你,我将绝不会容忍这种行为。

EXERCISES

I. Answer the following questions according to the reading text.

1. Glaucon said to Socrates, "Don't you describe as good something which is welcomed for its own sake, rather than because its consequences are desired?" From Glaucon's words, what are people's criteria to judge one thing as good or bad?

2. What is the third category of good things?

3. What is the origin and nature of morality?

4. What does Glaucon want to say through the example of the Lydian shepherd?

5. What does Glaucon want to say with the example of "a saint with a lifelong reputation as a sinner"?

6. According to Glaucon, what are gods' attitudes towards those moral persons?

7. What is the Socrates' view on morality?

II. Paraphrase the following sentences with your own words, and then translate them into Chinese.

1. Don't you describe as good something which is welcomed for its own sake, rather than because its consequences are desired? (Para. 3)

2. So that's the origin and nature of morality, on this view: it is a compromise between the ideal of doing wrong without having to pay for it, and the worst situation, which is having wrong done to one while lacking the means of exacting compensation. (Para. 17)

3. Here's what they'll say: for a moral person in the situation I've described, the future holds flogging, torture on the rack, imprisonment in chains, having his eyes burnt out, and every ordeal in the book, up to and including being impaled on a stake. (Para. 26)

4. Homer makes very similar claims: "As of some righteous king," he says, "who pleases the gods by upholding justice, and the dark earth bears wheat and barley, the trees hang heavy with fruit, the sheep steadily give birth, and the sea-waters yield fish." (Para. 32)

5. They all unanimously go on and on about how self-discipline and morality may be commendable, but are also difficult and troublesome, whereas self-indulgence and

immorality are enjoyable and easily gained, and it's only in people's minds and in convention that they are contemptible. (Para. 35)

6. I mean, I can accept the fact that others praise morality and criticize immorality in these terms, by eulogizing or abusing their reputations and rewards, but I won't put up with that form you (unless you insist), because this and this alone is what you've spent your whole life investigating. (Para. 45)

III. Figure out the meanings of the phrases in bold, and then make another sentence with each of the phrases.

1. At this point, I thought I'd be **exempt from** further talking but apparently that was only the preamble. (Para. 1)

2. "I'm aware of this view," I said, "and it's the reason why Thrasymachus has been **running** morality **down** all this time, and praising immorality." (Para. 12)

3. They then **set about** making laws and decrees, and from then on they use the terms "legal" and "right" to describe anything which is enjoined by their code. (Para. 17)

4. And we should **set** them **apart** from each other by leaving their respective immorality and morality absolutely intact, so that we make each of them a consummate professional. (Para. 22)

5. Now that we've **come up with** this sketch of an immoral person, we must conceive of a moral person to stand beside him—someone who is straightforward and principled. (Para. 23)

6. So if Glaucon here has left anything out, you should **back** him **up**. (Para. 30)

7. We find that not a single one of you self-styled supporters of morality has ever **found fault with** immorality or commended morality except in terms of the reputation, status, and rewards which follow from them. (Para. 43)

IV. The following are famous remarks from Plato's works. Read these remarks and share your understanding with your classmates.

1. a saint with a lifelong reputation as a sinner (Para. 23)

2. Then at last he'll realize that one's goal should be not actual morality, but the appearance of morality. (Para. 26)

3. Immorality is more rewarding than morality. (Para. 35)

4. The gods often assign misfortune and a terrible life to good people, and the opposite to

the other type of person. (Para. 36)

5. The first of these people to gain power is the first to behave immorally—and as immorally as he possibly can. (Para. 42)

V. The discussion about morality and immorality among Socrates, Glaucon, and Adeimantus is inclusive. Follow their discussion and write a conversation of your own, in which you should express your view on morality and immorality. Try to point out the defects in their arguments with no less than 200 words.

UNIT 5

Hamlet
A Drama

ORAL TASKS

1. How many Shakespeare's plays do you know? What are they?
2. Do you know some classical lines in *Hamlet*?

INTRODUCTION

Drama is a specific mode of fiction represented in a theatre. The term "drama" comes from a Greek word meaning "action", which is derived from "I do". In English, the word "play" was the standard term used to describe drama until William Shakespeare's time.

William Shakespeare (1564–1616) was an English playwright, actor and poet, also known as the "Bard of Avon" and often called England's national poet. His extant works, including collaborations, consist of approximately 39 plays, 154 sonnets, two long narrative poems, and a few other verses, some of uncertain authorship. His plays have been translated into every major living language and are performed more often than those of any other playwright.

Hamlet, Prince of Denmark, often shortened to *Hamlet*, is a tragedy written at an uncertain date between 1599 and 1602. Set in Denmark, the play dramatizes the revenge Prince Hamlet is called to wreak upon his uncle, Claudius, by the ghost of Hamlet's father, King Hamlet. Claudius had murdered his own brother and seized the throne, also marrying his deceased brother's widow.

Hamlet is Shakespeare's longest play, and is considered among the most powerful and influential works of world literature, and probably one of Shakespeare's most popular works during his lifetime.

PART 3

TEXTUAL READING[1]

ACT III
SCENE I. A room in the castle.

Enter KING, QUEEN, POLONIUS, OPHELIA, ROSENCRANTZ, GUILDENSTERN, LORDS[2]

Claudius:	And can you by no drift of circumstance	
	Get from him why he puts on this **confusion**,	**confusion:** 困惑
	Grating so harshly all his days of quiet	**grate:** 碾磨
	With **turbulent** and dangerous lunacy?[3]	**turbulent:** 动荡不安
5 **Rosencrantz:**	He does **confess** he feels himself **distracted**;	**confess:** 承认
	But from what cause he will by no means[4] speak.	**distracted:** 分心的
Guildenstern:	Nor do we find him forward to be sounded,	
	But with a **crafty** madness keeps **aloof**,	**crafty:** 狡猾的
	When we would bring him on to some confession	**aloof:** 冷淡的，置身事外的

---

1 本篇出自：William Shakespeare. *Hamlet, Prince of Denmark.* Philip Edwards ed. Cambridge: Cambridge University Press, 2003。

2 King 是现任国王 Claudius（克罗迪斯），Hamlet（哈姆雷特）的叔叔，在先王（哈姆雷特的父亲）去世后，娶了王后（哈姆雷特的母亲），也就成了哈姆雷特的继父。Queen 是 Gertrude（葛忒露德）王后，哈姆雷特的亲生母亲。Polonius（波乐纽斯）是克罗迪斯器重的大臣。Ophelia（莪菲丽亚）是波乐纽斯的女儿，也是哈姆雷特的女朋友。Rosencrantz（罗森克兰兹）和 Guildenstern（纪尔顿斯丹）是哈姆雷特的好朋友。（注：本篇译文来自卞之琳翻译的《莎士比亚悲剧四种》，北京：人民文学出版社，1989。下同。）

3 *And can you... dangerous lunacy* (Lines 1-4)：这四行构成一个完整的句子，句子的主体结构是 Can you get from him why he puts on this confusion。by no drift of circumstance 作为状语来限定 get，表示获取的方式；grating so harshly... and dangerous lunacy 用来补充说明 confusion。drift of circumstance 指"变换场景"，在这里表示"拐弯抹角，变着法子"的意思；quiet 在这里是名词，days of quiet 表示"安宁的日子"。可译为："你们用尽了迂回曲折的说法 / 还是探不出他为何这样子乱来，/ 这样子乱发他胡闹而危险的疯狂，/ 不去好好过平平静静的日子吗？"

4 *by no means*: 绝不，一点也不，在任何情况下都不。e.g. "Am I right in assuming that you two were at Miss Catterick's flat on the night in question?" "*By no means.*" "我想你们俩那天夜晚就在卡特里克小姐的寓所里吧！" "不，你完全错了！"

	10	Of his true state.[5]
	Gertrude:	Did he receive you well?
	Rosencrantz:	Most like a gentleman.
disposition: 性情	**Guildenstern:**	But with much forcing of his disposition.
niggard: 吝啬的	**Rosencrantz:**	Niggard of question; but, of our demands,
	15	Most free in his reply.[6]
assay: 试验	**Gertrude:**	Did you assay him?
pastime: 消遣		To any pastime?
	Rosencrantz:	Madam, it so fell out[7] that certain players
		We o'er-raught on the way;[8] of these we told him,
	20	And there did seem in him a kind of joy
court: 宫廷		To hear of it. They are about the court,
		And as I think, they have already order
		This night to play before him.
	Polonius:	'Tis[9] most true,
beseech: 恳请	25	And he beseeched me to entreat your majesties
majesty: 陛下		To hear and see the matter.
	Claudius:	With all my heart, and it doth[10] much content me
inclined: 倾向的		To hear him so inclined.
		Good gentlemen, give him a further edge,
	30	And drive his purpose on to these delights.
	Rosencrantz:	We shall, my lord.
		Exeunt Rosencrantz and Guildenstern
	Claudius:	Sweet Gertrude, leave us too,

---

5 *Nor do we find... Of his true state* (Lines 7-10): 该句的正常语序是 Nor do we find him forward to be sounded. But when we would bring him on to some confession of his true state, with a crafty madness (he) keeps aloof. 第8行中省略了主语 he, 即哈姆雷特。可译为: "他也不情愿让我们摸到底细，/ 每逢我们要引他吐露一点儿 / 他的真相，他就耍他的疯把戏，/ 躲闪了过去。"

6 *Niggard of question, ... Most free in his reply* (Lines 14-15): 这是一个省略句，完整的句子是 (He is) niggard of question, but of our demands (he is) most free in his reply. 可译为: "不大肯说话，可是我们问什么 / 他都肯回答。"

7 *fall out*: 碰巧。e.g. How did it fall out that the two men arrived to address the same meeting at the same time? 这两个人怎么会同时到同一个会上讲话呢?

8 *We o'er-raught on the way*: 我们路上恰巧赶上。*o'er*: over。

9 *'Tis*: It is。

10 *doth*: does。

	For we have closely sent for Hamlet hither¹¹,	
	That he, as 'twere¹² by accident, may here	
35	Affront Ophelia. Her father and myself,	**affront:** 面对
	lawful espials,	**lawful:** 合法的
	Will so bestow ourselves that, seeing unseen,	**espial:** 密探
	We may of their encounter frankly judge,	**bestow:** 赋予
	And gather by him, as he is behaved,	
40	If 't be th'affliction¹³ of his love or no	
	That thus he suffers for.¹⁴	
Gertrude:	I shall obey you.	
	And for your part Ophelia, I do wish	
	That your good beauties be the happy cause	**cause:** 原因
45	Of Hamlet's wildness. So shall I hope your virtues	
	Will bring him to his wonted way again,	**wonted:** 惯常的
	To both your honours.	
Ophelia:	Madam, I wish it may.	

Exit Gertrude with Lords

Polonius:	Ophelia, walk you here. —Gracious, so please you,	
50	We will bestow ourselves. —Read on this book,	
	That show of such an exercise may colour	
	Your loneliness. —We are oft to blame in this:	
	'Tis too much proved, that with devotion's visage,	**visage:** 面容
	And pious action, we do sugar o'er	**pious:** 虔诚
55	The devil himself.¹⁵	**sugar:** 粉饰

---

11 *hither*: 到这里。

12 *'twere*: it were。

13 *th'affliction*: the affliction。

14 *Her father and myself... That thus he suffers for* (Lines 35-41)：这些构成一个完整句子，her father and myself 是这个句子的主语；第 37 行中 that 引导宾语从句；第 40 行中 if 引导宾语从句做 judge 的宾语；第 41 行中 that 引导定语从句限定 affliction；第 37 行中的 seeing unseen 可以理解为 while we can see (seeing) them, we are not seen (unseen) by them。可译为："她的父亲跟我就权充密探，/ 躲好了看他们，不让他们看见，/ 好好注意他们会面的情形，/ 从他的一举一动，一言一语，/ 断定他是不是为了恋爱的痛苦 / 才这样发作的。"

15 *'Tis too much proved, ... The devil himself* (Lines 53-55)：这三行按照普通的书写方式比较容易理解，即 It is too much proved that with devotion's visage and pious action, we do sugar over the devil himself. 可译为："我们把真诚的面孔、/ 虔敬的动作，往往用作了糖衣 / 包裹了心里的魔鬼哩。"

lash: 鞭打
conscience: 良心
harlot: 娼妓

Claudius: (*Aside*) Oh, 'tis too true.
How smart a lash that speech doth give my conscience!
The harlot's cheek, beautied with plastering art,
Is not more ugly to the thing that helps it
60　Than is my deed to my most painted word.¹⁶
O heavy burthen!

Polonius: I hear him coming. Let's withdraw, my lord.

Exeunt Claudius and Polonius
Enter Hamlet

Hamlet: To be, or not to be, that is the question—
Whether 'tis nobler in the mind to suffer
outrageous: 粗暴的
65　The slings and arrows of outrageous fortune,
Or to take arms against a sea of troubles,
And by opposing end them.¹⁷ To die, to sleep—
No more; and by a sleep to say we end
The heart-ache and the thousand natural shocks

flesh: 肉体
heir: 继承者
consummation: 圆满
devoutly: 虔诚地
perchance: 可能
rub: 难处
coil: 纠缠

70　That flesh is heir to—'tis a consummation
Devoutly to be wished.¹⁸ To die, to sleep—
To sleep, perchance to dream. Ay, there's the rub,
For in that sleep of death what dreams may come,
When we have shuffled off ¹⁹ this mortal coil,

16　*The harlot's cheek, ... my most painted word* (Lines 58-60)：这个句子中有两个比喻，一是将娼妓的脸比作我的行为；二是将涂抹面颊的技艺比作我的花言巧语。the thing 指代的就是脂粉，it 指代脸蛋。意思是说，娼妓的面颊虽然丑陋，但是比不上涂抹面颊的脂粉那么丑陋。同样，我的行为虽然丑陋，但是我的花言巧语更加丑陋。可译为："娼妓的脸蛋，涂上了厚厚的脂粉，/ 要说丑陋不堪，/ 还是远远不及用花言巧语掩藏的我的行为！"

17　*Whether 'tis nobler... by opposing end them* (Lines 64-67)：该句的基本结构是 Whether it is nobler... to suffer..., or to take arms... (to) end them，表示在 to suffer 和 to take arms 两者之间选择。可译为："要做到高贵，究竟该忍气吞声 / 来承受狂暴的命运矢石交攻呢，/ 还是该挺身反抗无边的苦恼，扫它个干净？"或"到底是在脑海中承受 / 狂暴命运的弹弓与箭羽的攻击高贵呢？/ 还是拿起武器反抗无边的苦海，并通过反抗这苦海来终结它们呢？"

18　*by a sleep... devoutly to be wished* (Lines 68-71)：该句的正常语序是 It is a consummation... (that) by a sleep... we end the heart-ache and the thousand natural shocks...。devoutly to be wished 是 consummation 的定语，that flesh is heir to 是 natural shocks 的定语。可译为："而如果睡眠等于了结了 / 心痛以及千百种身体要担受的 / 皮痛肉痛，那该是天大的好事，/ 正求之不得啊！"

19　*shuffle off*: 摆脱，去掉。e.g. He shuffled off his old friends when he became famous. 他成名以后，抛弃了老朋友。

75	Must give us pause.[20] There's the respect	
	That makes calamity of so long life,	**calamity:** 灾难
	For who would bear the whips and scorns of time,	**whip:** 抽打
	Th' oppressor's wrong, the proud man's contumely,	**scorn:** 蔑视
	The pangs of despised love, the law's delay,	**oppressor:** 压迫者
80	The insolence of office, and the spurns	**contumely:** 无礼
	That patient merit of th' unworthy takes,	**pang:** 痛苦
	When he himself might his quietus make	**insolence:** 轻慢
	With a bare bodkin? Who would fardels bear,	**quietus:** 解脱；死亡
	To grunt and sweat under a weary life,	**fardel:** 重负
85	But that the dread of something after death,	**grunt:** 呻吟
	The undiscovered country from whose bourn	**weary:** 疲倦的
	No traveller returns, puzzles the will,	**bourn:** 界限；目的地
	And makes us rather bear those ills we have	
	Than fly to others that we know not of?[21]	
90	Thus conscience does make cowards of us all,	
	And thus the native hue of resolution	**hue:** 色调
	Is sicklied o'er with the pale cast of thought,	**resolution:** 决心
	And enterprises of great pith and moment	**pale:** 苍白
	With this regard their currents turn awry,	**enterprise:** 事业心
		pith: 精髓

---

20 *Ay, there's the rub, ... Must give us pause* (Lines 72-75): 该句的主体结构是 there's the rub, ... (which) must give us pause，其中 for 后面跟着原因状语从句，when 引导时间状语从句。可译为："这就麻烦了！／我们一旦摆脱了尘世的牵缠，／在死的睡眠里还会做些什么梦，／一想到就不能不踌躇。"意思是说，梦中（或者死后）的痛苦也许更多，这就让想死的人犹豫不决。

21 *There's the respect... Than fly to others that we know not of* (Lines 75-89): 这个句子较长，它的主体结构是 There's the respect / That makes calamity of so long life, / For who would bear... / When he himself might his quietus make / With a bare bodkin? Who would... bear..., / But that the dread... puzzles... and makes us...。这个长句中有两个 who would bear... 的并列结构，第一个 who would bear 后面跟了一系列的并列宾语成分，同时还有 when 引导的状语从句，表示"当他能够……的时候，谁愿意忍受（who would bear）……"。在 but 后面的从句中，有两个并列主语 the dread 和 the undiscovered country，两个并列谓语 puzzles 和 makes，其中还有一个 rather... than... 的结构。可译为："这一点顾虑／正好使灾难变成了长期的折磨。／谁甘心忍受人世的鞭挞和嘲弄，／忍受压迫者虐待、傲慢者凌辱，／忍受失恋者的痛苦、法庭的拖延、／衙门的横暴，做埋头苦干的大才、／被作威作福的小人一脚踢出去，／如果他只消自己来使一下尖刀／就可以得到解脱啊？谁甘心挑担子，／拖着疲累的生命，呻吟，流汗，／要不是怕一死就去了没有人回来的／那个从未发现的国土，怕那边／还不知会怎样，因此意志动摇了，／因此便宁愿忍受目前的灾殃，／而不愿投奔另一些未知的苦难？"

		95	And lose the name of action.²² Soft you now,
orison: 祈祷			The fair Ophelia. —Nymph, in thy **orisons**
			Be all my sins remembered.
	Ophelia:		Good my lord,
			How does your honour for this many a day?
humbly: 卑微地	**Hamlet:**	100	I **humbly** thank you, well, well, well.
remembrance: 纪念品	**Ophelia:**		My lord, I have **remembrances** of yours
			That I have longed long to re-deliver.
			I pray you now receive them.
	Hamlet:		No, not I,
aught: 任何事物		105	I never gave you **aught**.
	Ophelia:		My honoured lord, you know right well you did,
			And with them words of so sweet breath composed
perfume: 芬芳			As made the things more rich.²³ Their **perfume** lost,
			Take these again, for to the noble mind
wax: 转变为		110	Rich gifts **wax** poor when givers prove unkind.
			There, my lord.
	Hamlet:		Ha, ha, are you honest?
	Ophelia:		My lord?
	Hamlet:		Are you fair?
	Ophelia:	115	What means your lordship?
	Hamlet:		That if you be honest and fair, your honesty should admit no
discourse: 话语			**discourse** to your beauty.
	Ophelia:		Could beauty, my lord, have better commerce than with honesty?
bawd: 荡妇	**Hamlet:**	120	Ay, truly; for the power of beauty will sooner transform honesty from what it is to a **bawd** than the force of honesty

---

22　*Thus conscience does make... And lose the name of action* (Lines 90-95)：该部分由三个并列的句子组成，它们的主语分别是 conscience...，the native hue of resolution... 和 enterprises...，三个句子都是简单句。可译为："这样子，顾虑使我们都成了懦夫，/ 也就这样子，决断决行的本色 / 蒙上了惨白的一层思虑的病容；/ 本可以轰轰烈烈的大作大为，/ 由于这一点想不通，就出了别扭，/ 失去了行动的名分。"

23　*My honoured lord, ... As made the things rich* (Lines 106-108)：该句的主句是 you know right well you did，with 引导伴随结构，其中 as 是代词，指代 words。可译为："尊贵的殿下该分明知道是送过的；/ 殿下还附带说过些甜言蜜语 / 使礼物变得更贵重呢。"

	can translate beauty into his likeness. ²⁴ This was sometime a paradox, but now the time gives it proof. I did love you once.	**paradox:** 悖论
Ophelia:	Indeed my lord you made me believe so.	
125 Hamlet:	You should not have believed me, for virtue cannot so inoculate our old stock but we shall relish of it. I loved you not.	**inoculate:** 嫁接 **stock:** 树干 **relish:** 喜好
Ophelia:	I was the more deceived.	
Hamlet:	Get thee to a nunnery—why wouldst thou be a breeder of sinners? I am myself indifferent honest, but yet I could accuse	**thee:** 你（宾格） **nunnery:**尼姑庵
130	me of such things, that it were better my mother had not borne me.²⁵ I am very proud, revengeful, ambitious, with more offences at my beck²⁶ than I have thoughts to put them in, imagination to give them shape, or time to act them in. What should such fellows as I do crawling between earth and heaven? We are arrant knaves all, believe none of us. Go thy	**thou:** 你（主格） **breeder:** 哺育者 **crawl:** 爬行 **arrant:** 彻头彻尾的
135	ways to a nunnery. Where's your father?	**knave:** 无赖 **thy:** 你的
Ophelia:	At home my lord.	
Hamlet:	Let the doors be shut upon him, that he may play the fool nowhere but in's²⁷ own house. Farewell.	
Ophelia:	Oh help him you sweet heavens!	
140 Hamlet:	If thou dost²⁸ marry, I'll give thee this plague for thy dowry: be thou as chaste as ice, as pure as snow, thou shalt not escape calumny. Get thee to a nunnery, go. Farewell. Or, if thou wilt needs marry, marry a fool, for wise men know well enough what monsters you make of them. To a nunnery go, and quickly	**dowry:** 嫁妆 **chaste:** 贞洁的 **calumny:** 污蔑 **farewell:** 再见
145	too. Farewell.	

---

24 *for the power of beauty will sooner... beauty into his likeness* (Lines 120–122): 该句的主体结构是 sooner... than...，比较的是两个转变。一个是 transform... from... to...，其中的 what it is 是指（honesty）的"本来面目"；另外一个是 translate... into...，其中的 likeness 是指与 beauty 相同（美好的）东西。可译为："因为美丽的力量倒容易 / 把贞洁点化为淫荡，贞洁的力量可难 / 把美丽改成了像它自己的样子。"

25 *I am myself indifferent honest, ... my mother had not borne me* (Lines 129–131): 该句 but 引导的从句中，含 such... that... 的结构。such 是指前面提到的抚养的罪人，that 引导的是一个虚拟结构。可译为："我自己是相当洁身自好的；可是我还能指出 / 我的许多罪名，真害得我但愿母亲当初还是不要生我出来的好。"

26 *at my beck*: 大多数情况下用作 at one's beck and call，唯某人之命是从。e.g. He has many servants at his beck and call. 他有许多仆人供他使唤。

27 *in's*: in his。

28 *thou dost*: you do。

restore: 恢复	**Ophelia:**	O heavenly powers, restore him!
jig: 蹦跳，上下急动	**Hamlet:**	I have heard of your paintings too, well enough. God has given you one face, and you make yourselves another. You
amble: 从容地走		jig, you amble, and you lisp, and nickname God's creatures,
lisp: 口齿不清	150	and make your wantonness your ignorance. Go to, I'll no more
nickname: 给人取绰号		on't, it hath[29] made me mad. I say we will have no mo[30] marriages. Those that are married already, all but one, shall
wantonness: 放纵		live, the rest shall keep as they are. To a nunnery, go.
ignorance: 无知		*Exit*
	Ophelia:	O, what a noble mind is here o'erthrown!
courtier: 朝臣	155	The courtier's, soldier's, scholar's, eye, tongue, sword,
scholar: 学者		Th'expectancy and rose of the fair state,
expectancy: 期许		The glass of fashion and the mould of form,
mould: 模型		The observed of all observers, quite, quite down,[31]
deject: 使沮丧		And I of ladies most deject and wretched,
suck: 吸吮	160	That sucked the honey of his music vows,
sovereign: 至高无上的		Now see that noble and most sovereign reason, Like sweet bells jangled, out of tune and harsh;
jangle: 发刺耳之声		That unmatched form and feature of blown youth
blown: 充分发展的		Blasted with ecstasy.[32] Oh woe is me
blast: 冲击	165	T'have[33] seen what I have seen, see what I see.
ecstasy: 迷醉		Enter Claudius and Polonius
woe: 悲哀	**Claudius:**	Love? His affections do not that way tend;
affection: 感情		Nor what he spake, though it lacked form a little, Was not like madness. There's something in his soul
melancholy: 忧郁		O'er which his melancholy sits on brood;
brood: 沉思		

29 *hath*: has。

30 *mo*: more。

31 *The courtier's... quite down* (Lines 155-158): 这一系列句子都是用来代指哈姆雷特的，其中 the observed of all observers 中的 observed 指哈姆雷特，他是被观察模仿的对象。可译为："朝廷人士的眼睛、学者的舌头、军人的利剑，/ 国家的期望和花朵，/ 风流时尚的镜子、文雅的典范，/ 举世瞩目的中心，倒了，全倒了！"

32 *And I of ladies... Blasted with ecstasy* (Lines 159-164): 该句的主体结构是 I... see that... that...。第 159 和 160 行都是用来限定 I 的，其中包括一个 that 引导的定语从句。谓语 see 后面有两个 that 引导的宾语从句。可译为："我呢，最伤心、悲惨的女子，/ 从他盟誓的音乐里吸取过甜蜜，/ 如今却看着他高贵无上的理智/ 好像银铃儿搅乱了，失去了和谐；/ 看着他青春年少的无比风貌/ 叫疯狂一下子摧折了！"

33 *T'have*: To have。

170	And I do doubt the hatch and the disclose	
	Will be some danger; which for to prevent,	
	I have in quick determination	
	Thus set it down: he shall with speed to England	
	For the demand of our neglected tribute.	**tribute:** 贡物
175	Haply the seas and countries different,	**haply:** 或许
	With variable objects, shall expel	
	This something-settled matter in his heart,	
	Whereon his brains still beating puts him thus	**whereon:** 在……上面
	From fashion of himself.³⁴ What think you on't?	
180	**Polonius:** It shall do well. But yet do I believe	
	The origin and commencement of his grief	**commencement:** 发端
	Sprung from³⁵ neglected love. How now Ophelia?	
	You need not tell us what Lord Hamlet said,	
	We heard it all. My lord, do as you please,	
185	But if you hold it fit, after the play,	
	Let his queen mother all alone entreat him	
	To show his grief. Let her be round with him,	
	And I'll be placed, so please you, in the ear	
	Of all their conference. If she find him not,	
190	To England send him, or confine him where	
	Your wisdom best shall think.	
	Claudius: It shall be so.	
	Madness in great ones must not unwatched go.	
	Exeunt	

---

34 *Haply the seas, ... From fashion of himself* (Lines 175-179): 该句的主体结构是 the seas and countries different... shall expel... matter in his heart，whereon 引导的从句限定说明 heart。可译为："出洋过海，跑跑不同的国度，/ 看看新鲜的事物，/ 也许会排除掉 / 这种老是盘踞他心头的心事，/ 叫他的脑筋不再老是盘算它，/ 害得他疯头疯脑。"

35 *spring from:* 起源于，出于。e.g. He sprang from one of the best families in the north. 他出身于北方的一家望族。

EXERCISES

I. Answer the following questions according to the reading text.

1. What does the King want to find out about Hamlet?
2. What do Rosencrantz and Guildenstern comment upon Hamlet's behaviour?
3. How do the King and Polonius try to find out Hamlet's true state of mind?
4. From Hamlet's long monologue, "To be, or not to be, that is the question…", what is Hamlet's attitude towards his action? Why?
5. Do you think Ophelia and Hamlet love each other? Why?
6. Why does Hamlet suggest that Ophelia go to a nunnery?
7. How does Ophelia feel about Hamlet after her talk with Hamlet?
8. After overhearing the talk between Hamlet and Ophelia, how does the King think of Hamlet's madness?

II. Paraphrase the following lines with your own words, and then translate them into Chinese.

1. **(Lines 11–13)**   Did he receive you well?

   Most like a gentleman.

   But with much forcing of his disposition.

2. **(Lines 27–28)**   With all my heart, and it doth much content me

   To hear him so inclined.

3. **(Lines 43–47)**   I do wish

   That your good beauties be the happy cause

   Of Hamlet's wildness. So shall I hope your virtues

   Will bring him to his wonted way again,

   To both your honours.

4. **(Lines 108–110)**   Their perfume lost,

Take these again, for to the noble mind

Rich gifts wax poor when givers prove unkind.

5. (Lines 131–133) I am very proud, revengeful, ambitious, with more offences at my beck than I have thoughts to put them in, imagination to give them shape, or time to act them in.

6. (Lines 148–150) You jig, you amble, and you lisp, and nickname God's creatures, and make your wantonness your ignorance.

7. (Lines 168–171) There's something in his soul

O'er which his melancholy sits on brood;

And I do doubt the hatch and the disclose

Will be some danger;

III. Figure out the meanings of the phrases in bold, and then make another sentence with each of the phrases.

1. (Lines 33–35) For we have closely **sent for** Hamlet hither,

That he, as 'twere **by accident**, may here

Affront Ophelia.

2. (Line 118) Could beauty, my lord, **have** better **commerce** than **with** honesty?

3. (Lines 120–122) The power of beauty will sooner **transform** honesty **from** what it is **to** a bawd than the force of honesty can **translate** beauty **into** his likeness.

4. (Lines 129–131) I am myself indifferent honest, but yet I could **accuse** me **of** such things, that it were better my mother had not borne me.

5. (Lines 172–173) I have in quick determination

Thus **set** it **down**

6. (Lines 180–182) But yet do I believe

The origin and commencement of his grief

Sprung from neglected love.

IV. "To be, or not to be, that's the question" is a famous line in *Hamlet*. What is your understanding of it? Try to illustrate your understanding with your own experience.

UNIT 6

The History of England
A History

ORAL TASKS

1. How much do you know about the history of England?
2. Have you heard of the Glorious Revolution? What's the significance of it?

INTRODUCTION

History is the study of the past as it is described in written documents. The concept of history raises the possibility of "learning from history". And it suggests the possibility of better understanding ourselves in the present, by understanding the forces, choices, and circumstances that brought us to our current situation.

The History of England from the Accession of James II is the full title of the five-volume work. It covers the history from 1685 to 1702, encompassing the reign of James II, the Glorious Revolution, the co-regency of William III and Mary II, and up to William III's death. *The History* is famous for its brilliant, ringing prose and its confident, sometimes dogmatic emphasis on a progressive model of British history.

Sir Thomas James Babington Macaulay, generally known as Baron Macaulay (1800–1859), was a British historian and Whig politician. His books on British history have been hailed as literary masterpieces. Macaulay played a major role in introducing English and western concepts to the education in India. He supported the replacement of Persian by English as the official language, the use of English as the medium of instruction in all schools, and the training of English-speaking Indians as teachers. This led to Macaulayism in India.

This part is a description of William III, who is essential to the Glorious Revolution that changes the history of England.

PART 3

TEXTUAL READING[1]

Chapter VII

1▸ The place which William Henry, Prince of Orange Nassau[2], occupies in the history of England and of mankind is so great that it may be desirable to portray with some minuteness the strong lineaments of his character.

2▸ He was now in his thirty-seventh year. But both in body and in mind he was older than other men of the same age. Indeed it might be said that he had never been young. His external appearance is almost as well known to us as to his own captains and counsellors. Sculptors, painters, and medallists exerted their utmost skill in the work of transmitting his features to posterity; and his features were such as no artist could fail to seize, and such as, once seen, could never be forgotten. His name at once calls up before us a slender and feeble frame, a lofty and ample forehead, a nose curved like the beak of an eagle, an eye rivalling that of an eagle in brightness and keenness, a thoughtful and somewhat sullen brow, a firm and somewhat peevish mouth, a cheek pale, thin, and deeply furrowed by sickness and by care.[3] That pensive, severe, and solemn aspect could scarcely have belonged to a happy or a good-humoured man. But it indicates in a manner[4] not to be mistaken

portray: 描绘
minuteness: 详细
lineament: 轮廓
counsellor: 顾问
exert: 发挥
utmost: 最大的
posterity: 后代
slender: 修长的
feeble: 虚弱的
frame: 体格
ample: 宽阔的
beak: 鸟嘴
rival: 与……相匹敌
sullen: 阴沉
peevish: 暴躁的
furrow:（使）起皱纹
pensive: 沉思的
severe: 严肃的
solemn: 庄重的
good-humoured: 脾气好的

---

1 本篇出自：Lord Macaulay. *The History of England.* Edited and abridged with an introduction by Hugh Trevor-Roper. London: Penguin Books, 1986。

2 *Orange Nassau*：奥兰治–拿骚，拿骚王室。荷兰自 1815 年 3 月 16 日实行君主制，一直由奥兰治–拿骚王室统治。The House of Orange-Nassau 又称橙色王朝。

3 *His name... by care*: 该句由不同的片段组成，分别描绘威廉的 forehead, nose, eyes, brow, mouth 和 cheek。可译为："他的名字马上让我们的眼前浮现出这样一个人：他体格修长虚弱，前额高而宽，鼻子像鹰的嘴巴一样弯曲，眼睛像鹰一样明亮敏锐，眉毛让人感觉到他在沉思，有时显得阴沉，嘴巴透着刚毅，也有些暴躁，他的面颊苍白瘦削，满是疾病和操劳留下的皱纹。"（注：本篇译文由编者自译。下同。）

4 *in a manner*: 在某种意义上。e.g. His mild inquiries were answered snappishly and in a manner not to the point. 他和善的询问得到的却是不耐烦的回答，而且在某种意义上说是答非所问。

fortitude: 坚韧
reverse: 挫折

endow: 赋予

disheartened: 沮丧的
pretension: 抱负
aversion: 厌恶
oligarchy: 寡头统治集团
supreme: 至高无上的
fondly: 充满感情地
mortal: 不共戴天的
feigned: 虚假的
civility: 礼仪
domestic: 家仆
remonstrate: 抗议
vigilant: 警觉的

capacity equal to the most arduous enterprises, and *fortitude* not to be shaken by *reverses* or dangers. ⁵

3 ▸ Nature had largely *endowed* William with the qualities of a great ruler; and education had developed those qualities in no common degree. With strong natural sense, and rare force of will, he found himself, when first his mind began to open, a fatherless and motherless child, the chief of a great but depressed and *disheartened* party, and the heir to vast and indefinite *pretensions*, which excited the dread and *aversion* of the *oligarchy* then *supreme* in the United Provinces⁶,⁷. The common people, *fondly* attached during a century to his house, indicated, whenever they saw him, in a manner not to be mistaken, that they regarded him as their rightful head. The able and experienced ministers of the republic, *mortal* enemies of his name, came every day to pay their *feigned civilities* to him, and to observe the progress of his mind. The first movements of his ambition were carefully watched: every unguarded word uttered by him was noted down; nor had he near him any adviser on whose judgment reliance could be placed. He was scarcely fifteen years old when all the *domestics* who were attached to his interest, or who enjoyed any share of his confidence, were removed from under his roof by the jealous government. He *remonstrated* with energy beyond his years, but in vain. *Vigilant* observers saw the tears more than once rise in the eyes of the young state prisoner. His health, naturally

---

5　*But it indicates... shaken by reverses or dangers*: 该句的主体结构是 it indicates... capacity..., and fortitude...，其中 capacity 有一个前置定语 not to be mistaken 和一个后置定语 equal to the most arduous enterprises，fortitude 有一个后置定语 not to be shaken by reverses or dangers。可译为："但它以无可辨驳的方式表明，他具备能够胜任艰巨事业的能力和不为失败或者危险动摇的坚韧。"

6　*the United Provinces*: 联合省，大致相当于现在的荷兰。历史上第一个资本主义国家，在 17 世纪（即威廉生活的年代）达到鼎盛时期，是海上霸主，被誉为"海上马车夫"。

7　*With strong natural sense... in the United Provinces*: 该句的主体结构是 he found himself... a... child, the chief..., and the heir...，即"他发现自己是一个孩子，一位负责人，一位继承人"，其余的都是附属成分。with strong natural sense, and (with) rare force of will 是伴随状语成分，when first his mind began to open 是时间状语从句，这两个状语成分都是限定主句的 he found；which 引导的定语从句限定 pretensions，then supreme in the United Province 是后置定语成分来限定 the oligarchy。可译为："他具有天然禀赋和罕见的意志力，当他的心智初开，他发现自己没有父亲和母亲，他发现自己是一个伟大但消沉低落的政党的领袖，他发现自己是巨大而无限的抱负的继承人。这些抱负激起了当时在联合省权倾一时的寡头集团的恐惧和厌恶。"

delicate, sank for a time under the emotions which his desolate situation had produced. Such situations bewilder and unnerve the weak, but call forth all the strength of the strong. Surrounded by snares in which an ordinary youth would have perished, William learned to tread at once warily and firmly. Long before he reached manhood he knew how to keep secrets, how to baffle curiosity by dry and guarded answers, how to conceal all passions under the same show of grave tranquillity.

4▸ Meanwhile he made little proficiency in fashionable or literary accomplishments. The manners of the Dutch nobility of that age wanted the grace which was found in the highest perfection among the gentlemen of France, and which, in an inferior degree, embellished the Court of England; and his manners were altogether Dutch.[8] Even his countrymen thought him blunt. To foreigners he often seemed churlish. In his intercourse with the world in general he appeared ignorant or negligent of those arts which double the value of a favour and take away the sting of a refusal.[9] He was little interested in letters or science. The discoveries of Newton and Leibnitz[10], the poems of Dryden[11] and Boileau[12], were unknown to him. Dramatic performances tired him; and he was glad to turn away from the stage and to talk about public affairs, while Orestes was raving, or while Tartuffe[13] was pressing Elmira's hand. He had indeed some talent for sarcasm, and not

delicate: 虚弱的
desolate: 凄苦的
bewilder: 使迷惑
unnerve: 吓坏
snare: 陷阱
perish: 消亡
tread: 行走
baffle: 抑制
grave: 沉重的
tranquillity: 平静
nobility: 贵族
want: 缺乏
embellish: 装饰
blunt: 迟钝的
churlish: 乡巴佬气的
intercourse: 交流
sting: 刺痛

sarcasm: 挖苦

---

8 *The manners ... altogether Dutch*: 该句中有两个 which 引导的定语从句，in the highest perfection 和 in an inferior degree 分别是这两个定语从句中的插入成分，是表示程度的状语。可译为："那个时代的荷兰贵族缺乏一种优雅，这种优雅完美地体现在了法国绅士身上，（这种优雅在）英国稍逊一筹，但也装饰了宫廷。他的行为举止完全是荷兰式的。"

9 *In his intercourse... of a refusal*: 该句中，which 引导的定语从句限定 those arts，其中有两个并列谓语 double 和 take away。可译为："在他与一般世界的交流中，他对为人处世之道茫然无知，而那些为人处世之道能够使他在给人恩惠的时候，让人倍感温暖，在拒绝别人的时候，不让别人感到受伤害。"

10 *Leibnitz*: 戈特弗里德·威廉·凡·莱布尼兹（Gottfried Wilhelm von Leibniz）。德国自然科学的天才，与牛顿齐名，也是著名哲学家，被誉为17世纪的亚里士多德。

11 *Dryden*: 约翰·德莱顿（John Dryden）。英国古典主义时期戏剧家、批评家，王政复辟时期的桂冠诗人，著有《论戏剧诗》《悲剧批评的基础》等，是英国文学批评的创始人，他所创造的"英雄偶句诗体"成为英国诗歌的主要形式之一。

12 *Boileau*: 尼古拉·布瓦洛·德普雷奥（Nicolas Boileau Despreaux）。法国古典主义诗人、文学理论家，其著作《诗的艺术》对法国和英国古典主义产生深远影响，被誉为古典主义文学理论的经典。

13 *Tartuffe*: 塔尔士夫。法国著名喜剧作家莫里哀的同名喜剧的主人公，后以Tartuffe喻指伪君子。

quaint: 古怪的
affect: 喜欢
orator: 演说者
strenuous: 奋发的
sagacious: 有远见的
geometry: 几何
singularly: 异常地
comprehend: 理解

intelligibly: 可理解地
qualification: 资质

philosophical: 哲学的

municipal: 市政的

seldom employed, quite unconsciously, a natural rhetoric, quaint, indeed, but vigorous and original. He did not, however, in the least affect the character of a wit or of an orator. His attention had been confined to those studies which form strenuous and sagacious men of business. From a child he listened with interest when high questions of alliance, finance, and war were discussed. Of geometry he learned as much as was necessary for the construction of a ravelin or a hornwork. Of languages, by the help of a memory singularly powerful, he learned as much as was necessary to enable him to comprehend and answer without assistance everything that was said to him, and every letter which he received.[14] The Dutch was his own tongue. With the French he was not less familiar. He understood Latin, Italian, and Spanish. He spoke and wrote English and German, inelegantly, it is true, and inexactly, but fluently and intelligibly. No qualification could be more important to a man whose life was to be passed in organizing great alliances, and in commanding armies assembled from different countries.

5 ▸ One class of philosophical questions had been forced on his attention by circumstances, and seems to have interested him more than might have been expected from his general character. Among the Protestants[15] of the United Provinces, as among the Protestants of our island, there were two great religious parties which almost exactly coincided with two great political parties. The chiefs of the municipal oligarchy were Arminians[16], and

---

14 *Of languages, by the help... he received*：该句的主体结构是 he learned... to comprehend and answer... everything... and every letter...。as much as was necessary 作为插入成分，表示他所学的程度。可译为："谈到语言，借助异常强大的记忆力，他的所学足以使他在不依赖外界帮助的情况下理解并答复别人对他说的每一句话，收到的每一封信。"

15 *Protestant*：新教徒，即 protest（抗议）罗马天主教的信徒。最初指马丁·路德宗教改革中的信徒，后来由于对罗马天主教的抗议方式和教义不同，而产生了不同的新教派别，甚至彼此之间相互对立。其中比较有名的是马丁·路德创立的路德宗、加尔文创立的归正宗和作为英国国教的安立甘宗。

16 *Arminian*：阿米尼乌斯教派信徒。由荷兰神学家雅各布斯·阿米尼乌斯（Jacobus Arminius）创立，反对预定论，强调普世性的救赎和人的责任与意志自由，与加尔文派观点相左。简单地说，阿米尼乌斯教派认为人具有自由意志，能够通过自己的行为，即在现世的功德，改变甚至决定自己能否获得救赎。

were commonly regarded by the multitude as little better than Papists[17]. The princes of Orange had generally been the patrons of the Calvinistic divinity[18], and owed no small part of their popularity to their zeal for the doctrines of election and final perseverance, a zeal not always enlightened by knowledge or tempered by humanity.[19] William had been carefully instructed from a child in the theological system to which his family was attached, and regarded that system with even more than the partiality which men generally feel for a hereditary faith.[20] He had ruminated on the great enigmas which had been discussed in the Synod of Dort[21], something which suited his intellect and his temper. That example of intolerance indeed which some of his predecessors had set he never imitated. For all persecution he felt a fixed aversion, which he avowed, not only where the avowal was obviously politic, but on occasions where it seemed that his interest would have been promoted

multitude: 大众
patron: 支持者
divinity: 神学
zeal: 热情
doctrine: 教义
perseverance: 持久
enlighten: 启蒙
humanity: 人性
theological: 神学的
partiality: 偏爱
hereditary: 遗传的
ruminate: 反复思考
intellect: 才智
predecessor: 先辈
persecution: 迫害
avowal: 誓言

---

17 *Papist*: 罗马天主教教徒，教皇制的信奉者。天主教认为，信徒具有自由意志，可以通过教会和自己的行为获得上帝的恩宠，从而获得救赎。这些行为包括行善积德、向教会捐献等。在这一点上，天主教与阿米尼乌斯教派的区别在于，天主教徒的救赎必须通过教会。

18 *the Calvinistic divinity*：加尔文主义神学，或加尔文教派。信奉法国宗教改革家约翰·加尔文（John Calvin）的神学观点，又称归正宗神学。1536 年加尔文发表《基督教要义》，系统清晰地阐明了他的主要神学观点，成为基督教神学里程碑式的巨著。在自由意志问题上，加尔文教派与天主教和阿米尼乌斯教派不同，前者反对人有自由意志，认为人的一切是上帝预先安排好了的，无论人行善还是做恶，都无法改变人的救赎。

19 *The princes of Orange... by humanity*: 该句较长，但主体结构明晰。主语是 the princes of Orange，有两个并列谓语 had been... 和 owed...，最后一部分的 a zeal not always... 说明前面 zeal。可译为："奥兰治家族的君主通常都是加尔文主义神学的支持者，他们受欢迎是在很大程度上得益于他们对于上帝选拔和上帝持续恩典的热情，这种热情往往并非是受到知识的启蒙或者是受到人性的影响。"

20 *William had been... a hereditary faith*: 该句的主语 William 有两个并列谓语 had been... 和 regard...，因此可以分成两个部分来理解，在后一部分中，which 引导定语从句限定 partiality。可译为："威廉自幼就在家族信仰的神学体系中接受认真的教导，他对于那种体系的偏爱远胜于一般人对于世袭信仰的偏爱。"

21 *the Synod of Dort*: 多特大会。1610 年阿米乌斯抗辩派发表抗辩宣言，质疑改革宗神学传统。这篇抗辩文引发强烈的争议，改革宗教会在多特举行了有史以来最大的一次会议，以解决这一纷争。来自荷兰、苏格兰、英格兰、比利时、德国、瑞士、法兰西等全世界各地改革宗的代表参加此次议会，但是议会采取了加尔文的信仰传统，抗辩派的提案被否决，最终的结果是通过一份文件，即后来称之为"多特正典"的信仰文件。文件包括对预定论、肯定的赎罪、全然的败坏、有效的恩典和上帝对圣徒的保守的阐释。

dissimulation:
装糊涂

predestination:
预定论

keystone: 基调

superintend:
主管，监督

providence: 天意

Epicurean:
享乐主义者

sap: 活力

speculative:
推测的

conduct: 行为

blossom:
繁荣

precocious:
早熟的

diplomatist:
外交家

weighty: 重大的

lad: 小伙子

composure: 镇静

imperturbable:
泰然自若的

judicious:
明智的

by dissimulation or by silence.²² His theological opinions, however, were even more decided than those of his ancestors. The tenet of predestination²³ was the keystone of his religion. He often declared that, if he were to abandon that tenet, he must abandon with it all belief in a superintending Providence, and must become a mere Epicurean²⁴.

6 ▸ Except in this single instance, all the sap of his vigorous mind was early drawn away from the speculative to the practical. The faculties which are necessary for the conduct of important business ripened in him at a time of life when they have scarcely begun to blossom in ordinary men. Since Octavius²⁵ the world had seen no such instance of precocious statesmanship. Skilful diplomatists were surprised to hear the weighty observations which at seventeen the Prince made on public affairs, and still more surprised to see a lad, in situations in which he might have been expected to betray strong passion, preserve a composure as imperturbable as their own.²⁶ At eighteen he sat among the fathers of the commonwealth, grave, discreet, and judicious as the oldest among them. At twenty-one, in a day of gloom and terror, he was placed at the head of the administration. At twenty-three he was renowned throughout Europe as a soldier and a politician. He had put

....

22 *For all persecution... or by silence*: 该句的主句是 he felt a fixed aversion，其余的都是限定成分，which 是限定 aversion 的定语从句，其中有两个 where 引导的状语从句，说明 avowed 的场合。可译为："他对所有的迫害都感到一种固执的厌恶，对此，不仅是在誓言具有明显政治色彩的场合，而且还在一些装糊涂或者不说话或许更符合他的利益的场合，他都曾经发过誓。"

23 *the tenet of predestination*：预定论，加尔文派的重要神学观点。加尔文从上帝的主权出发，认为上帝在创世之前就按自己的意志拣选（预定）那些会得救的人。

24 *Epicurean*: 伊比鸠鲁派，享乐主义者。伊比鸠鲁学派是古希腊著名哲学家、思想家伊比鸠鲁（Epicurus）所创建的一个哲学流派，他发展了苏格拉底学生阿瑞斯提普斯的享乐主义观点，并与德谟克利特的原子论观点结合起来。因其认为最大的善是驱逐恐惧，追求快乐，以达到宁静自由的状态，故后世又以 Epicurean 指称享乐主义者。

25 *Octavius*: 盖乌斯·屋大维·奥古斯都（Gaius Octavius Augustus），罗马帝国的第一位君主，凯撒的外孙。公元前 43 年，凯撒被刺，屋大维登上政治舞台。他击败其他对手，掌控大权，并于公元前 30 年被元老院赐封"奥古斯都"的称号，即"神圣伟大"之意。

26 *Skilful diplomatists... as their own*: 该句的主语是 skilful diplomatists，有两个并列的谓语成分，即 were surprised to hear 和 still more surprised to see。第一个谓语成分后面跟着一个宾语，宾语中有一个定语从句；第二个谓语成分中，有 in situations in which... 的插入成分做状语。可译为："高明的外交家非常惊讶地听到这位年仅 17 岁的君主在公共事务上做出的重大判断，而且更加惊讶地发现，在别人都认为他必定无法控制强烈的情绪下，这位小伙子能够像他们一样保持镇定自若。"

domestic factions under his feet: he was the soul of a mighty coalition; and he had contended with honour in the field against some of the greatest generals of the age.

faction: 内讧
coalition: 联合政府
contend: 斗争
warrior: 斗士

7 ▸ His personal tastes were those rather of a warrior than of a statesman: but he, like his great-grandfather, the silent Prince[27] who founded the Batavian commonwealth[28], occupies a far higher place among statesmen than among warriors. The event of battles, indeed, is not an unfailing test of the abilities of a commander; and it would be peculiarly unjust to apply this test to William: for it was his fortune to be almost always opposed to captains who were consummate masters of their art, and to troops far superior in discipline to his own.[29] Yet there is reason to believe that he was by no means equal, as a general in the field, to some who ranked far below him in intellectual powers. To those whom he trusted he spoke on this subject with the magnanimous frankness of a man who had done great things, and who could well afford to acknowledge some deficiencies. He had never, he said, served an apprenticeship to the military profession. He had been placed, while still a boy, at the head of an army. Among his officers there had been none competent to instruct him. His own blunders and their consequences had been his only lessons. "I would give," he once exclaimed, "a good part of my estates to have served a few campaigns under the Prince of Condé[30] before I had to command against him." It is not improbable that the circumstance which prevented William from attaining any eminent dexterity in strategy may

magnanimous: 慷慨的
frankness: 坦诚
deficiency: 不足
apprenticeship: 学徒
blunder: 错误
dexterity: 灵活

27　*the silence Prince*: 威廉一世。他曾出使法国，法王亨利二世向其讲述了将基督教新教徒赶出尼德兰的计划，威廉虽大为震惊，却缄口不提反对意见，从而获得"沉默者"绰号。威廉一世反对西班牙统治，为自由独立而战，独立革命后就任尼德兰联省共和国首任执政，1584 年遇刺身亡。

28　*the Batavian commonwealth*：联省共和国，又称荷兰共和国。1579 年荷兰北方六省宣布组成联盟，1581 年威廉一世就任首任执政，1594 年格罗宁根省加入，总共有七省，史称尼德兰联省共和国。

29　*The event of battles, ... to his own*: 该句由三部分组成，其中 to captains 与 to troops 并列。可译为："的确，战争事件并非是检验指挥官能力的屡试不爽的手段；以此来测试威廉尤其不公：因为命中注定他的对手要么是战术超群的长官，要么是纪律远比自己队伍严明的队伍。"

30　*the Prince of Condé*: 路易二世·德·波旁（Louis II de Bourbon），第四代孔代亲王。孔代亲王为法国波旁王朝时期的贵族称号。路易二世·德·波旁被认为是 17 世纪最伟大的军事家和杰出的统帅。在法荷战争中为法国军队的统帅，1674 年在塞纳夫战役中击败当时的奥兰治亲王威廉。因此麦考利在下文中称其为"伟大的孔代亲王""威廉最杰出的对手"。

have been favourable to the general vigour of his intellect. If his battles were not those of a great tactician, they entitled him to be called a great man. No disaster could for one moment deprive him of his firmness or of the entire possession of all his faculties. His defeats were repaired with such marvellous celerity that, before his enemies had sung the Te Deum[31], he was again ready for conflict; nor did his adverse fortune ever deprive him of the respect and confidence of his soldiers.[32]

8 ▸ That respect and confidence he owed in no small measure to his personal courage. Courage, in the degree which is necessary to carry a soldier without disgrace through a campaign, is possessed, or might, under proper training, be acquired, by the great majority of men. But courage like that of William is rare indeed. He was proved by every test; by war, by wounds, by painful and depressing maladies, by raging seas, by the imminent and constant risk of assassination, a risk which has shaken very strong nerves, a risk which severely tried even the adamantine fortitude of Cromwell[33].[34] Yet none could ever discover what that thing was which the Prince of Orange feared. His advisers could with difficulty induce him to take any precaution against the pistols and daggers of conspirators. Old sailors were amazed at the composure which he preserved amidst roaring breakers on a perilous coast. In battle his bravery made him conspicuous even among tens of thousands of brave warriors, drew forth the generous applause of hostile armies, and was scarcely ever questioned even by the injustice of hostile factions. During his first campaigns he exposed himself like a man who sought for death, was always foremost in the charge and last in the retreat, fought, sword in hand, in the thickest press, and, with a musket ball in his arm and the blood streaming over his cuirass, still stood his ground and waved his hat under the hottest

---

tactician: 战术家

celerity: 迅速
adverse: 逆境的

malady: 疾病
imminent: 迫近的
assassination: 暗杀
adamantine: 坚定不移的
induce: 引诱
precaution: 预防
pistol: 手枪
dagger: 匕首
conspirator: 阴谋者
perilous: 危险的
conspicuous: 显而易见的
applause: 喝彩
hostile: 敌方的
cuirass: 胸甲

---

31 *the Te Deum*: 基督教的颂歌，赞美诗，弥赛。Te Deum 来自于拉丁文 Te Deum laudamus 的字首，意为 "噢，上帝，我们赞美"。

32 *His defeats were repaired... confidence of his soldiers*: 该句中含 such... that... 的结构。可译为："他迅速重振旗鼓，以至于在敌人唱赞歌之前，他又准备反击了；他的逆境也没有让他失去对士兵们的尊重和信心。"

33 *Cromwell*: 奥利弗·克伦威尔（Oliver Cromwell）。英国资产阶级革命领袖，杰出的政治家、军事家、宗教领袖，是英国内战时期议会军的军事统帅和共和时期的护国公。

34 *He was proved... fortitude of Cromwell*: 该句由几个并列结构组成，其中一组是由六个 by 组成的，另外一组是由两个 a risk which 的定语从句组成，用来解释前面的 risk of assassination。可译为："他经受住了各种考验，战争、伤痛、痛苦与压抑的疾病、波涛汹涌的大海，以及迫在眉睫且无时不在的暗杀风险，这种风险让强者也为之震撼，甚至曾极大地考验了克伦威尔坚定不移的刚毅。"

fire.³⁵ His friends adjured him to take more care of a life invaluable to his country; and his most illustrious antagonist, the great Condé, remarked, after the bloody day of Seneff, that the Prince of Orange had in all things borne himself like an old general, except in exposing himself like a young soldier. William denied that he was guilty of temerity. It was, he said, from a sense of duty and on a cool calculation of what the public interest required that he was always at the post of danger. The troops which he commanded had been little used to war, and shrank from a close encounter with the veteran soldiery of France. It was necessary that their leader should show them how battles were to be won. And in truth more than one day which had seemed hopelessly lost was retrieved by the hardihood with which he rallied his broken battalions and cut down with his own hand the cowards who set the example of flight. Sometimes, however, it seemed that he had a strange pleasure in venturing his person. It was remarked that his spirits were never so high and his manners never so gracious and easy as amidst the tumult and carnage of a battle. Even in his pastimes he liked the excitement of danger. Cards, chess, and billiards gave him no pleasure. The chase was his favourite recreation; and he loved it most when it was most hazardous. His leaps were sometimes such that his boldest companions did not like to follow him. He seems even to have thought the most hardy field sports of England effeminate, and to have pined in the Great Park of Windsor³⁶ for the game which he had been used to drive to bay in the forests of Guelders³⁷, wolves, and wild boars, and huge stags with sixteen antlers.³⁸

adjure: 恳请
illustrious: 显赫的
antagonist: 敌手
temerity: 鲁莽

veteran: 富有经验的
soldiery: 军队
retrieve: 挽回
hardihood: 刚毅
rally: 召集
battalion: 大军
gracious: 优雅的
tumult: 喧闹
carnage: 残杀
chase: 追逐
recreation: 娱乐
hazardous: 危险的
leap: 跳越
effeminate: 柔弱的
pine: 渴望

---

35 *During his first campaigns... under the hottest fire*: 该句较长，who 所引导的定语从句较为复杂，who 在从句中作主语；sought for..., was always foremost..., fought, still stood... 四个动词或系表结构并置，作谓语；sword in hand, in the thickest press, and with a musket ball in his arm and the blood streaming over his cuirass 三个短语作伴随状语，修饰 fought。可译为："在他的第一场战役中，他以这样的面目展示在众人之前：他不畏生死，冲锋时在最前面，撤退时却是最后一个，在厮杀的人群中，他利剑在手、子弹上膛、胸甲上淌着血，却仍坚守阵地，纷飞战火中挥舞着他的帽子。"

36 *the Great Park of Windsor*: 温莎大公园，温莎古堡外的大公园。

37 *the forests of Guelders*: 荷兰的格德司森林国家公园。

38 *He seems even to... with sixteen antlers*: 该句中有两个并列成分 seems... to have thought..., and to have pined...。后一个成分中含有 which 引导的定语从句，限定 the game。可译为："他似乎甚至认为英格兰最勇敢的田野运动也是柔弱的，在温莎大公园中他渴望着曾经在格德司森林将狼群、野猪，以及共有 16 只鹿角的巨大牡鹿们围困起来的游戏。"

9 ▸ The audacity of his spirit was the more remarkable because his physical organization was unusually delicate. From a child he had been weak and sickly. In the prime of manhood his complaints had been aggravated by a severe attack of smallpox. He was asthmatic and consumptive. His slender frame was shaken by a constant hoarse cough. He could not sleep unless his head was propped by several pillows, and could scarcely draw his breath in any but the purest air. Cruel headaches frequently tortured him. Exertion soon fatigued him. The physicians constantly kept up the hopes of his enemies by fixing some date beyond which, if there were anything certain in medical science, it was impossible that his broken constitution could hold out.[39] Yet, through a life which was one long disease, the force of his mind never failed, on any great occasion, to bear up his suffering and languid body.

10 ▸ He was born with violent passions and quick sensibilities: but the strength of his emotions was not suspected by the world. From the multitude his joy and his grief, his affection and his resentment, were hidden by a phlegmatic serenity, which made him pass for the most coldblooded of mankind. Those who brought him good news could seldom detect any sign of pleasure. Those who saw him after a defeat looked in vain for any trace of vexation. He praised and reprimanded, rewarded and punished, with the stern tranquillity of a Mohawk[40] chief: but those who knew him well and saw him near were aware that under all this ice a fierce fire was constantly burning. It was seldom that anger deprived him of power over himself. But when he was really enraged the first outbreak of his passion was terrible. It was indeed scarcely safe to approach him. On these rare occasions, however, as soon as he regained his self command, he made such ample reparation to those whom he had wronged as tempted them to wish that he would go into a fury again. His affection was as impetuous as his wrath. Where he loved, he loved with the whole energy of his strong mind. When death separated him from what he loved, the few who witnessed his agonies trembled for his reason and his life. To a very small circle of intimate friends, on whose fidelity and secrecy he could absolutely depend, he was a different man from the reserved and stoical William whom the multitude supposed to be destitute

---

39　*The physicians constantly kept up... could hold out*: 该句中 beyond which... 作定语从句，修饰 some date。在从句中，if 所引导的条件句插入句中，which 在句中作 hold out 的宾语。可译为："医生们宣布：如果没有医疗奇迹发生，他糟糕的身体不可能熬过某一个期限，这些消息时不时地给他的敌人带去希望。"

40　*Mohawk*: 莫霍克部落，居住在现在的纽约州北部的土著部落。

of human feelings.⁴¹ He was kind, cordial, open, even convivial and jocose, would sit at table many hours, and would bear his full share in festive conversation.

cordial: 热忱的
convivial: 欢快的
jocose: 诙谐的
festive: 喜庆的

11 ▸ Highest in his favour stood a gentleman of his household named Bentinck, sprung from a noble Batavian race, and destined to be the founder of one of the great patrician houses of England. The fidelity of Bentinck had been tried by no common test. It was while the United Provinces were struggling for existence against the French power that the young Prince on whom all their hopes were fixed was seized by the smallpox. That disease had been fatal to many members of his family, and at first wore, in his case, a peculiarly malignant aspect. The public consternation was great. The streets of the Hague⁴² were crowded from daybreak to sunset by persons anxiously asking how his Highness was. At length his complaint took a favourable turn. His escape was attributed partly to his own singular equanimity, and partly to the intrepid and indefatigable friendship of Bentinck. From the hands of Bentinck alone William took food and medicine. By Bentinck alone William was lifted from his bed and laid down in it. "Whether Bentinck slept or not while I was ill," said William to Temple, with great tenderness, "I know not. But this I know, that, through sixteen days and nights, I never once called for anything but that Bentinck was instantly at my side." Before the faithful servant had entirely performed his task, he had himself caught the contagion. Still, however, he bore up against drowsiness and fever till his master was pronounced convalescent. Then, at length, Bentinck asked leave to go home. It was time: for his limbs would no longer support him. He was in great danger, but recovered, and, as soon as he left his bed, hastened to the army, where, during many sharp campaigns, he was ever found, as he had been in peril of a different kind, close to William's side.⁴³

patrician: 贵族的

malignant: 恶性的
consternation: 恐慌
equanimity: 镇静
intrepid: 无畏的
indefatigable: 牢不可破的

contagion: 传染病
drowsiness: 瞌睡
convalescent: 恢复中的

---

41 *To a very small circle... of human feelings*: 该句的主体结构是 he was a different man from the reserved and stoical William，前面 whose 引导的定语从句是说明对于什么样的人他是不一样的，后面 whom 引导的定语从句是说明普通人是怎么看他的。可译为："他有一小圈知心好友，忠诚可靠、严格保密；面对这些朋友，他完全不是普通大众所认为的缺乏人情味、沉默寡言、清心寡欲的威廉。"

42 *Hague*: 海牙，荷兰的一座城市。

43 *He was in great danger... close to William's side*: 除 he was in great danger 之外，其余部分的主句是 (he) hastened to the army。在 where 引导的定语从句中，he was ever found... close to William's side 是主句。可译为："他身处极度危险中，但是一旦恢复，一旦离开床，他就匆忙忙赶到部队；人们不难发现，在许多艰苦的战役中，就像他曾经经历过的各种危险一样，他一直紧紧地站在威廉的身旁。"

descendant: 后代

frigid: 冷酷的
ingenuousness: 天真
impart: 坦露
mingle: 结合

carousal: 喧闹的酒宴

procure: 获取

devotional: 虔诚的
amiable: 亲切的
garrulity: 饶舌
sedate: 沉静的
effusion: 倾诉
felicity: 幸福

12▶ Such was the origin of a friendship as warm and pure as any that ancient or modern history records. The descendants of Bentinck still preserve many letters written by William to their ancestor: and it is not too much to say that no person who has not studied those letters can form a correct notion of the Prince's character. He whom even his admirers generally accounted the most distant and frigid of men here forgets all distinctions of rank, and pours out all his thoughts with the ingenuousness of a schoolboy.44 He imparts without reserve secrets of the highest moment. He explains with perfect simplicity vast designs affecting all the governments of Europe. Mingled with his communications on such subjects are other communications of a very different, but perhaps not of a less interesting kind. All his adventures, all his personal feelings, his long runs after enormous stags, his carousals on St. Hubert's day45, the growth of his plantations, the failure of his melons, the state of his stud, his wish to procure an easy pad nag for his wife, his vexation at learning that one of his household, after ruining a girl of good family, refused to marry her, his fits of seasickness, his coughs, his headaches, his devotional moods, his gratitude for the divine protection after a great escape, his struggles to submit himself to the divine will after a disaster, are described with an amiable garrulity hardly to have been expected from the most discreet and sedate statesman of the age.46 Still more remarkable is the careless effusion of his tenderness, and the brotherly interest which he takes in his friend's domestic felicity. When an heir is born to Bentinck, "he will live, I hope," says William, "to be as good a fellow as you are; and,

---

44 *He whom even his admirers... ingenuousness of a schoolboy*: 该句的主体结构是 He... forgets..., and pours out..., whom 引导的宾语从句说明主语 he。可译为：“甚至他的仰慕者一般也认为他是最难以接近的冷酷的人，但是在这里，他忘记了所有的社会地位，以一个孩子的天真倾诉了全部的心思。”

45 *St. Hubert's day*: 圣·休伯特斋戒日。圣·休伯特（Saint Hubertus or Huber），列日（比利时城市）主教，猎人、数学家、眼镜商、金属工人的守护神。11 月 3 日被定为圣·休伯特斋戒日。

46 *All his adventures, ... statesman of the age*: 该句中，从 all his adventures 到 after a disaster 都是这个句子的主语，其中包括 15 个并列的 his 描述他的状态。hardly to have been expected from 用来限定 garrulity。可译为："他所有的冒险、他所有的个人情感、他长途追逐巨大的牡鹿、他在圣·休伯特斋戒日的喧闹、他种植园的长势、他西瓜种植的失败、他种马的状况、他希望为夫人弄到一匹好骑的款步马、他在听到一位家人玷污了良家女子又不愿意娶她后的烦恼、他晕船发作的情形、他的咳嗽、他的头痛、他虔诚的情绪、他在大撤退后对圣灵保护的感激、他在灾难后使自己屈从神圣意志的挣扎等，都在亲切的喋喋不休中讲述出来，很难想象这些是出自这个时代最谨慎稳重的政治家之手。"

if I should have a son, our children will love each other, I hope, as we have done." Through life he continues to regard the little Bentincks with paternal kindness. He calls them by endearing diminutives: he takes charge of them in their father's absence, and, though vexed at being forced to refuse them any pleasure, will not suffer them to go on a hunting party, where there would be risk of a push from a stag's horn, or to sit up late at a riotous supper. When their mother is taken ill during her husband's absence, William, in the midst of business of the highest moment, finds time to send off several expresses in one day with short notes containing intelligence of her state. On one occasion, when she is pronounced out of danger after a severe attack, the Prince breaks forth into fervent expressions of gratitude to God. "I write," he says, "with tears of joy in my eyes." There is a singular charm in such letters, penned by a man whose irresistible energy and inflexible firmness extorted the respect of his enemies, whose cold and ungracious demeanour repelled the attachment of almost all his partisans, and whose mind was occupied by gigantic schemes which have changed the face of the world.⁴⁷

diminutives: 昵称

riotous: 喧闹的

fervent: 热烈的

extort: 强求
demeanour: 行为方式
repel: 驱走

13 ▶ His kindness was not misplaced. Bentinck was early pronounced by Temple to be the best and truest servant that ever prince had the good fortune to possess, and continued through life to merit that honourable character. The friends were indeed made for each other. William wanted neither a guide nor a flatterer. Having a firm and just reliance on his own judgment, he was not partial to counsellors who dealt much in suggestions and objections. At the same time he had too much discernment, and too much elevation of mind, to be gratified by sycophancy. The confidant of such a prince ought to be a man, not of inventive genius or commanding spirit, but brave and faithful, capable of executing orders punctually, of keeping secrets inviolably, of observing facts vigilantly, and of reporting them truly; and such a man was Bentinck.⁴⁸

merit: 值得

flatterer: 阿谀奉承者

discernment: 辨别力
elevation: 高度
gratified: 称心的
sycophancy: 奉承
confidant: 心腹
inventive: 别出心裁的
inviolably: 神圣地

---

47 *There is a singular charm... the face of the world*: 该句中有三个并列的 whose 引导的定语从句来限定 a man，说明写那些信的是什么样的人。可译为："这些信中有一种独特的魅力，写信人不可抑止的精力和不变的坚定意志使他的敌人也不得不敬他三分，他冷酷粗野的行为方式使几乎所有该党的支持者都无法亲近他，他脑袋里只想着改变世界面貌的巨大计划。"

48 *The confidant of such a prince... was Bentinck*: 这句话较长，not of... but... 作后置定语修饰 a man；capable of 后接四个短语，与 brave and faithful 并置，共同说明 Bentinck 的能力。可译为："这位王子的密友应该是这样的：他并非天生的天才或指挥官，却勇敢、忠诚，他能如期执行命令，能保证机密不外泄，能留心观察事物并能如实汇报。本廷顿就是这样一个人。"

14▸ William was not less fortunate in marriage than in friendship. Yet his marriage had not at first promised much domestic happiness. His choice had been determined chiefly by political considerations: nor did it seem likely that any strong affection would grow up between a handsome girl of sixteen, well disposed indeed, and naturally intelligent, but ignorant and simple, and a bridegroom who, though he had not completed his twenty-eighth year, was in constitution older than her father, whose manner was chilling, and whose head was constantly occupied by public business or by field sports.[49] For a time William was a negligent husband. He was indeed drawn away from his wife by other women, particularly by one of her ladies, Elizabeth Villiers, who, though destitute of personal attractions, and disfigured by a hideous squint, possessed talents which well fitted her to partake his cares. He was indeed ashamed of his errors, and spared no pains to conceal them: but, in spite of all his precautions, Mary well knew that he was not strictly faithful to her. Spies and talebearers, encouraged by her father, did their best to inflame her resentment. A man of a very different character, the excellent Ken, who was her chaplain at the Hague during some months, was so much incensed by her wrongs that he, with more zeal than discretion, threatened to reprimand her husband severely.[50] She, however, bore her injuries with a meekness and patience which deserved, and gradually obtained, William's esteem and gratitude.

15▸ Yet there still remained one cause of estrangement. A time would probably come when the Princess, who had been educated only to work embroidery, to play on the spinet, and to read the Bible and *The Whole Duty of Man*[51], would

---

bridegroom: 新郎
constitution: 体格
chilling: 冷漠的

disfigure: 使变丑
hideous: 可怕的
squint: 斜视
partake: 分享
talebearer: 告密者
inflame: 煽动
chaplain: 牧师
incense: 激怒
meekness: 温顺

estrangement: 疏远
embroidery: 刺绣

---

49 *nor did it seem... public business or by field sports*: 该句较长，well deposed, naturally intelligent, ignorant and simple 三个形容词或分词短语作后置定语修饰 a handsome girl of 16，who 和 whose 所引导的定语从句修饰 a bridegroom。可译为：" 新娘是一位16岁的端庄少女，性情好，聪明但却无知、简单；新郎呢，虽然才28岁，体质却还不如新娘的父亲，而且性情冷漠，头脑里整天装的都是公事或野外运动，这两人之间会滋生任何强烈的爱情才怪呢。"

50 *A man of a very different character, ... her husband severely*: 该句的主体结构是 A man... was so... that he... threatened...。可译为："杰出的肯恩是一位性格与众不同的人，有几个月他是她在海牙的牧师，她所受到的冤屈使他极其愤怒，他甚至情绪化地威胁要严厉申斥她的丈夫。"

51 *The Whole Duty of Man*:《人所当尽的本分》。新教的祷告书，1658年由亨利·哈蒙德引入，标题来自于《传道书》12章第13节（*Ecclesiastes 12:13*）"让我们听一听整件事的结论：敬畏神，谨守他的诫命，这是人所当尽的本分。"（"Let us hear the conclusion of the whole matter: Fear God, and keep his commandments: for this is the whole duty of man."）

be the chief of a great monarchy, and would hold the balance of Europe, while her lord, ambitious, versed in affairs, and bent on great enterprises, would find in the British government no place marked out for him, and would hold power only from her bounty and during her pleasure.[52] It is not strange that a man so fond of authority as William, and so conscious of a genius for command, should have strongly felt that jealousy which, during a few hours of royalty, put dissension between Guildford Dudley[53] and the Lady Jane[54], and which produced a rupture still more tragical between Darnley[55] and the Queen of Scots[56]. The Princess of Orange had not the faintest suspicion of her husband's feelings. Her preceptor, Bishop Compton, had instructed her carefully in religion, and had especially guarded her mind against the arts of Roman Catholic divines, but had left her profoundly ignorant of the English constitution and of her own position. She knew that her marriage vow bound her to obey her husband; and it had never occurred to her that the relation in which they stood to each other might one day be inverted. She had been nine years married before she discovered the cause of William's discontent; nor would she ever have learned it from himself. In

dissension: 不和
rupture: 裂缝
faint: 微小的
preceptor: 指导老师

constitution: 宪法
vow: 誓言
invert: 反转
discontent: 不满

---

52 *A time would probably come... during her pleasure*: 该句较长，while 所引导的让步状语从句中，her lord 指 "威廉"，ambitious, versed in affairs, and bent on great enterprises，这三个形容词、分词短语作后置定语，修饰 the lord。可译为："玛丽公主所接受的教育就是学习刺绣、弹钢琴、读《圣经》和《人所当尽的本分》，可有朝一日她却要成为一个巨大王室的首脑，要维持欧洲的平衡。当这一刻到来之时，她那野心勃勃、精通事务、立志建立一番伟业的丈夫却发现，在英国的政府里没有为他而设的位置，他要获得权力只能靠玛丽的慷慨，只能来自于她高兴之时。"

53 *Guildford Dudley*: 吉尔福德·达德利，诺森伯兰公爵的儿子，简·格雷的丈夫。

54 *the Lady Jane*: 简·格雷（Jane Grey），在位九天的英国女皇。诺森伯兰公爵谋划将简·格雷嫁给自己的儿子，推动简·格雷于 1553 年登上王位，继而试图将自己的儿子推上王位。爱德华六世惧怕死后罗马天主教掌控英国，拟定《继承法》，将王位传于新教徒身份的简·格雷，而将同父异母的姐姐玛丽和伊丽莎白排除在外。玛丽一世登基后将简·格雷和吉尔福德·达德利囚禁于伦敦塔，要求格雷放弃其新教信仰以换取求生的机会，遭其拒绝。格雷和达德利死于 1554 年 2 月。

55 *Darnley*: 达恩利勋爵，亨利·斯图亚特，玛丽的表兄，玛丽女王的第二任丈夫。达恩利贪求权力，要求玛丽在他的头衔上赠以 "国王"，后死于阴谋。玛丽一世被疑为幕后黑手，并在被囚于英格兰时受伊丽莎白女王质询，但质询方最后得出的结论是：没有足够的证据证明玛丽是有罪的。此处，麦考莱引用典故类比威廉与吉尔福德·达德利、达恩利勋爵相似的身份和心态。

56 *the Queen of Scots*: 苏格兰女王玛丽一世，玛丽·斯图亚特（Mary Stuart），苏格兰的统治者。1558 年同法国王子弗朗西斯结婚，1559 年成为法国王后，弗朗西斯去世后返回苏格兰亲政，因其天主教信仰而为苏格兰加尔文教徒所不满。1565 年嫁给亨利·斯图亚特。1567 年被废黜，次年逃入英格兰，被英格兰女王伊丽莎白软禁，并于 1587 年被处死。

reconciliation:
和解

general his temper inclined him rather to brood over his griefs than to give utterance to them; and in this particular case his lips were sealed by a very natural delicacy. At length a complete explanation and reconciliation were brought about by the agency of Gilbert Burnet.[57]

PART 4

EXERCISES

I. Answer the following questions according to the reading text.

1. What does William III look like?
2. During his younger years, how did William III live his life? What's the influence upon his life?
3. What does William III like to do during his spare time?
4. Why does William III love Calvinistic divinity so much?
5. How does William III acquire his ability to command?
6. In his daily life, what kind of person is William III?
7. Why is Bentinck so much trust-worthy by William III?
8. What kind of person is Mary? What is special in the relationship between Mary and William?

II. Paraphrase the following sentences with your own words, and then translate them into Chinese.

1. Sculptors, painters, and medallists exerted their utmost skill in the work of transmitting his features to posterity; and his features were such as no artist could fail to seize, and such as, once seen, could never be forgotten. (Para. 2)

2. Nature had largely endowed William with the qualities of a great ruler; and education had developed those qualities in no common degree. (Para. 3)

---

57 *Gilbert Burnet*: 吉尔伯特·伯内特，苏格兰神学家、历史学家，精通多国语言，1689年被威廉三世任命为索尔兹伯里主教。

3. No qualification could be more important to a man whose life was to be passed in organizing great alliances, and in commanding armies assembled from different countries. (Para. 4)

4. To those whom he trusted he spoke on this subject with the magnanimous frankness of a man who had done great things, and who could well afford to acknowledge some deficiencies. (Para. 7)

5. Courage, in the degree which is necessary to carry a soldier without disgrace through a campaign, is possessed, or might, under proper training, be acquired, by the great majority of men. (Para. 8)

III. Figure out the meanings of the phrases in bold, and then make another sentence with each of the phrases.

1. Such situations bewilder and unnerve the weak, but **call forth** all the strength of the strong. (Para. 3)

2. Dramatic performances tired him; and he was glad to **turn away from** the stage and to talk about public affairs, while Orestes was raving, or while Tartuffe was pressing Elmira's hand. (Para. 4)

3. From the multitude his joy and his grief, his affection and his resentment, were hidden by a phlegmatic serenity, which made him **pass for** the most coldblooded of mankind. (Para. 10)

4. Highest in his favour stood a gentleman of his household named Bentinck, **sprung from** a noble Batavian race. (Para. 11)

5. Still, however, he **bore up against** drowsiness and fever till his master was pronounced convalescent. (Para. 11)

6. He **takes charge of** them in their father's absence. (Para. 12)

7. In general his temper inclined him rather to **brood over** his griefs than to give utterance to them. (Para. 15)

IV. Religious conflicts were important causes for historical changes in England. Consult dictionaries and write down your understandings of the following religions in your own words.

1. Papist or Catholicism

2. Protestant

3. Lutheranism
4. Calvinistic divinity
5. The tenet of predestination
6. Arminianism

V. Write down your impression of William III in your own words. Your writing can emphasize on one aspect of his life, such as his childhood, his interests, his commanding ability, his friendship, his marriage, etc.

An Inquiry into the Nature and Causes of the Wealth of Nations
An Essay

ORAL TASKS

1. How much do you know about *The Wealth of Nations*?
2. What is your understanding of the division of labour? Can you give us an example to show your division of labour in your daily life?

INTRODUCTION

An essay is, generally, a piece of formal writing that gives the author's own argument, which is characterized by "serious purpose, logical organization and length". It is commonly concerned with the author's learned arguments, observations of daily life, recollections, and reflections.

An Inquiry into the Nature and Causes of the Wealth of Nations (*The Wealth of Nations* for short) is one of the world's first collected descriptions of what builds nations' wealth, and is today a fundamental work in classical economics. First published in 1776, the book touches upon such broad topics as the division of labour, productivity, and free markets.

Adam Smith (1723–1790) was a Scottish pioneer of political economy and a key figure during the Scottish Enlightenment era. Smith is best known for his two classic works, *An Inquiry into the Nature and Causes of the Wealth of Nations* (1776) and *The Theory of Moral Sentiments* (1759). Educated at the University of Glasgow and Balliol College, Oxford, Smith laid the foundations of classical free market economic theory. *The Wealth of Nations* was a precursor to modern academic discipline of economics.

This excerpt is about the division of labour. Huge efficiencies can be gained by breaking production down into many small tasks, each undertaken by specialist hands. This leaves producers with a surplus that they can exchange with others, or to invest in new and even more efficient labour-saving machinery.

An Inquiry into the Nature and Causes of the Wealth of Nations: An Essay UNIT 7

TEXTUAL READING[1]

BOOK I

Of the Causes of Improvement in the Productive Powers of Labour, and of the Order According to Which Its Produce Is Naturally Distributed Among the Different Ranks of the People

Chapter I: Of the Division of Labour

1 ▸ The greatest improvement in the productive powers of labour, and the greater part of the skill, dexterity, and judgment with which it is any where directed, or applied, seem to have been the effects of the division of labour.[2]

division: 分工

2 ▸ The effects of the division of labour, in the general business of society, will be more easily understood by considering in what manner it operates in some particular manufactures. It is commonly supposed to be carried furthest in some very trifling ones; not perhaps that it really is carried further in them than in others of more importance: but in those trifling manufactures which are destined to supply the small wants of but a small number of people, the whole number of workmen must necessarily be small; and those employed in every different branch of the work can often be collected into the same workhouse, and placed at once under the view of the spectator.[3]

manufacture: 行业

trifling: 微小的

workhouse: 济贫院

spectator: 观察者

---

1 本篇出自：Adam Smith. *The Wealth of Nations*, introd. Edwin R. A. Seligman. New York: J. M. Dent & Sons 1910。

2 *The greatest improvement... the division of labour*: 该句的主体结构是 The greatest improvement... seem to have been the effects of the division of labour，其中 which 引导的定语从句限定前面的 the greater part of skill, dexterity and judgment。可译为："劳动生产力上最大的增进，以及运用劳动时所表现的更大的技巧、熟练和判断力，似乎都是分工的结果。"（注：本篇部分译文参考了郭自力翻译的《一本书读懂国富论》，哈尔滨：黑龙江科学技术出版社，2012。下同。）

3 *It is commonly supposed... under the view of the spectator*: 该句较长，其主句是 It is commonly supposed to be carried furthest in some very trifling ones，后面由两个分号分隔的句子解释这个主句。第一个分号后面的句子中包含一个 not... but... 的结构。可译为："一般认为，规模小的制造业分工的程度最高；实际上，这些小规模的制造业，分工的程度也许不会比其他比较重要的制造业来得高。但是，那些旨在供给少数人少量需求的制造业，所雇用的劳工人数必然不多，而在不同部门工作的工人，往往可集中在同一个工厂内工作，让旁观者一眼就能综观全局。"

In those great manufactures, on the contrary, which are destined to supply the great wants of the great body of the people, every different branch of the work employs so great a number of workmen that it is impossible to collect them all into the same workhouse. We can seldom see more, at one time, than those employed in one single branch. Though in such manufactures, therefore, the work may really be divided into a much greater number of parts than in those of a more trifling nature, the division is not near so obvious, and has accordingly been much less observed.[4]

3▸ To take an example, therefore, from a very trifling manufacture; but one in which the division of labour has been very often taken notice of, the trade of the pin-maker; a workman not educated to this business (which the division of labour has rendered a distinct trade), nor acquainted with the use of the machinery employed in it (to the invention of which the same division of labour has probably given occasion), could scarce, perhaps, with his utmost industry, make one pin in a day, and certainly could not make twenty.[5] But in the way in which this business is now carried on, not only the whole work is a peculiar trade, but it is divided into a number of branches, of which the greater part are likewise peculiar trades.[6] One man draws out the wire, another straights it, a third cuts it, a fourth points it, a fifth grinds it at the top for receiving the head; to make the head requires two or three distinct operations; to put it on is a peculiar business, to whiten the pins is another; it is even a trade by itself to put them into the paper; and the important business of making a pin is, in this manner, divided into about eighteen distinct operations, which, in some manufactories, are all performed by distinct hands, though in others the same man will sometimes perform two or three

---

pin-maker: 别针制造商
render: 使……变为
distinct: 单独的；不同的
acquaint: 熟悉
machinery: 机器
scarce: 缺乏的，不足的
industry: 勤劳
wire: 铁丝
whiten: 染白

---

4 *Though in such manufactures, ... much less observed*: 该句为让步状语从句，其中包含一个比较结构。可译为："所以在大的制造业中，虽然工作分配的部门比起小作坊的部门要多得多，但分工的方式却没有那么明显，因此旁观者不太容易一眼看穿。"

5 *a workman not educated... could not make twenty*: 该句的主体结构是 a workman... make one pin... could not make twenty。其中，not educated... 和 nor acquainted with... 都是用来限定 a workman。可译为："一位没有接受过这项职业（劳动分工使得该职业成为一个单独的行业）教育的人，一位不熟悉其中机器（机器的发明也极有可能同样是劳动分工造成的）使用的人，也许尽其最大的努力，一天也难以做出 1 颗大头针，更别说做出 20 颗了。"

6 *But in the way... peculiar trades*: 该句中，it 指 the whole work，也就是 a peculiar trade；第二个 which 指 a number of branches。可译为："但按照现在经营的方法，不但这种作业全部已经成为专门职业，而且这种职业分成若干部门，其中有大多数也同样成为专门职业。"

An Inquiry into the Nature and Causes of the Wealth of Nations: An Essay

of them. I have seen a small manufactory of this kind where ten men only were employed, and where some of them consequently performed two or three distinct operations. But though they were very poor, and therefore but indifferently accommodated with the necessary machinery, they could, when they exerted themselves, make among them about twelve pounds of pins in a day. There are in a pound upwards of four thousand pins of a middling size. Those ten persons, therefore, could make among them upwards of forty-eight thousand pins in a day. Each person, therefore, making a tenth part of forty-eight thousand pins, might be considered as making four thousand eight hundred pins in a day. But if they had all wrought separately and independently, and without any of them having been educated to this peculiar business, they certainly could not each of them have made twenty, perhaps not one pin in a day; that is, certainly, not the two hundred and fortieth, perhaps not the four thousand eight hundredth part of what they are at present capable of performing, in consequence of a proper division and combination of their different operations.[7]

manufactory: 工厂

indifferently: 漠不关心地

wrought: 工作（work 的过去式或过去分词）

combination: 结合

4 ▶ In every other art and manufacture, the effects of the division of labour are similar to what they are in this very trifling one; though, in many of them, the labour can neither be so much subdivided, nor reduced to so great a simplicity of operation. The division of labour, however, so far as it can be introduced, occasions, in every art, a proportionable increase of the productive powers of labour.[8] The separation of different trades and employments from one another, seems to have taken place, in consequence of this advantage. This separation, too, is generally carried furthest in those countries which enjoy the highest degree of industry and improvement; what is the work of one man in a rude state of society being generally that of several in an improved one.[9] In every improved society, the farmer is generally nothing

subdivide: 细分
simplicity: 简化
proportionable: 成比例的

rude: 落后的

7　*that is, ... of their different operations*: 该句中，in consequence of 引导的短语用来说明前面 what 引导的从句。可译为："也就是说，不到他们当前完成数量的1/240，或许连1/4800都不到，而目前所完成的数量是不同行业之间恰当的分工与和合作的结果。"

8　*The division of labour... the productive powers of labour*: 该句的主体结构是 The division of labour... occasions... a proportionable increase..., 其中 occasion 为动词，意为"引发，导致（一种增长）"。可译为："然而在任何一个行业，若能引进分工，都会因分工而使劳动生产力得到相当比例的提高。"

9　*what is the work... in an improved one*: 该句中附属结构 being generally that... 的主语是 what，其中 that 指前面的 the work。可译为："在落后国家里单个人的工作在发达的国家通常有好几个人来完成。"

but a farmer; the manufacturer, nothing but a manufacturer. The labour, too, which is necessary to produce any one complete manufacture is almost always divided among a great number of hands. How many different trades are employed in each branch of the linen and woollen manufactures from the growers of the flax and the wool, to the bleaches and smoothers of the linen, or to the dyers and dressers of the cloth! The nature of agriculture, indeed, does not admit of so many subdivisions of labour, nor of so complete a separation of one business from another, as manufactures. It is impossible to separate so entirely the business of the grazier from that of the corn-farmer as the trade of the carpenter is commonly separated from that of the smith. The spinner is almost always a distinct person from the weaver; but the ploughman, the harrower, the sower of the seed, and the reaper of the corn, are often the same. The occasions for those different sorts of labour returning with the different seasons of the year, it is impossible that one man should be constantly employed in any one of them. This impossibility of making so complete and entire a separation of all the different branches of labour employed in agriculture is perhaps the reason why the improvement of the productive powers of labour in this art does not always keep pace with their improvement in manufactures.[10] The most opulent nations, indeed, generally excel all their neighbours in agriculture as well as in manufactures; but they are commonly more distinguished by their superiority in the latter than in the former.[11] Their lands are in general better cultivated, and having more labour and expense bestowed upon them, produce more in proportion to the extent and natural fertility of the ground. But this superiority of produce is seldom much more than in proportion to the superiority of labour and expense.[12] In agriculture, the labour of the rich country is not always much

linen: 亚麻制品
woollen: 羊毛制品
flax: 亚麻
dyer: 染工
grazier: 放牧者
carpenter: 木匠
smith: 铁匠
spinner: 纺纱工人
weaver: 织布工
ploughman: 农夫
harrower: 耙地者
reaper: 收割者

opulent: 丰饶的
excel: 超越
distinguished: 显著的
cultivate: 开垦
fertility: 肥沃
produce: 农作物

---

10 *This impossibility of making... in manufactures*: 该句的主体结构是 This impossibility... is... the reason why...，impossibility 后的 of making... in agriculture 作为它的限定成分；why 引导的从句中 in this art 指前面的 agriculture。可译为："在农业中，无法将所有不同分支的劳动进行完全和全面的分离，也许就是在这个领域的劳动生产力的提高无法与制造业同步提高的原因。"

11 *The most opulent nations, ... than in the former*: 该句中的 their，they 和 their 都指 the most opulent nations；the latter 指 manufacture；the former 指 agriculture。可译为："现在最富裕的一些国家的确在农业和制造业方面都优于邻国；但他们在制造业方面的优越程度，通常大于农业方面的优越程度。"

12 *But this superiority... the superiority of labour and expense*: 该句是两个 superiority 之间按照比例的比较。可译为："但农作物的这种优势鲜有超越相应比例的劳力和费用上的优势。也就是说，这种农作物上的优势源自劳力和开销上的优势，与劳动分工关系不大。"

more productive than that of the poor; or, at least, it is never so much more productive as it commonly is in manufactures. The corn of the rich country, therefore, will not always, in the same degree of goodness, come cheaper to market than that of the poor. The corn of Poland, in the same degree of goodness, is as cheap as that of France, notwithstanding the superior opulence and improvement of the latter country. The corn of France is, in the corn provinces, fully as good, and in most years nearly about the same price with the corn of England, though, in opulence and improvement, France is perhaps inferior to England. The corn-lands of England, however, are better cultivated than those of France, and the corn-lands of France are said to be much better cultivated than those of Poland. But though the poor country, notwithstanding the inferiority of its cultivation, can, in some measure, rival the rich in the cheapness and goodness of its corn, it can pretend to no such competition in its manufactures; at least if those manufactures suit the soil, climate, and situation of the rich country.[13] The silks of France are better and cheaper than those of England, because the silk manufacture, at least under the present high duties upon the importation of raw silk, does not so well suit the climate of England as that of France. But the hardware and the coarse woollens of England are beyond all comparison superior to those of France, and much cheaper too in the same degree of goodness. In Poland there are said to be scarce any manufactures of any kind, a few of those coarser household manufactures excepted, without which no country can well subsist.

notwithstanding: 尽管
opulence: 富饶

duty: 关税
importation: 进口

subsist: 维持

5 ▸ This great increase of the quantity of work which, in consequence of the division of labour, the same number of people are capable of performing, is owing to three different circumstances; first, to the increase of dexterity in every particular workman; secondly, to the saving of the time which is commonly lost in passing from one species of work to another; and lastly, to the invention of a great number of machines which facilitate and abridge labour, and enable one man to do the work of many.

facilitate: 促进
abridge: 缩短

---

13 *But though the poor country... the rich country*: 该句的主体结构是 though the poor country... can... rival the rich in..., it can pretend to...; ... if..., 其余都是辅助成分。可译为:"但是,尽管贫穷的国家耕作技术低劣,但其玉米质优价廉,在某种程度上仍然能够与富裕的国家匹敌。然而,它不大可能在制造业达到这种竞争性,至少如果那些制造业适合富裕国家的土地、气候和地形的话。"

6 ▶ First, the improvement of the dexterity of the workman necessarily increases the quantity of the work he can perform; and the division of labour, by reducing every man's business to some one simple operation, and by making this operation the sole employment of his life, necessarily increases very much the dexterity of the workman.¹⁴ A common smith, who, though **accustomed** to handle the **hammer**, has never been used to make nails, if upon some particular occasion he is obliged to attempt it, will scarce, I am assured, be able to make above two or three hundred nails in a day, and those too very bad ones. A smith who has been accustomed to make nails, but whose **sole** or **principal** business has not been that of a nailer, can seldom with his utmost **diligence** make more than eight hundred or a thousand nails in a day. I have seen several boys under twenty years of age who had never exercised any other trade but that of making nails, and who, when they exerted themselves, could make, each of them, **upwards of** two thousand three hundred nails in a day. The making of a nail, however, is by no means one of the simplest operations. The same person blows the **bellows**, stirs or mends the fire as there is occasion, heats the iron, and forges every part of the nail: in forging the head too he is obliged to change his tools. The different operations into which the making of a pin, or of a metal button, is subdivided, are all of them much more simple, and the dexterity of the person, of whose life it has been the sole business to perform them, is usually much greater.¹⁵ The rapidity with which some of the operations of those manufactures are performed, **exceeds** what the human hand could, by those who had never

---

14 *First, the improvement... the dexterity of the workman*: 该句由两个句子组成，由分号隔开。第一个句子的主体结构是 the improvement... increases the quantity...，第二个句子的主体结构是 the division of labour... increases... the dexterity...。第二个句子中含有两个 by 引导的方式状语，by reducing... 和 by making...。可译为："首先，一个人熟练度的增加，必然能够提升他能完成的任务数量；而且分工使每个人终其一生集中于一项简单的操作上，这势必使这个人的熟练度大大地增加。"

15 *The different operations... usually much greater*: 该句由两个并列句组成，前者的主体结构是 The different operations... are all of them much more simple，其中含有 which 引导的定语从句限定 operations；后者的主体结构是 the dexterity of the person... is usually much greater，其中 whose 引导的定语从句说明 the person。可译为："做别针或扣子的任务可以分解成不同的操作，这些操作都大为简化，而且，终其一生以其中一项工作为业的人，他的熟练度通常高得多。"

An Inquiry into the Nature and Causes of the Wealth of Nations: An Essay UNIT 7

seen them, be supposed capable of acquiring.[16]

7 ▶ Secondly, the advantage which is gained by saving the time commonly lost in passing from one sort of work to another is much greater than we should at first view be *apt* to imagine it.[17] It is impossible to pass very quickly from one kind of work to another that is carried on in a different place and with quite different tools. A country weaver, who cultivates a small farm, must lose a good deal of time in passing from his loom to the field, and from the field to his loom. When the two trades can be carried on in the same workhouse, the loss of time is no doubt much less. It is even in this case, however, very *considerable*. A man commonly *saunters* a little in turning his hand from one sort of employment to another. When he first begins the new work he is seldom very keen and *hearty*; his mind, as they say, does not go to it, and for some time he rather *trifles* than applies to good purpose. The habit of sauntering and of *indolent* careless application, which is naturally, or rather necessarily acquired by every country workman who is obliged to change his work and his tools every half hour, and to apply his hand in twenty different ways almost every day of his life, renders him almost always *slothful* and lazy, and incapable of any vigorous application even on the most pressing occasions.[18] Independent, therefore, of his deficiency in point of dexterity, this cause alone must always reduce considerably the quantity of work which he is capable of performing.

apt: 恰当的

considerable: 可观的

saunter: 闲逛

hearty: 精神饱满的

trifle: 糊弄

indolent: 懒惰的

slothful: 迟钝的

---

16 *The rapidity... capable of acquiring*: 该句的主体结构是 The rapidity... exceeds what the human hand could... be supposed capable of acquiring，其中包含 what 引导的宾语从句，谓语前是 which 引导的定语从句来限定 rapidity，谓语后是插入成分 by those who...，其中 who 引导的是定语从句。可译为："这些制造业中某些操作的速度之快，若非亲眼所见，你很难相信。"

17 *the advantage... be apt to imagine it*: 该句的主体结构是 the advantage... is much greater than...，其中 which 引导定语从句。可译为："通过节省从一项工作转向另一项工作所耗费的时间，分工所获得的优势远远大于我们乍看之下所能想象的程度。"

18 *The habit... on the most pressing occasions*: 该句的主体结构是 The habit... renders him... slothful and lazy, and incapable...。在这个句子中, of sauntering and of indolent... application 和 which is... acquired by... workman 是限定前面的 habit，而 workman 后面也接着一个定语从句，其中 to change 和 to apply 并列。可译为："这种闲逛、做事懒散马虎的习惯是每一位乡村工人自然都有，或者说必定会获得的一个习惯。乡村工人每半个小时就不得不变换他的工作和工具，在其一生中，几乎每天都要有 20 种不同的方式来运用他的双手，这使得他几乎总是迟钝、懒散，甚至在最紧迫的情况下也无法精力充沛地做任何事情。"

8 ▶ Thirdly, and lastly, every body must be sensible how much labour is facilitated and abridged by the application of proper machinery. It is unnecessary to give any example. I shall only observe, therefore, that the invention of all those machines by which labour is so much facilitated and abridged seems to have been originally owing to the division of labour. Men are much more likely to discover easier and readier methods of attaining any object, when the whole attention of their minds is directed towards that single object than when it is *dissipated* among a great variety of things. But in consequence of the division of labour, the whole of every man's attention comes naturally to be directed towards some one very simple object. It is naturally to be expected, therefore, that some one or other of those who are employed in each particular branch of labour should soon find out easier and readier methods of performing their own particular work, wherever the nature of it admits of such improvement. A great part of the machines made use of in those manufactures in which labour is most subdivided, were originally the inventions of common workmen, who, being each of them employed in some very simple operation, naturally turned their thoughts towards finding out easier and readier methods of performing it.[19] Whoever has been much accustomed to visit such manufactures, must frequently have been shewn very pretty machines, which were the inventions of such workmen in order to facilitate and quicken their own particular part of the work. In the first fire-engines, a boy was constantly employed to open and shut alternately the *communication* between the *boiler* and the *cylinder*, according as the *piston* either ascended or descended. One of those boys, who loved to play with his *companions*, observed that, by tying a *string* from the handle of the *valve* which opened this communication to another part of the machine, the valve would open and shut without his *assistance*, and leave him at *liberty* to *divert* himself with his play-fellows. One of the greatest improvements that has been made upon this machine, since it was first invented, was in this manner the discovery of a boy who wanted to save his own labour.

---

19 *A great part... methods of performing it*: 该句的主体结构是 A great part... were originally the inventions of common workmen，其中 made use of in those manufactures 用来限定前面的 machines，in which 引导的定语从句限定前面的 manufacture；workmen 后面是由 who 引导的非限定性定语从句，其中 being each of... 作为插入语，也用来说明 workmen。可译为："在那些劳动被最大限度细分了的工厂中使用的大部分机器最初都是由普通工人发明的。这些工人各自从事一些非常简单的操作，自然会将他们的注意力放到找出更简单更便捷的操作方法上。"

An Inquiry into the Nature and Causes of the Wealth of Nations: An Essay UNIT 7

9▸ All the improvements in machinery, however, have by no means been the inventions of those who had occasion to use the machines. Many improvements have been made by the ingenuity of the makers of the machines, when to make them became the business of a peculiar trade; and some by that of those who are called philosophers or men of speculation, whose trade it is not to do anything, but to observe everything; and who, upon that account, are often capable of combining together the powers of the most distant and dissimilar objects.[20] In the progress of society, philosophy or speculation becomes, like every other employment, the principal or sole trade and occupation of a particular class of citizens. Like every other employment too, it is subdivided into a great number of different branches, each of which affords occupation to a peculiar tribe or class of philosophers; and this subdivision of employment in philosophy, as well as in every other business, improves dexterity, and saves time.[21] Each individual becomes more expert in his own peculiar branch, more work is done upon the whole, and the quantity of science is considerably increased by it.

10▸ It is the great multiplication of the productions of all the different arts, in consequence of the division of labour, which occasions, in a well-governed society, that universal opulence which extends itself to the lowest ranks of the people.[22] Every workman has a great quantity of his own work to dispose of beyond what he himself has occasion for; and every other workman being exactly in the same situation, he is enabled to exchange a great quantity of

ingenuity: 独创性

speculation: 思索

tribe: 一伙；一类

philosophy: 思想体系；哲学

multiplication: 增加

universal: 普遍的

extend: 延伸

dispose: 处理

---

20 *Many improvements... the most distant and dissimilar objects*: 该句中，第一个分号前是一个完整的句子，分号后是一个伴随结构，也是一个省略结构。some (improvements are made by the ingenuity of) philosophers or men of speculation，随后的 whose trade 和 who 引导的定语从句用来限定 philosophers or men of speculation；upon that account 表示"基于那个理由"。可译为："许多改进是专门钻研机械的发明家的独创，还有些来自哲学家或思想家。这些人的职业并不是具体实施，而是观测事物，因此能够把看似最不相关的事物联系起来。"

21 *Like every other employment too, ... and saves time*: 该句较长，但是结构相对简单。分号将其分为两个并列的成分。前者中 which 引导定语从句，which 指的是 different branches；后者的主体结构是 this subdivision... improves dexterity and saves time。可译为："如同其他各行各业一样，它也可以细分为不同的分支，每个分支都为特定的一伙人或者一群思想者提供职业；这种在思想体系内的职业细分，和其他行业的一样，提高了灵巧度，并节省了时间。"

22 *It is the great multiplication... the lowest ranks of the people*: 该句的主体结构是一个强调句式。主干部分为 Multiplication occasions opulence；句中的第二个 which 引导的定语从句限定前面的 opulence。可译为："在管理良好的社会里，正是这种分工所造成的各行各业产量的成倍增长促使了普及大众的整体富裕。"

151

his own goods for a great quantity, or, what comes to the same thing, for the price of a great quantity of theirs. He supplies them **abundantly** with what they have occasion for, and they **accommodate** him as **amply** with what he has occasion for, and a general plenty **diffuses** itself through all the different ranks of the society.

11 ▸ Observe the accommodation of the most common **artificer** or day-labourer in a civilized and thriving country, and you will **perceive** that the number of people of whose industry a part, though but a small part, has been employed in procuring him this accommodation, exceeds all **computation**.²³ The woollen coat, for example, which covers the day-labourer, as coarse and rough as it may appear, is the produce of the joint labour of a great multitude of workmen. The shepherd, the sorter of the wool, the wool-comber or carder, the dyer, the scribbler, the spinner, the weaver, the fuller, the dresser, with many others, must all join their different arts in order to complete even this **homely** production. How many **merchants** and **carriers**, besides, must have been employed in transporting the materials from some of those workmen to others who often live in a very distant part of the country! How much commerce and navigation in particular, how many ship-builders, sailors, sail-makers, rope-makers, must have been employed in order to bring together the different drugs made use of by the dyer, which often come from the remotest corners of the world! What a variety of labour, too, is necessary in order to produce the tools of the **meanest** of those workmen! To say nothing of such **complicated** machines as the ship of the sailor, the **mill** of the fuller, or even the loom of the weaver, let us consider only what a variety of labour is **requisite** in order to form that very simple machine, the **shears** with which the shepherd **clips** the wool. The miner, the builder of the **furnace** for **smelting** the **ore**, the seller of the **timber**, the burner of the **charcoal** to be made use of in the smelting-house, the **brick-maker**, the **brick-layer**, the workmen who attend the furnace, the **mill-wright**, the **forger**, the smith, must all of them join their different arts in order to produce them. Were we to examine, in the same manner, all the different parts of his dress

---

abundantly: 大量地

accommodate: 供应

amply: 充足地

diffuse: 扩散

artificer: 技工

perceive: 觉察到

computation: 计算

homely: 平凡的

merchant: 商人

carrier: 运送者

mean: 低端的，平庸的

complicated: 复杂的

mill: 作坊

requisite: 必需的

shear: 修剪

clip: 修剪

furnace: 熔炉

smelt: 熔炼

ore: 矿石

timber: 木材

charcoal: 木炭

brick-maker: 制砖者

brick-layer: 泥瓦匠

mill-wright: 工厂技工

forger: 铁匠

---

23 *Observe... exceeds all computation*: 该句的主体结构是 Observe..., and you will perceive that the number... exceeds all computation。Observe... 是一个祈使句，perceive 后面是一个宾语从句，其中 whose 引导的定语从句来限定 the number of people。可译为："让我们观察一下文明繁荣的国度里那些最普通的技工和散工的食宿，你会发觉：这些日常用品凝结了多少劳动的心血。"

An Inquiry into the Nature and Causes of the Wealth of Nations: An Essay UNIT 7

and household furniture, the coarse linen shirt which he wears next his skin, the shoes which cover his feet, the bed which he lies on, and all the different parts which compose it, the kitchen-grate at which he prepares his victuals, the coals which he makes use of for that purpose, dug from the bowels of the earth, and brought to him perhaps by a long sea and a long land carriage, all the other utensils of his kitchen, all the furniture of his table, the knives and forks, the earthen or pewter plates upon which he serves up and divides his victuals, the different hands employed in preparing his bread and his beer, the glass window which lets in the heat and the light, and keeps out the wind and the rain, with all the knowledge and art requisite for preparing that beautiful and happy invention, without which these northern parts of the world could scarce have afforded a very comfortable habitation, together with the tools of all the different workmen employed in producing those different conveniences;[24] if we examine, I say, all these things, and consider what a variety of labour is employed about each of them, we shall be sensible that, without the assistance and co-operation of many thousands, the very meanest person in a civilised country could not be provided, even according to what we very falsely imagine the easy and simple manner in which he is commonly accommodated.[25] Compared, indeed, with the more extravagant luxury of the great, his accommodation must no doubt appear extremely

furniture: 家具

kitchen-grate: 壁炉

victual: 食物

bowel: 内部，最深处

utensil: 用具

pewter: 青灰色的

habitation: 居所

convenience: 便利

extravagant: 过度的

luxury: 奢侈

---

24 *Were we to examine, ... producing those different conveniences*: 这部分内容虽多，但并不是一个完整的句子，而是各种日常生活用品的罗列，为后面的句子 if we examine... 做准备。整个部分的主体是 were we to examine 这个虚拟结构，随后的各项都是 examine 的宾语，其中许多宾语后都跟随有 which 引导的定语从句，用来限定说明各项宾语。可译为："假如我们用同样的方式来考察他的衣着和家具，他贴身穿的粗亚麻衬衣、裹脚的鞋子，他所躺的床的所有不同部分及其构成部分，他准备食物的壁炉，壁炉中所需的煤炭是从地心挖出来，也许还经过了长途的海陆运输才运到他那里，他厨房里所有餐具，他桌上所有器具，刀具、叉子，用来盛放食物的陶器或青花盘，在准备面包和啤酒所需要的不同人手、准备透入光和热并阻隔风雨的玻璃窗，以及准备那个欢快迷人的发明所必备的知识和技艺，缺少了玻璃窗，世界北部的人将难以有一个非常舒适的居所，再加上所有不同工人在生产那些不同便利之物之时所使用的工具。"

25 *if we examine, ... is commonly accommodated*: 该句的主体结构是 if we examine..., and consider..., we shall be sensible that... the very meanest person... could not be provided, ...。consider 后跟随着 what 引导的宾语从句，sensible 后是 that 引导的宾语从句，其中 without... 是插入成分，even 表示程度，according to 后面跟随 what 引导的宾语从句，该从句中还包含由 which 引导的定语从句，限定 manner。可译为："我的意思是，如果我们考察所有这些事情，并将其中每一件所涉及的各种劳动考虑在内，我们就会意识到，没有成千上万的劳动者的支持和相互合作，在一个文明的国度中，连最卑微的人也无法生活，甚至根据我们极端错误地想象到的、他能够维系一般生活的简单朴素方式也无法做到。"

frugal: 节俭的

simple and easy; and yet it may be true, perhaps, that the accommodation of an European prince does not always so much exceed that of an industrious and frugal peasant as the accommodation of the latter exceeds that of many an African king, the absolute master of the lives and liberties of ten thousand naked savages.

PART 4

EXERCISES

I. Answer the following questions according to the reading text.

1. What are the effects of the division of labour?
2. How many operations are there in making a pin? What are they?
3. As to the improvement of productive labour, are there any differences between agriculture and manufacture? Why?
4. Through the comparisons among agriculture and silk manufactures among France, England, and Poland, what does the writer want to say?
5. As a result of the division of labour, what are the reasons for the great increase of the quantity of work?
6. Can one common smith make more nails than each one of a group of boys under twenty years of age? Why?
7. Through the division of labour, how can time be saved?
8. Through the example of the boy of fire engine, what does Adam Smith, the author, want to say?
9. Who are involved in the production of a woolen coat of a day-labour?
10. What does Adam Smith, the author, want to say when he compares the accommodation of an industrious peasant, an European prince, and an African king at the end of the chapter?

II. Paraphrase the following sentences with your own words, and then translate them into Chinese.

1. The nature of agriculture, indeed, does not admit of so many subdivisions of labour, nor of so complete a separation of one business from another, as manufactures. (Para. 4)

2. Their lands are in general better cultivated, and having more labour and expense bestowed upon them, produce more in proportion to the extent and natural fertility of the ground. (Para. 4)

3. A common smith, who, though accustomed to handle the hammer, has never been used to make nails, if upon some particular occasion he is obliged to attempt it, will scarce, I am assured, be able to make above two or three hundred nails in a day, and those too very bad ones. (Para. 6)

4. The habit of sauntering and of indolent careless application, which is naturally, or rather necessarily acquired by every country workman who is obliged to change his work and his tools every half hour, and to apply his hand in twenty different ways almost every day of his life, renders him almost always slothful and lazy, and incapable of any vigorous application even on the most pressing occasions. (Para. 7)

5. One of the greatest improvements that has been made upon this machine, since it was first invented, was in this manner the discovery of a boy who wanted to save his own labour. (Para. 8)

6. In the progress of society, philosophy or speculation becomes, like every other employment, the principal or sole trade and occupation of a particular class of citizens. (Para. 9)

7. And yet it may be true, perhaps, that the accommodation of an European prince does not always so much exceed that of an industrious and frugal peasant as the accommodation of the latter exceeds that of many an African king, the absolute master of the lives and liberties of ten thousand naked savages. (Para. 11)

III. Figure out the meanings of the phrases in bold, and then make another sentence with each of the phrases.

1. The separation of different trades and employments from one another, seems to have taken place, **in consequence of** this advantage. (Para. 4)

2. But though the poor country, notwithstanding the inferiority of its cultivation, can, **in some measure**, rival the rich in the cheapness and goodness of its corn, it can **pretend to** no such competition in its manufactures; at least if those manufactures suit the soil, climate, and situation of the rich country. (Para. 4)

3. This great increase of the quantity of work which, in consequence of the division of labour, the same number of people are capable of performing, is **owing to** three different circumstances. (Para. 5)

4. I have seen several boys under twenty years of age who had never exercised any other trade but that of making nails, and who, when they exerted themselves, could make, each of them, **upwards of** two thousand three hundred nails in a day. (Para. 6)

5. When the two trades can be **carried on** in the same workhouse, the loss of time is **no doubt** much less. (Para. 7)

6. It is naturally to be expected, therefore, that some one or other of those who are employed in each particular branch of labour should soon find out easier and readier methods of performing their own particular work, wherever the nature of it **admits of** such improvement. (Para. 8)

7. Every workman has a great quantity of his own work to **dispose of** beyond what he himself has occasion for. (Para. 10)

8. **To say nothing of** such complicated machines as the ship of the sailor, the mill of the fuller, or even the loom of the weaver, let us consider only what a variety of labour is requisite in order to form that very simple machine, the shears with which the shepherd clips the wool. (Para. 11)

IV. Explain the following phrases in your own words.

1. productive power of labour
2. division of labour
3. men of speculation

V. Write a division of labour in your daily life and explain its advantages with no less than 200 words.

The Communist Manifesto
A Pamphlet

Oral tasks

1. When did you hear of *The Communist Manifesto*, and what came to your mind first?
2. Do you think our Chinese students' understanding of *The Communist Manifesto* will be different from that of students in other countries? What will be the differences?

Introduction

A pamphlet is a non-periodical printed publication of at least 5 but not more than 48 pages, exclusive of the cover pages, published in a particular country and made available to the public.

The Communist Manifesto (short for *Manifesto*) is an 1848 political pamphlet by German philosophers Karl Marx and Friedrich Engels. Commissioned by the Communist League and originally published in London just as the revolution of 1848 began to erupt, the *Manifesto* was later recognised as one of the world's most influential political documents. It presents an analytical approach to the class struggle (historical and then-present) and the problems of capitalism and the capitalist mode of production.

Karl Marx (1818–1883) was a German philosopher and political theorist. When he was in London, England, he developed his thought in collaboration with German thinker Friedrich Engels and published various works, of which the two most well-known are the 1848 pamphlet *The Communist Manifesto* and the three-volume *Das Kapital.* Friedrich Engels (1820–1895) was a German philosopher, social scientist, and businessman. Engels founded Marxist theory together with Karl Marx and in 1845 published *The Condition of the Working Class in England,* based on personal observations and research in Manchester.

The Communist Manifesto: A Pamphlet UNIT 8

PART 3

TEXTUAL READING[1]

The Communist Manifesto

1 ▸ A spectre is haunting Europe—the spectre of communism. All the powers of old Europe have entered into a holy alliance to exorcise this spectre: Pope and Tsar, Metternich[2] and Guizot[3], French Radicals and German police-spies.

2 ▸ Where is the party in opposition that has not been decried as communistic by its opponents in power? Where is the opposition that has not hurled back the branding reproach of communism, against the more advanced opposition parties, as well as against its reactionary adversaries?[4]

3 ▸ Two things result from this fact:

4 ▸ I. Communism is already acknowledged by all European powers to be itself a power.

5 ▸ II. It is high time[5] that Communists should openly, in the face of the whole world, publish their views, their aims, their tendencies, and meet this nursery tale of the Spectre of Communism with a manifesto of the party itself.

spectre: 幽灵
exorcise: 驱除
Pope: 教皇
Tsar: 沙皇
radical: 激进分子
police-spy: 间谍
decry: 贬损；谴责
opponent: 反对者
hurl: 愤慨地指责
reactionary: 反动的
adversary: 敌手，对手

---

1 本篇出自：Karl Marx & Friedrich Engels. *The Communist Manifesto*. Translated by Samuel Moore (1888). Edited and introduced. by Gareth Stedman Jones. London: Penguin Books (Penguin Classics), 2002。

2 *Metternich*: 克莱门斯·梅特涅（Klemens Wenzel von Metternich）。1809 年开始任奥地利帝国的外交大臣，1821 年起兼任奥地利帝国首相。他反对一切民族主义、自由主义和革命运动，是"神圣同盟"的重要人物，在欧洲形成了以"正统主义"和"大国均势"为核心的梅特涅体系。

3 *Guizot*: 弗朗索瓦·皮埃尔·吉尧姆·基佐（François Pierre Guillaume Guizot），1847 年至 1848 年间任法国首相。他是一名保守派人士，未能留心民间的疾苦。他推行的国内和国外政策引起了国内外的不满。

4 *Where is the opposition... against its reactionary adversaries*: 该句的主句是 Where is the opposition...，that 后面的部分是限定说明 opposition 的定语从句，其中 hurled back... against..., as well as against... 三个部分并列。可译为："又有哪一个反对党不拿共产主义这个罪名去回敬更进步的反对党人和自己的反动敌人呢？"（注：本篇译文来自马克思、恩格斯，《共产党宣言》，北京：人民出版社，2015。下同。）

5 *high time*: 是……的时候；正是应该……的时候。e.g. John's suit is old and it is high time he buy a new one. 约翰的衣服穿旧了，是该买一套新衣服的时候了。

nationality: 民族
sketch: 草拟

6 ▸ To this end, Communists of various nationalities have assembled in London and sketched the following manifesto, to be published in the English, French, German, Italian, Flemish and Danish languages.

Chapter I. Bourgeois and Proletarians

bourgeois: 资产阶级分子
proletarian: 无产阶级分子
hitherto: 至今
plebeian: 平民
lord: 领主，贵族
serf: 农奴
guild-master: 行会师傅
journeyman: 雇佣工，学徒工
revolutionary: 革命的
reconstitution: 重构
epoch: 时代
manifold: 多重的
gradation: 分级，等级
knight: 骑士
feudal: 封建的
vassal: 封臣
apprentice: 学徒
subordinate: 从属的
sprout: 萌芽
antagonism: 对立
hostile: 敌对的

7 ▸ The history of all hitherto existing society is the history of class struggles.

8 ▸ Freeman and slave, patrician and plebeian, lord and serf, guild-master and journeyman, in a word, oppressor and oppressed, stood in constant opposition to one another, carried on an uninterrupted, now hidden, now open fight, a fight that each time ended, either in a revolutionary reconstitution of society at large, or in the common ruin of the contending classes.⁶

9 ▸ In the earlier epochs of history, we find almost everywhere a complicated arrangement of society into various orders, a manifold gradation of social rank. In ancient Rome we have patricians, knights, plebeians, slaves; in the Middle Ages, feudal lords, vassals, guild-masters, journeymen, apprentices, serfs; in almost all of these classes, again, subordinate gradations.

10 ▸ The modern bourgeois society that has sprouted from the ruins of feudal society has not done away with⁷ class antagonisms. It has but established new classes, new conditions of oppression, new forms of struggle in place of the old ones.

11 ▸ Our epoch, the epoch of the bourgeoisie, possesses, however, this distinct feature: it has simplified class antagonisms. Society as a whole is more and more splitting up into two great hostile camps, into two great classes directly facing each other—Bourgeoisie and Proletariat.

---

6 *Freeman and slave, ... the contending classes*: 该句由多个并列成分构成，freeman and slave, patrician and plebeian, lord and serf, guild-master and journeyman, in a word, oppressor and oppressed 共同构成主语，其中 in a word, oppressor and oppressed 是对其前面的概括。stood 和 carried on 是并列的谓语，now hidden 和 now open fight 是并列状语。在 that 引导的定语从句中，either... or... 同样引导两个并列的状语。可译为：“自由民和奴隶、贵族和平民、领主和农奴、行会师傅和帮工，一句话，压迫者和被压迫者，始终处于相互对立的地位，进行不断的、有时隐蔽有时公开的斗争，而每一次斗争的结局都是整个社会受到革命改造或者斗争的各阶级同归于尽。"

7 *do away with*: 废除；取消；摆脱。e.g. It is time to do away with some of the old laws. 该是废除那些陈旧的法规的时候了。

12 ▸ From the serfs of the Middle Ages sprang the chartered burghers of the earliest towns.⁸ From these burgesses the first elements of the bourgeoisie were developed.

13 ▸ The discovery of America, the rounding of the Cape, opened up fresh ground for the rising bourgeoisie. The East-Indian and Chinese markets, the colonisation of America, trade with the colonies, the increase in the means of exchange and in commodities generally, gave to commerce, to navigation, to industry, an impulse never before known, and thereby, to the revolutionary element in the tottering feudal society, a rapid development.⁹

14 ▸ The feudal system of industry, in which industrial production was monopolised by closed guilds, now no longer sufficed for the growing wants of the new markets. The manufacturing system took its place. The guild-masters were pushed on one side by the manufacturing middle class; division of labour between the different corporate guilds vanished in the face of division of labour in each single workshop.

15 ▸ Meantime the markets kept ever growing, the demand ever rising. Even manufacturer no longer sufficed. Thereupon, steam and machinery revolutionised industrial production. The place of manufacture was taken by the giant, Modern Industry; the place of the industrial middle class by industrial millionaires, the leaders of the whole industrial armies, the modern bourgeois.

16 ▸ Modern industry has established the world market, for which the discovery of America paved the way. This market has given an immense development to commerce, to navigation, to communication by land. This development has, in its turn, reacted on the extension of industry; and in proportion as industry, commerce, navigation, railways extended, in the

chartered: 特许的

burgher: 市民

burgess: 自由民，自治市民

colonisation: 殖民

commodity: 商品

tottering: 摇摇欲坠的

monopolise: 垄断

suffice: 满足

corporate: 法人的，团体的

---

8 *From the serfs... of the earliest towns*：该句和下一句都是倒装句，其正常语序应该是 the chartered burghers... sprang from the serfs of the Middle Ages。可译为："从中世纪的农奴中产生了初期城市的城关市民。"

9 *The East-Indian and Chinese markets, ... a rapid development*：该句由多个并列成分构成，the East-Indian and Chinese markets, the colonisation of America, trade with the colonies, the increase in the means of exchange and in commodities 这几个并列成分构成了该句的主语；gave 是该句的谓语，接有两个宾语，分别是 an impulse never before known 和 a rapid development。可译为："东印度和中国的市场，美洲的殖民化，对殖民地的贸易、交换方式和一般商品的增加，使商业、航海业和工业空前高涨，因而使正在崩溃的封建社会内部的革命因素迅速发展。"

same proportion the bourgeoisie developed, increased its capital, and pushed into the background every class handed down from the Middle Ages.[10]

17 ▸ We see, therefore, how the modern bourgeoisie is itself the product of a long course of development, of a series of revolutions in the modes of production and of exchange.

18 ▸ Each step in the development of the bourgeoisie was accompanied by a corresponding political advance of that class. An oppressed class under the sway of the feudal nobility, an armed and self-governing association in the medieval commune: here independent urban republic (as in Italy and Germany); there taxable "third estate" of the monarchy (as in France); afterwards, in the period of manufacturing proper, serving either the semi-feudal or the absolute monarchy as a counterpoise against the nobility, and, in fact, cornerstone of the great monarchies in general, the bourgeoisie has at last, since the establishment of Modern Industry and of the world market, conquered for itself, in the modern representative State, exclusive political sway.[11] The executive of the modern state is but a committee for managing the common affairs of the whole bourgeoisie.

19 ▸ The bourgeoisie, historically, has played a most revolutionary part.

20 ▸ The bourgeoisie, wherever it has got the upper hand[12], has put an end

accompany: 伴随

corresponding: 相应的

medieval: 中世纪的

commune: 社团

monarchy: 君主制

counterpoise: 平衡

cornerstone: 基石

conquer: 征服

exclusive: 专有的

executive: 执行者

committee: 委员会

---

10 *This development has... from the Middle Ages*: 该句的后一部分是 in proportion as... in the same proportion... 的结构，是指按照同样比例发展的。可译为："这种发展又反过来促进了工业的扩展，同时，随着工业、商业、航海业和铁路的扩展，资产阶级也在同一程度上得到发展，增加自己的资本，把中世纪遗留下来的一切阶级都排挤到后面去。"

11 *An oppressed class... exclusive political sway*: 该句介绍了三个阶段的情况，可分成三部分来理解。一是 under the sway of the feudal nobility；二是 in the period of manufacturing proper；三是 since the establishment of Modern Industry and of the world market。可译为："它在封建主统治下是被压迫的等级，在公社里是武装的和自治的团体，在一些地方组成独立的城市共和国（如意大利和德国），在另一些地方组成君主国中的纳税的第三等级（如法国）；后来，在工场手工业时期，它是等级君主国或专制君主国中同贵族抗衡的势力，而且是大君主国的主要基础；最后，从大工业和世界市场建立的时候起，它在现代的代议制国家里夺得了独占的政治统治。"

12 *get the upper hand*: 控制；取得优势；占……上风；胜过。e.g. I try to be cool and sensible but sometimes my feelings get the upper hand of me. 我试图保持冷静和理智，但有时我又感情用事。

to[13] all feudal, patriarchal, idyllic relations. It has pitilessly torn asunder the motley feudal ties that bound man to his "natural superiors", and has left remaining no other nexus between man and man than naked self-interest, than callous "cash payment". It has drowned the most heavenly ecstasies of religious fervour, of chivalrous enthusiasm, of philistine sentimentalism, in the icy water of egotistical calculation.[14] It has resolved personal worth into exchange value, and in place of the numberless indefeasible chartered freedoms, has set up that single, unconscionable freedom—Free Trade. In one word, for exploitation, veiled by religious and political illusions, it has substituted naked, shameless, direct, brutal exploitation.

21 ▶ The bourgeoisie has stripped of its halo every occupation hitherto honoured and looked up to with reverent awe. It has converted the physician, the lawyer, the priest, the poet, the man of science, into its paid wage labourers.

22 ▶ The bourgeoisie has torn away from the family its sentimental veil, and has reduced the family relation to a mere money relation.

23 ▶ The bourgeoisie has disclosed how it came to pass that the brutal display of vigour in the Middle Ages, which reactionaries so much admire, found its fitting complement in the most slothful indolence. It has been the first to show what man's activity can bring about. It has accomplished wonders far surpassing Egyptian pyramids, Roman aqueducts[15], and Gothic cathedrals; it has conducted expeditions that put in the shade[16] all former

patriarchal: 父权的

idyllic: 田园牧歌的

pitilessly: 无情地

asunder: 撕裂，分开

motley: 混杂的

nexus: 纽带

callous: 无情的

drown: 淹没

fervour: 狂热

chivalrous: 骑士的

philistine: 俗气的；平庸的

sentimentalism: 伤感主义

egotistical: 自我中心的

indefeasible: 不可剥夺的

unconscionable: 肆无忌惮的；不合理的

exploitation: 剥削

veil: 隐蔽

substitute: 取代

strip: 剥去

reverent: 尊敬的

awe: 畏惧

convert: 转换

physician: 医生

vigour: 活力

complement: 补充

surpass: 超越

aqueduct: 水渠

expedition: 远征

---

13 *put an end to*: 结束；制止；消灭。e.g. We ought to find some way of putting an end to that noise. 我们应该寻找某种办法来防止那种噪声。

14 *It has drowned... water of egotistical calculation*：该句的主体结构是 It has drowned the most heavenly ecstasies... in the icy water...。可译为："它把宗教虔诚、骑士热忱、小市民伤感这些情感的神圣发作，淹没在利己主义打算的冰水之中。"

15 *Roman aqueduct*: 罗马水道。为了保证罗马城的用水，古罗马城历代花费巨大的人力、财力和物力，建设了罗马水道，在水源的开发、调蓄、分引、输水和保证城市用水方面均有显著成就。供水干渠是从郊外水源地用高架水槽引至城内的，城内配水管道遍布于街道、小巷，供人民饮用、洗涤、沐浴等生活需求及消防用水。

16 *put in the shade*: 使逊色；使相形见绌。e.g. We thought the first singer was very good, but the second one put her in the shade. 我们以为第一个歌唱家唱得很好，可是，第二个唱得更好，使她大为逊色。

Exoduses of nations and crusades.[17]

24 ▸ The bourgeoisie cannot exist without constantly revolutionising the instruments of production, and thereby the relations of production, and with them the whole relations of society. Conservation of the old modes of production in unaltered form, was, on the contrary, the first condition of existence for all earlier industrial classes. Constant revolutionising of production, uninterrupted disturbance of all social conditions, everlasting uncertainty and agitation distinguish the bourgeois epoch from all earlier ones. All fixed, fast-frozen relations, with their train of ancient and venerable prejudices and opinions, are swept away, all new-formed ones become antiquated before they can ossify.[18] All that is solid melts into air, all that is holy is profaned, and man is at last compelled to face with sober senses his real conditions of life, and his relations with his kind.

25 ▸ The need of a constantly expanding market for its products chases the bourgeoisie over the entire surface of the globe. It must nestle everywhere, settle everywhere, establish connexions everywhere.

26 ▸ The bourgeoisie has through its exploitation of the world market given a cosmopolitan character to production and consumption in every country. To the great chagrin of Reactionists, it has drawn from under the feet of industry the national ground on which it stood. All old-established national industries have been destroyed or are daily being destroyed. They are dislodged by new industries, whose introduction becomes a life and death question for all civilised nations, by industries that no longer work up indigenous raw material, but raw material drawn from the remotest zones; industries whose products are consumed, not only at home, but in every quarter of the globe. In place of the old wants, satisfied by the production of the country, we find new wants, requiring for their satisfaction the products of distant lands and climes. In place of the old local and national seclusion and self-sufficiency, we have intercourse in every direction, universal

---

17　*It has accomplished... nations and crusades*: 该句中的专有名词较多。可译为："它创造了完全不同于埃及金字塔、罗马水道和哥特式教堂的奇迹；它完成了完全不同于民族大迁徙和十字军征讨的远征。"

18　*All fixed... they can ossify*: 该句由两个完整的句子并列而成，前句的主体结构是 All... relations... are swept away。可译为："一切固定的僵化的关系以及与之相适应的素被尊崇的观念和见解都被消除了，一切新形成的关系等不到固定下来就陈旧了。"

inter-dependence of nations. And as in material, so also in intellectual production. The intellectual creations of individual nations become common property. National one-sidedness and narrow-mindedness become more and more impossible, and from the numerous national and local literatures, there arises a world literature.

27 ▸ The bourgeoisie, by the rapid improvement of all instruments of production, by the immensely facilitated means of communication, draws all, even the most barbarian, nations into civilisation. The cheap prices of commodities are the heavy artillery with which it batters down[19] all Chinese walls, with which it forces the barbarians' intensely obstinate hatred of foreigners to capitulate.[20] It compels all nations, on pain of extinction, to adopt the bourgeois mode of production; it compels them to introduce what it calls civilisation into their midst, i.e., to become bourgeois themselves. In one word, it creates a world after its own image.

barbarian: 野蛮的；未开化的
artillery: 炮弹
intensely: 极度地
obstinate: 顽固的
capitulate: 屈服
extinction: 灭绝

28 ▸ The bourgeoisie has subjected the country to the rule of the towns. It has created enormous cities, has greatly increased the urban population as compared with the rural, and has thus rescued a considerable part of the population from the idiocy of rural life. Just as it has made the country dependent on the towns, so it has made barbarian and semi-barbarian countries dependent on the civilised ones, nations of peasants on nations of bourgeois, the East on the West.

subject: 使屈从于

idiocy: 愚昧行为

29 ▸ The bourgeoisie keeps more and more doing away with the scattered state of the population, of the means of production, and of property. It has agglomerated population, centralised the means of production, and has concentrated property in a few hands. The necessary consequence of this was political centralisation. Independent, or but loosely connected provinces, with separate interests, laws, governments, and systems of taxation, became lumped together into one nation, with one government, one code of laws,

agglomerate: 聚集

lump: 聚集，合并

---

19 *batter down*：（不断用重物撞击而）摧毁（某物），冲垮，打垮。It was commonly deployed in urban environments, where its mass could batter down obstacles and building. 它通常被部署在城市环境里，在那里，其重量能粉碎障碍和建筑。

20 *The cheap prices... foreigners to capitulate*：该句中有两个 with which 构成的并列定语从句，其先行词都是 artillery。可译为："它的商品的低廉价格，是用来摧毁一切城墙、征服野蛮人最顽强的仇外心理的重炮。"

one national class-interest, one frontier, and one customs-tariff.²¹

30 ▸ The bourgeoisie, during its rule of scarce one hundred years, has created more massive and more colossal productive forces than have all preceding generations together. Subjection of Nature's forces to man, machinery, application of chemistry to industry and agriculture, steam-navigation, railways, electric telegraphs, clearing of whole continents for cultivation, canalisation of rivers, whole populations conjured out of the ground—what earlier century had even a presentiment that such productive forces slumbered in the lap of social labour?²²

31 ▸ We see then: the means of production and of exchange, on whose foundation the bourgeoisie built itself up, were generated in feudal society. At a certain stage in the development of these means of production and of exchange, the conditions under which feudal society produced and exchanged, the feudal organisation of agriculture and manufacturing industry, in one word, the feudal relations of property became no longer compatible with the already developed productive forces;²³ they became so many fetters. They had to be burst asunder; they were burst asunder.

telegraph: 电报
canalisation: 开凿运河
conjure: 念咒召唤，变戏法般凭空出现
presentiment: 预感
slumber: 蛰伏

compatible: 兼容的
fetter: 枷锁，脚镣

---

21 *Independent, or but loosely... and one customs-tariff*: 该句的主体结构是 provinces... lumped together into one nation with...。主体结构之外的省略部分由多个并列成分构成。可译为："各自独立的、几乎只有同盟关系的、各有不同利益、不同法律、不同政府、不同关税的各个地区，现在已经结合为一个拥有统一的政府、统一的法律、统一的民族阶级利益和统一的关税的统一民族。"

22 *Subjection of Nature's forces to man... of social labour*: 破折号前是几个并列结构，即 subjection... application... clearing... canalisation... whole population...。conjured out of the ground 用作限定 whole population；破折号后 that 引导的定语从句限定 presentiment。可译为："自然力的征服，机器的采用，化学在工业和农业中的应用，轮船的行驶，铁路的通行，电报的使用，整个大陆的开垦，河川的通航，仿佛用法术从地下呼唤出来的大量人口——过去哪一个世纪料想到在社会劳动里蕴藏有这样的生产力呢？"

23 *At a certain stage... productive forces*: 该句中，the conditions... the feudal organisation... the feudal relations... 构成并列主语，其中 under which 引导的定语从句限定 the conditions；句子开始部分的介词短语 at a certain stage... 作状语。可译为："在这些生产资料和交换手段发展到一定阶段上，封建社会的生产和交换在其中进行的关系，封建的农业和工场手工业组织。简言之，封建的所有制关系已不再适应已经发展了的生产力。"

32 ▸ Into their place stepped free competition, accompanied by a social and political constitution adapted in it, and the economic and political sway of the bourgeois class.

sway: 势力

33 ▸ A similar movement is going on before our own eyes. Modern bourgeois society, with its relations of production, of exchange and of property, a society that has conjured up such gigantic means of production and of exchange, is like the sorcerer who is no longer able to control the powers of the nether world whom he has called up by his spells. For many a decade past the history of industry and commerce is but the history of the revolt of modern productive forces against modern conditions of production, against the property relations that are the conditions for the existence of the bourgeois and of its rule.[24] It is enough to mention the commercial crises that by their periodical return put the existence of the entire bourgeois society on its trial, each time more threateningly. In these crises, a great part not only of the existing products, but also of the previously created productive forces, are periodically destroyed. In these crises, there breaks out an epidemic that, in all earlier epochs, would have seemed an absurdity—the epidemic of over-production. Society suddenly finds itself put back into a state of momentary barbarism; it appears as if a famine, a universal war of devastation, had cut off the supply of every means of subsistence; industry and commerce seem to be destroyed; and why? Because there is too much civilisation, too much means of subsistence, too much industry, too much commerce. The productive forces at the disposal of society no longer tend to further the development of the conditions of bourgeois property; on the contrary, they have become too powerful for these conditions, by which they are fettered, and so soon as they overcome these fetters, they bring disorder into the whole of bourgeois society, endanger

sorcerer: 巫师
nether: 地下的
revolt: 反叛

periodically: 周期性地
epidemic: 传染病
absurdity: 无稽之谈
momentary: 瞬间的
famine: 饥荒
devastation: 毁灭
subsistence: 生存
disposal: 安排，处置

---

24. *For many a decade past... of the bourgeois and of its rule*：该句的主体结构是 the history... is but the history of the revolt... against..., against the property relations that...，最后的 that 引导定语从句限定前面的 the property relations。可译为：“几十年来的工业和商业的历史，只不过是现代生产力反抗现代生产关系，反抗作为资产阶级及其统治的存在条件的所有制关系的历史。"

the existence of bourgeois property.²⁵ The conditions of bourgeois society are too narrow to comprise the wealth created by them. And how does the bourgeoisie get over these crises? On the one hand by enforced destruction of a mass of productive forces; on the other, by the conquest of new markets, and by the more thorough exploitation of the old ones. That is to say, by paving the way for²⁶ more extensive and more destructive crises, and by diminishing the means whereby crises are prevented.

enforced: 强制的

extensive: 广泛的

diminish: 降低，减少

fell: 打倒

34 ▸ The weapons with which the bourgeoisie felled feudalism to the ground are now turned against the bourgeoisie itself.

35 ▸ But not only has the bourgeoisie forged the weapons that bring death to itself; it has also called into existence²⁷ the men who are to wield those weapons—the modern working class—the proletarians.

36 ▸ In proportion as the bourgeoisie, i.e., capital, is developed, in the same proportion is the proletariat, the modern working class, developed—a class of labourers, who live only so long as they find work, and who find work only so long as their labour increases capital. These labourers, who must sell themselves piecemeal, are a commodity, like every other article of commerce, and are consequently exposed to all the vicissitudes of competition, to all the fluctuations of the market.²⁸

piecemeal: 零碎地

vicissitude: 变化

fluctuation: 波动

37 ▸ Owing to the extensive use of machinery, and to the division of labour, the work of the proletarians has lost all individual character, and, consequently,

---

25 *The productive forces... the existence of bourgeois property*: 该句较长，由三个独立的句子组成。on the contrary 和 so soon as 中间是一个独立的句子，其中 by which 限定前面的 these conditions。在后面的部分中，bring 和 endanger 做并列谓语。该句中的 they 都是指代 the productive forces。可译为："社会所拥有的生产力已经不能再促进资产阶级文明和资产阶级所有制关系的发展；相反，生产力已经强大到这种关系所不能适应的地步，它已经受到这种关系的阻碍；而它一着手克服这种障碍，就使整个资产阶级社会陷入混乱，就使资产阶级所有制的存在受到威胁。"

26 *pave the way for*: 为……铺平道路；为……做好准备；为……奠定基础。e.g. The scientific discoveries fo the eighteenth century paved the way for the Industrial Revolution in Britain. 18世纪的科学发现为英国工业革命奠定了基础。

27 *call into existence*: 使形成；实现。e.g. The Second World War called the atomic bomb into existence. 第二次世界大战出现了原子弹。

28 *These labourers... of the market*: 该句的主体结构是 These labourers... are a commodity, ... and are consequently exposed to... to...。可译为："这些不得不把自己零星出卖的工人，像其他任何货物一样，也是一种商品，所以他们同样地受到竞争的一切变化、市场的一切波动的影响。"

all charm for the workman. He becomes an appendage of the machine, and it is only the most simple, most monotonous, and most easily acquired knack, that is required of him. Hence, the cost of production of a workman is restricted, almost entirely, to the means of subsistence that he requires for maintenance, and for the propagation of his race. But the price of a commodity, and therefore also of labour, is equal to its cost of production. In proportion, therefore, as the repulsiveness of the work increases, the wage decreases. Nay more, in proportion as the use of machinery and division of labour increases, in the same proportion the burden of toil also increases, whether by prolongation of the working hours, by the increase of the work exacted in a given time or by increased speed of machinery, etc.[29]

38 ▸ Modern Industry has converted the little workshop of the patriarchal master into the great factory of the industrial capitalist. Masses of labourers, crowded into the factory, are organised like soldiers. As privates of the industrial army they are placed under the command of a perfect hierarchy of officers and sergeants. Not only are they slaves of the bourgeois class, and of the bourgeois State; they are daily and hourly enslaved by the machine, by the overlooker, and, above all, by the individual bourgeois manufacturer himself. The more openly this despotism proclaims gain to be its end and aim, the more petty, the more hateful and the more embittering it is.

39 ▸ The less the skill and exertion of strength implied in manual labour, in other words, the more modern industry becomes developed, the more is the labour of men superseded by that of women.[30] Differences of age and sex have no longer any distinctive social validity for the working class. All are instruments of labour, more or less expensive to use, according to their age and sex.

appendage: 附属物

monotonous: 单调的

knack: 技能

propagation: 繁衍

repulsiveness: 反感度

toil: 劳苦

prolongation: 延长

private: 列兵

hierarchy: 等级

sergeant: 军士

enslave: 奴役

despotism: 专制制度

embitter: 使苦恼

exertion: 强加，施加

supersede: 替代

distinctive: 区别性的

validity: 有效性

29　*Nay more, in proportion as... by increased speed of machinery, etc*: 该句中的两个 in proportion 表示同步变化。whether 后面的三个 by 引导的短语，并列做状语，修饰前面的 increases。可译为："不仅如此，机器越推广，分工越细致，劳动量也就越增加，这或者是由于工作时间的延长，或者是由于在一定时间内所要求的劳动的增加，机器运转的加速，等等。"

30　*The less the skill... by that of women*：该句的主体结构是三个比较结构，即 The less... the more... the more...，其中，implied in manual labour 用来限定 strength。可译为："手工操作所要求的技巧和气力越少，换句话说，现代工业越发达，男工也就越受到女工的排挤。"

40 ▸ No sooner is the exploitation of the labourer by the manufacturer, so far, at an end, that he receives his wages in cash, than he is set upon[31] by the other portions of the bourgeoisie, the landlord, the shopkeeper, the pawnbroker, etc.[32]

41 ▸ The lower strata of the middle class—the small tradespeople, shopkeepers, and retired tradesmen generally, the handicraftsmen and peasants—all these sink gradually into the proletariat, partly because their diminutive capital does not suffice for the scale on which Modern Industry is carried on, and is swamped in the competition with the large capitalists, partly because their specialised skill is rendered worthless by new methods of production.[33] Thus the proletariat is recruited from all classes of the population.

42 ▸ The proletariat goes through various stages of development. With its birth begins its struggle with the bourgeoisie. At first the contest is carried on by individual labourers, then by the workpeople of a factory, then by the operative of one trade, in one locality, against the individual bourgeois who directly exploits them. They direct their attacks not against the bourgeois conditions of production, but against the instruments of production themselves; they destroy imported wares that compete with their labour, they smash to pieces machinery, they set factories ablaze, they seek to restore by force the vanished status of the workman of the Middle Ages.

43 ▸ At this stage, the labourers still form an incoherent mass scattered over the whole country, and broken up by their mutual competition. If anywhere they unite to form more compact bodies, this is not yet the consequence of

---

portion: 部分
pawnbroker: 当铺老板
strata: 阶层
tradespeople: 店主
handicraftsman: 手艺人
diminutive: 微小的
swamp: 陷入困境
recruit: 招募
operative: 有经验的工人，技工
locality: 地点
ware: 器件
smash: 粉碎
ablaze: 着火
incoherent: 支离破碎的
mutual: 相互的
compact: 紧密的

---

31 *set upon*: 攻击，袭击。e.g. Two masked men set upon him as he was going down a dark side street. 当他走在一条黑暗的小路上时，两个蒙面人袭击了他。

32 *No sooner is... the pawnbroker, etc.*：该句的主体结构是 no sooner... than...，其中，that he... in cash 用来说明被剥削的 end。可译为："当工厂主对工人的剥削告一段落，工人领到了用现钱支付的工资的时候，马上就有资产阶级中的另一部分人——房东、小店主、当铺老板等等向他们扑来。"

33 *The lower strata... by new methods of production*：该句的主体结构是 all these sink gradually into the proletariat, partly because... partly because...。其中，all these 指的是前面的 the lower strata...，在第一个 because 引导的从句中，does not suffice 和 is swamped... 做 capital 的并列谓语。可译为："以前的中间等级的下层，即小工业家、小商人和小食利者，手工业者和农民——所有这些阶级都降落到无产阶级的队伍里来了，有的是因为他们的小资本不足以经营大工业，经不起较大的资本家的竞争；有的是因为他们的手艺已经被新的生产方法弄得不值钱了。"

their own active union, but of the union of the bourgeoisie, which class, in order to attain its own political ends, is compelled to set the whole proletariat in motion[34], and is moreover yet, for a time, able to do so.[35] At this stage, therefore, the proletarians do not fight their enemies, but the enemies of their enemies, the remnants of absolute monarchy, the landowners, the non-industrial bourgeois, the petty bourgeois. Thus, the whole historical movement is concentrated in the hands of the bourgeoisie; every victory so obtained is a victory for the bourgeoisie.

remnant: 残余
absolute: 绝对的

44 ▸ But with the development of industry, the proletariat not only increases in number; it becomes concentrated in greater masses, its strength grows, and it feels that strength more. The various interests and conditions of life within the ranks of the proletariat are more and more equalised, in proportion as machinery obliterates all distinctions of labour, and nearly everywhere reduces wages to the same low level.[36] The growing competition among the bourgeois, and the resulting commercial crises, make the wages of the workers ever more fluctuating. The increasing improvement of machinery, ever more rapidly developing, makes their livelihood more and more precarious; the collisions between individual workmen and individual bourgeois take more and more the character of collisions between two classes. Thereupon, the workers begin to form combinations (Trades' Unions) against the bourgeois; they club together in order to keep up the rate of wages; they found permanent associations in order to make provision beforehand for these occasional revolts. Here and there, the contest breaks out into riots.

rank: 阶层
obliterate: 消除

fluctuate: 变化不定
livelihood: 生活状况
precarious: 不稳固的
collision: 冲突
permanent: 永久的
provision: 供给物
beforehand: 预先的
riot: 骚乱

45 ▸ Now and then the workers are victorious, but only for a time. The real fruit of their battles lies, not in the immediate result, but in the ever expanding union of the workers. This union is helped on by the improved means of

---

34 *set... in motion*: 使开动，调动，行动。e.g. Put this handle towards you to set the machine in motion. 将这个把手朝你一拉，机器便开动了。

35 *If anywhere they unite... able to do so*: 该句是由 If 引导的条件状语从句，主句基本结构是 not... but... 句型，其中，which 引导定语从句，其先行词 bourgeoisie 在从句中作主语，其后接两个并列的谓语，一个是 is compelled to...，另一个是 is... able to do so。可译为："工人的大规模集结，还不是他们自己联合的结果，而是资产阶级联合的结果，当时资产阶级为了达到自己的政治目的必须而且暂时还能够把整个无产阶级发动起来。"

36 *The various interests... the same low level*：该句中有 as 引导的原因状语从句，其中有两个并列句。可译为："机器使劳动的差别越来越小，使工资几乎到处都降到同样低的水平，因而无产阶级内部的利益、生活状况也越来越趋于一致。"

communication that are created by modern industry, and that place the workers of different localities in contact with one another. It was just this contact that was needed to centralise the numerous local struggles, all of the same character, into one national struggle between classes. But every class struggle is a political struggle. And that union, to attain which the burghers of the Middle Ages, with their miserable highways, required centuries, the modern proletarian, thanks to railways, achieve in a few years.

46 ▶ This organisation of the proletarians into a class, and, consequently into a political party, is continually being upset again by the competition between the workers themselves. But it ever rises up again, stronger, firmer, mightier. It compels legislative recognition of particular interests of the workers, by taking advantage of the divisions among the bourgeoisie itself. Thus, the ten-hours' bill[37] in England was carried.

47 ▶ Altogether collisions between the classes of the old society further, in many ways, the course of development of the proletariat. The bourgeoisie finds itself involved in a constant battle. At first with the aristocracy; later on, with those portions of the bourgeoisie itself, whose interests have become antagonistic to the progress of industry; at all time with the bourgeoisie of foreign countries. In all these battles, it sees itself compelled to appeal to the proletariat, to ask for help, and thus, to drag it into the political arena. The bourgeoisie itself, therefore, supplies the proletariat with its own elements of political and general education, in other words, it furnishes the proletariat with weapons for fighting the bourgeoisie.

48 ▶ Further, as we have already seen, entire sections of the ruling class are, by the advance of industry, precipitated into the proletariat, or are at least threatened in their conditions of existence. These also supply the proletariat with fresh elements of enlightenment and progress.

49 ▶ Finally, in times when the class struggle nears the decisive hour, the progress of dissolution going on within the ruling class, in fact within the whole range of old society, assumes such a violent, glaring character, that a

---

37　*the ten-hours' bill*：《十小时工作日法案》。英国工人阶级经过30年惊人的顽强斗争，争得了《十小时工作日法案》。《十小时工作日法案》是英国议会在1847年6月8日通过的，1848年5月1日起作为法律生效，该法律将妇女和少年的日劳动时间限制为10小时。《十小时工作日法案》不仅是一个重大的实际的成功，而且是一个原则的胜利：资产阶级政治经济学第一次在工人阶级政治经济学面前公开投降了。

small section of the ruling class cuts itself adrift, and joins the revolutionary class, the class that holds the future in its hands.[38] Just as, therefore, at an earlier period, a section of the nobility went over to the bourgeoisie, so now a portion of the bourgeoisie goes over to the proletariat, and in particular, a portion of the bourgeois ideologists, who have raised themselves to the level of comprehending theoretically the historical movement as a whole.[39]

adrift: 脱离开来

ideologist: 理论家

theoretically: 理论地

50 ▸ Of all the classes that stand face to face with the bourgeoisie today, the proletariat alone is a really revolutionary class. The other classes decay and finally disappear in the face of Modern Industry; the proletariat is its special and essential product.

decay: 衰败

51 ▸ The lower middle class, the small manufacturer, the shopkeeper, the artisan, the peasant, all these fight against the bourgeoisie, to save from extinction their existence as fractions of the middle class. They are therefore not revolutionary, but conservative. Nay more, they are reactionary, for they try to roll back the wheel of history. If by chance, they are revolutionary, they are only so in view of their impending transfer into the proletariat; they thus defend not their present, but their future interests, they desert their own standpoint to place themselves at that of the proletariat.[40]

artisan: 工匠

conservative: 保守的

impending: 即将发生的

desert: 舍弃

standpoint: 立场

52 ▸ The "dangerous class", [lumpenproletariat] the social scum, that passively rotting mass thrown off by the lowest layers of the old society, may, here and there, be swept into the movement by a proletarian revolution; its conditions of life, however, prepare it far more for the part of a bribed tool of

scum: 浮渣

passively: 消极地

rotting: 腐败的

sweep: 席卷

bribe: 贿赂

38　*Finally, in times when... the future in its hands*：该句的主体结构是 when..., the progress... assumes such... that...。when 引导时间状语从句，that 引导的从句中有两个并列谓语。可译为："最后，在阶级斗争接近决战的时期，统治阶级内部的、整个旧社会内部的瓦解过程，就达到非常强烈、非常尖锐的程度，甚至使得统治阶级中的一小部分人脱离统治阶级而归附于革命的阶级，即掌握着未来的阶级。"

39　*Just as, therefore, ... the historical movement as a whole*：该句中 in particular 后面部分与前面的 a portion of the bourgeoisie 的成分一样，具有强调的作用。可译为："所以，正像过去贵族中有一部分人转到资产阶级方面一样，现在资产阶级中也有一部分人，特别是已经提高到从理论上认识整个历史运动这一水平的一部分资产阶级思想家，转到无产阶级方面来了。"

40　*If by chance, ... that of the proletariat*：该句由三个独立的句子构成。可译为："如果说他们是革命的，那是鉴于他们行将转入无产阶级的队伍，这样，他们就不是维护他们目前的利益，而是维护他们将来的利益，他们就离开自己原来的立场，而站到无产阶级的立场上来。"

	reactionary intrigue.⁴¹
intrigue: 阴谋	
virtually: 事实上	53 ▸ In the condition of the proletariat, those of old society at large are already virtually swamped. The proletarian is without property; his relation to his wife and children has no longer anything in common with the bourgeois family relations; modern industry labour, modern subjection to capital, the same in England as in France, in America as in Germany, has stripped him of every trace of national character. Law, morality, religion, are to him so many bourgeois prejudices, behind which lurk in ambush just as many bourgeois interests.
subjection: 屈从	
prejudice: 偏见	
lurk: 隐匿	
ambush: 埋伏	
preceding: 前面的	54 ▸ All the preceding classes that got the upper hand sought to fortify their already acquired status by subjecting society at large to their conditions of appropriation. The proletarians cannot become masters of the productive forces of society, except by abolishing their own previous mode of appropriation, and thereby also every other previous mode of appropriation. They have nothing of their own to secure and to fortify; their mission is to destroy all previous securities for, and insurances of, individual property.
seek: 追求	
fortify: 巩固	
appropriation: 占用，占有	
abolish: 废除	
insurance: 保险，保障	
	55 ▸ All previous historical movements were movements of minorities, or in the interest of minorities. The proletarian movement is the self-conscious, independent movement of the immense majority, in the interest of the immense majority. The proletariat, the lowest stratum of our present society, cannot stir, cannot raise itself up, without the whole superincumbent strata of official society being sprung into the air.
substance: 实质	56 ▸ Though not in substance, yet in form, the struggle of the proletariat with the bourgeoisie is at first a national struggle. The proletariat of each country must, of course, first of all settle matters with its own bourgeoisie.
trace: 追踪	57 ▸ In depicting the most general phases of the development of the proletariat, we traced the more or less veiled civil war, raging within existing society, up to the point where that war breaks out into open revolution, and where the violent overthrow of the bourgeoisie lays the foundation for the sway of the

---

41　The "dangerous class", ... reactionary intrigue：该句由两个并列句组成，由分号分开。第一个句子的基本构成是 the social scum... may... be swept into...，其余的都是相应的修饰成分。可译为："流氓无产阶级是旧社会最下层中消极的腐化的部分，他们在一些地方也被无产阶级革命卷到运动里来，但是，由于他们的整个生活状况，他们更甘心于被人收买，去干反动的勾当。"

proletariat.⁴²

58 ▸ Hitherto, every form of society has been based, as we have already seen, on the antagonism of oppressing and oppressed classes. But in order to oppress a class, certain conditions must be assured to it under which it can, at least, continue its slavish existence. The serf, in the period of serfdom, raised himself to membership in the commune, just as the petty bourgeois, under the yoke of the feudal absolutism, managed to develop into a bourgeois. The modern labourer, on the contrary, instead of rising with the process of industry, sinks deeper and deeper below the conditions of existence of his own class. He becomes a pauper, and pauperism develops more rapidly than population and wealth. And here it becomes evident, that the bourgeoisie is unfit any longer to be the ruling class in society, and to impose its conditions of existence upon society as an over-riding law. It is unfit to rule because it is incompetent to assure an existence to its slave within his slavery, because it cannot help letting him sink into such a state, that it has to feed him, instead of being fed by him.⁴³ Society can no longer live under this bourgeoisie, in other words, its existence is no longer compatible with society.

slavish: 奴隶般的

yoke: 束缚

pauper: 穷人
pauperism: 贫民
impose: 强加
over-riding: 高于一切的
incompetent: 不胜任的，无资格的

59 ▸ The essential conditions for the existence and for the sway of the bourgeois class is the formation and augmentation of capital; the condition for capital is wage-labour. Wage-labour rests exclusively on competition between the labourers. The advance of industry, whose involuntary promoter is the bourgeoisie, replaces the isolation of the labourers, due to competition, by the revolutionary combination, due to association.⁴⁴ The development of Modern Industry, therefore, cuts from under its feet the very foundation on

augmentation: 增加

involuntary: 无意识的
promoter: 推动者

---

42 *In depicting... the sway of the proletariat*：该句的主句是 we traced the more or less veiled civil war，后面的 raging within existing society 是说明 civil war 的范围，up to the point 及其后面的限定成分都是来说明程度的。可译为："在叙述无产阶级发展的最一般的阶段的时候，我们循序探讨了现存社会内部或多或少隐蔽着的国内战争，直到这个战争爆发为公开的革命，无产阶级用暴力推翻资产阶级而建立自己的统治。"

43 *It is unfit to rule... being fed by him*：该句的难点在于第二个 because 引导的从句中有 such... that... 的结构。可译为："资产阶级不能统治下去了，因为它甚至不能保证自己的奴隶维持奴隶的生活，因为它不得不让自己的奴隶沦落到不能养活它反而要它来养活的地步。"

44 *The advance of industry... due to association*：该句的主体结构是 The advance of industry... replaces the isolation...，due to competition 说明 isolation 的原因，by... due to... 说明 replace 的方式和原因。可译为："资产阶级无意中造成而又无力抵抗的工业进步，使工人通过结社而达到的革命联合代替了他们由于竞争而造成的分散状态。"

which the bourgeoisie produces and appropriates products. What the bourgeoisie therefore produces, above all, are its own grave-diggers. Its fall and the victory of the proletariat are equally inevitable.

EXERCISES

I. Answer the following questions according to the reading text.

1. What does it mean when the communism is compared to a spectre?
2. Where does the modern bourgeois society come from? In what aspects is the modern bourgeois the same as previous societies?
3. From what aspects can we find the bourgeoisie's revolutionary part?
4. Why does the *Manifesto* say that "The bourgeoisie, during its rule of scarce one hundred years, has created more massive and more colossal productive forces than have all preceding generations together"?
5. While the bourgeoisie destroyed the feudalism, what did it give birth to?
6. Why does the proletariats' strength increases with the development of industry?
7. Why do the proletariats lose their national character?
8. Why is the bourgeoisie unfit to be the ruling class?

II. Paraphrase the following sentences with your own words, and then translate them into Chinese.

1. In the earlier epochs of history, we find almost everywhere a complicated arrangement of society into various orders, a manifold gradation of social rank. (Para. 9)
2. Society as a whole is more and more splitting up into two great hostile camps, into two great classes directly facing each other—Bourgeoisie and Proletariat. (Para. 11)
3. In one word, for exploitation, veiled by religious and political illusions, it has substituted naked, shameless, direct, brutal exploitation. (Para. 20)
4. The bourgeoisie has torn away from the family its sentimental veil, and has reduced the family relation to a mere money relation. (Para. 22)

5. It has created enormous cities, has greatly increased the urban population as compared with the rural, and has thus rescued a considerable part of the population from the idiocy of rural life. (Para. 28)

6. Into their place stepped free competition, accompanied by a social and political constitution adapted in it, and the economic and political sway of the bourgeois class. (Para. 32)

7. The weapons with which the bourgeoisie felled feudalism to the ground are now turned against the bourgeoisie itself. (Para. 34)

8. Further, as we have already seen, entire sections of the ruling class are, by the advance of industry, precipitated into the proletariat, or are at least threatened in their conditions of existence. (Para. 48)

III. Figure out the meanings of the phrases in bold, and then make another sentence with each of the phrases.

1. It is high time that Communists should openly, in the face of the whole world, publish their views, their aims, their tendencies, and meet this **nursery tale** of the Spectre of Communism with a manifesto of the party itself. (Para. 5)

2. Division of labour between the different corporate guilds vanished **in the face of** division of labour in each single workshop. (Para. 14)

3. Modern industry has established the world market, for which the discovery of America **paved the way**. (Para. 16)

4. The bourgeoisie has stripped of its halo every occupation hitherto honoured and **looked up to with** reverent awe. (Para. 21)

5. The bourgeoisie keeps more and more **doing away with** the scattered state of the population, of the means of production, and of property. (Para. 29)

6. The conditions of bourgeois society are too narrow to comprise the wealth created by them. And how does the bourgeoisie **get over** these crises? (Para. 33)

7. They are reactionary, for they try to **roll back** the wheel of history. (Para. 51)

8. All the preceding classes that **got the upper hand** sought to fortify their already acquired status by subjecting society at large to their conditions of appropriation. (Para. 54)

IV. Explain the following words and phrases in your own words.

1. Holy alliance
2. The Middle Ages
3. Gothic
4. Exoduses of nations
5. Crusade

V. Explain one of our present social phenomena using the key points mentioned in *The Communist Manifesto*. Write down your understanding with no less than 200 words.

Pride and Prejudice
A Novel

Oral tasks

1. How much do you know about *Pride and Prejudice*?
2. Talk about the history and social life in Britain in the 19th century.
3. What's your view on love and marriage?

Introduction

A novel is a relatively long work of narrative fiction, and typically published as a book. It is generally suggested that the novel first came into being in the early 18th century.

Pride and Prejudice is a romantic novel by Jane Austen, first published in 1813. The story charts the emotional development of the protagonist, Elizabeth Bennet, who learns the error of making hasty judgments and comes to appreciate the difference between the superficial and the essential. The comedy of the writing lies in the depiction of manners, education, marriage, and money during the British Regency period. Jane Austen's opening line, "It is a truth universally acknowledged, that a single man in possession of a good fortune, must be in want of a wife", is a sentence filled with irony and playfulness. The novel revolves around the importance of marrying for love, not simply for money, despite the social pressures of making a good (i.e., wealthy) match.

Jane Austen (1775–1817) was an English novelist known primarily for her six major novels of sensibility (love or marriage), which interpret, critique and comment upon the British landed gentry at the end of the 18th century. Her use of biting irony, along with her realism and social commentary, has earned her acclaim among critics and scholars.

PART 3

TEXTUAL READING[1]

Volume I
Chapter I

1▸ It is a truth universally acknowledged, that a single man in possession of a good fortune, must be in want of a wife.[2]

fortune: 财富

2▸ However little known the feelings or views of such a man may be on his first entering a neighborhood, this truth is so well fixed in the minds of the surrounding families, that he is considered as the rightful property of some one or other of their daughters.[3]

rightful: 合法的

3▸ "My dear Mr. Bennet,"[4] said his lady to him one day, "have you heard that Netherfield Park is let at last?"

4▸ Mr. Bennet replied that he had not.

5▸ "But it is," returned she; "for Mrs. Long has just been here, and she told me all about it."

---

1 本篇出自：Jane Austen. *Pride and Prejudice*. New York: Norton, 2001。

2 *It is a truth… in want of a wife*: 该句是英语写作中一个比较经典的句子，由一个主句和一个从句构成。that 引导的从句是整个句子的实际主语，it 是该句的形式主语；介词短语 in possession of a good fortune 是 a single man 的限定成分。可译为："有个道理众所周知：家财万贯的单身男子，肯定是需要一位太太的。"（注：本篇译文来自李继宏翻译的《傲慢与偏见》，天津：天津人民出版社，2016。下同。）

3 *However little known... of their daughters*: 该句较长，包含 so... that... 结构，意为"如此……以至于……"。可译为："这个真理早已深深扎根于人们的心中，所以每当这样一个男子初到一地，左邻右舍即使对他的感受和想法还一无所知，也总会把他视为自己某个女儿应得的一份财产。"

4 20 世纪以前，家庭成员关系不如现代亲密，欧洲贵族阶级家庭尤其如此。就夫妻关系而言，像本尼特先生这种乡绅阶层，房子通常很大，夫妻有各自的房间和佣人，除了一起吃饭，每天相处的时间极少，所以彼此关系较为疏远。至于父母和子女的关系，乡绅阶层并不亲自照顾自己的子女，而是将这件事交给奶妈和其他佣人负责，再加上极高的婴儿死亡率等原因，父母与子女之间的感情非常淡漠，特别是作为一家之长的丈夫和父亲，更多的是以威严而非亲切的形象存在。本尼特太太在这里尊称自己的丈夫为 Mr. Bennet 而非直呼其名，以及后文几个女儿经常称他为"阁下"，只有撒娇的时候才叫"爸爸"，无不反映了这种疏远的家庭关系。

6▸ Mr. Bennet made no answer.

7▸ "Do not you want to know who has taken it?" cried his wife impatiently.

8▸ "You want to tell me, and I have no objection to hearing it."

9▸ This was invitation enough.

10▸ "Why, my dear, you must know, Mrs. Long says that Netherfield is taken by a young man of large fortune from the north of England; that he came down on Monday in a chaise and four[5] to see the place, and was so much delighted with it that he agreed with Mr. Morris immediately; that he is to take possession before Michaelmas[6], and some of his servants are to be in the house by the end of next week."

11▸ "What is his name?"

12▸ "Bingley."

13▸ "Is he married or single?"

14▸ "Oh! single, my dear, to be sure! A single man of large fortune; four or five thousand a year.[7] What a fine thing for our girls!"

15▸ "How so? how can it affect them?"

---

5 *a chaise and four*：一辆驷马大轿车。四驱翠轼，由四匹马拉动，车厢是封闭式的，有四个轮子，属于大型豪华马车。19 世纪中期以前，铁路尚未出现，马车是英国的主要交通工具，但饲养马匹的费用相当高昂。作者在 1799 年 6 月 19 日写给其姐姐卡桑德拉的信里提到，她们的哥哥爱德华用六十几尼（约 63 英镑）买了两匹不算高大的黑马。可以作为参照的是，那时一个熟练工匠的年收入大概是 55 英镑。此外维护车辆的成本也很高，只有富人才能用得起私家马车。作者的父亲乔治·奥斯汀曾在 1784 年买了一辆便宜的马车，但由于养护费太高，到 1798 年只好搁置不用。当年的马车和现在的汽车一样，也是款式繁多，高中低档都有，除了本书提到的翠轼（chaise）、辉腾（phaeton）、卡里克尔（curricle）、巴罗赫（barouche）等，常见的马车尚有其他上百种。

6 *Michaelmas*：米迦勒节，是纪念天使长米迦勒的节日。西方基督教会定于每年的 9 月 29 日，东正教会定于 11 月 8 日。其日期恰逢西欧许多地区秋收季节，节日纪念活动十分隆重。尤其在中世纪，许多民间传统习俗都与它有关。爱尔兰人过节时把戒指杂糅于饼馅中，谁吃到这枚戒指，被认为即将有结婚之喜。英格兰人有在此节食鹅肉的习俗，据称这是为了保证来年生活富裕。米迦勒节是英国四个年度四分节（Quarter Days）的第三个，其他三个分别是圣母节（3 月 25 日）、仲夏节（6 月 24 日）和圣诞节（12 月 25 日）。依照英国旧俗，四分节是签订租约或者雇佣合同的起止日。

7 19 世纪初期，英格兰和威尔士大概有 220 万个家庭，每年收入在 4000 英镑以上的家庭约 2300 户，这意味着宾格利的收入比 99.9% 的英国家庭高；考虑到他尚未成家，无须抚养子女，实际上可支配的财富相对更加惊人。

16 ▶ "My dear Mr. Bennet," replied his wife, "how can you be so tiresome! You must know that I am thinking of his marrying one of them."

tiresome: 无聊的

17 ▶ "Is that his design in settling here?"

18 ▶ "Design! Nonsense, how can you talk so! But it is very likely that he may fall in love with one of them, and therefore you must visit him as soon as he comes."

19 ▶ "I see no occasion for that. You and the girls may go, or you may send them by themselves, which perhaps will be still better, for as you are as handsome as any of them, Mr. Bingley might like you the best of the party."[8]

20 ▶ "My dear, you flatter me. I certainly have had my share of beauty, but I do not pretend to be any thing extraordinary now. When a woman has five grown up daughters,[9] she ought to give over thinking of her own beauty."

flatter: 奉承

extraordinary: 不同寻常的

21 ▶ "In such cases, a woman has not often much beauty to think of."

22 ▶ "But, my dear, you must indeed go and see Mr. Bingley when he comes into the neighbourhood."

23 ▶ "It is more than I engage for, I assure you."

24 ▶ "But consider your daughters. Only think what an establishment it would be for one of them. Sir William and Lady Lucas[10] are determined to

---

8 *You and the girls may go... the best of the party*: 该句中的 which 是指前面所说的 You and the girls may go, ... still better, for 引导了一个从句，表示原因。可译为："你和姑娘们去就行了，或者你让她们自己去，那样也许更好，因为你和她们一样漂亮，说不定宾格利先生最喜欢的反而是你。"

9 本尼特太太这是在说她自己。依照 1754 年 3 月 25 日在英格兰和威尔士生效的《1753 年婚姻法》，凡年满 21 岁者，即可不经父母同意而结婚，所以当时法定的成年标准是 21 岁。本尼特家五姐妹，只有 22 岁的简算是成年人。本尼特太太甚至把最小的女儿丽迪雅（15 岁）也算进去，体现了她恨不得早日把所有女儿都嫁出去的迫切心情。根据剑桥大学某研究小组对英国 12 个堂区的历史文献的分析结果，从 1775 年到 1799 年，英国女性平均初婚年龄是 24.7 岁，但终身未婚的男女加起来约占总人口的四分之一，作者本人及其姐姐卡桑德拉便终身未嫁，所以本尼特太太的急切虽然有些夸张，却也非不可理解。

10 *Sir William and Lady Lucas*: 威廉·卢卡斯夫妇。英国爵位分为公（Duke）、侯（Marquis）、伯（Earl）、子（Viscount）和男（Baron）五等，另设有从男爵（Baronet）和骑士（Knight）两种荣誉封号。男爵可世袭，但和骑士一样不入英国上议院，因此不算真正的贵族，且在男爵以上的贵族看来与平民无异。普通人对从男爵或者骑士的专用称谓是在其名字前加上"爵士（Sir）"，称呼其妻子则是在其姓氏前加上"夫人（Lady）"。

go, merely on that account, for in general you know they visit no new comers. Indeed you must go, for it will be impossible for us to visit him, if you do not."[11]

scrupulous:
谨慎的

25 ▸ "You are over scrupulous surely. I dare say Mr. Bingley will be very glad to see you; and I will send a few lines by you to assure him of my hearty consent to his marrying which ever he chuses[12] of the girls; though I must throw in a good word for my little Lizzy."[13]

26 ▸ "I desire you will do no such thing. Lizzy is not a bit better than the others; and I am sure she is not half so handsome as Jane, nor half so good humoured as Lydia. But you are always giving her the preference."

27 ▸ "They have none of them much to recommend them," replied he; "they are all silly and ignorant like other girls; but Lizzy has something more of quickness than her sisters."

compassion:
同情

28 ▸ "Mr. Bennet, how can you abuse your own children in such a way? You take delight in vexing me. You have no compassion on my poor nerves."[14]

29 ▸ "You mistake me, my dear. I have a high respect for your nerves. They are my old friends. I have heard you mention them with consideration these twenty years at least."

---

11 宾格利是单身汉，这意味着其家里没有女眷。依照当时的风俗，只有在本尼特先生先去拜访宾格利之后，他家里的女眷才能去。

12 *chuse*: 选择，古语，等同于 choose。

13 *and I will send... for my little Lizzy*: 该句中 throw in 意为额外奉送，外加。e.g. The shop advertised that with every suit of clothes they would throw in a pair of leather gloves. 这家商店做广告说买一套衣服，他们额外奉送一双皮手套。可译为："我可以写张字条让你带去，告诉他无论他看中哪个姑娘，我都衷心愿意招他当女婿；不过我得替丽兹多说几句好话。"

14 本尼特太太宣称自己神经有问题是为了引起别人的关注。在 18 世纪，英国生理学家认为许多疾病是由神经系统引起的，有艺术天赋的人神经比较敏感，从而容易罹患各种疾病。例如，托马斯·特罗特在其代表作《神经气质论》第 92 页中指出："勤于思考的学者和认真刻苦的学生往往脸色苍白，也许是因为他们深居简出，从而导致消化不良或者血液含氧量不足。大学里许多喜欢学习、热爱文学的年轻人都患有胃病，而且今后永远无法治愈。音乐爱好者一般而言神经敏锐，感情丰富，性格沉静，他们通常也受这些病痛折磨。其实这句话适用于所有文学艺术爱好者。这种人无论男女都容易患上神经疾病。"该理论导致当时许多人喜欢宣称自己患有神经疾病，以至于英国学者希瑟·毕替称其为"时髦病"。本尼特太太多次提及自己患有神经疾病，目的在于暗示自己拥有高人一等的特殊气质。

30 ▸ "Ah! you do not know what I suffer."

31 ▸ "But I hope you will get over[15] it, and live to see many young men of four thousand a year come into the neighbourhood."

32 ▸ "It will be no use to us, if twenty such should come since you will not visit them."

33 ▸ "Depend upon it, my dear, that when there are twenty, I will visit them all."

34 ▸ Mr. Bennet was so odd a mixture of quick parts, sarcastic humour, reserve, and caprice, that the experience of three and twenty years had been insufficient to make his wife understand his character.[16] Her mind was less difficult to develop. She was a woman of mean understanding, little information, and uncertain temper. When she was discontented she fancied herself nervous. The business of her life was to get her daughters married; its solace was visiting and news.

sarcastic: 冷嘲热讽的

caprice: 反复无常的

insufficient: 不足的

fancy: 想象

solace: 安慰

Chapter II

35 ▸ Mr. Bennet was among the earliest of those who waited on Mr. Bingley. He had always intended to visit him, though to the last always assuring his wife that he should not go; and till the evening after the visit was paid, she had no knowledge of it. It was then disclosed in the following manner. Observing his second daughter employed in trimming a hat,[17] he suddenly addressed her with,

36 ▸ "I hope Mr. Bingley will like it, Lizzy."

---

15 *get over*: 克制（感情等），克服（困难）。e.g. The singer had to learn to get over her fear of the public. 歌唱演员必须学会克服对观众的恐惧心理。

16 *Mr. Bennet was so odd... understand his character*: 该句的主体结构含 so... that...，其中有由 quick parts, sarcastic humour, reserve, and caprice 四个并列的名词词组作 a mixture of 的宾语。可译为："本尼特先生这人有点古怪，他既机敏诙谐，喜欢冷嘲热讽，又保守矜持，让人捉摸不定。所以他妻子虽然和他同床共枕 23 年，却依然不是很了解他的性格。"

17 工业革命以前，服装是昂贵的商品，时尚潮流又日新月异，每当流行款式发生变化，人们通常会修改原有的衣服和帽子，而不是另外买新款的，有时甚至会把原有的衣服重新染色。1799 年 6 月 2 日，简·奥斯汀在写给其姐姐卡桑德拉的信里提到，她的外套价值 2 英镑，她在商店看到一顶缀有樱桃和葡萄的帽子卖 5 先令。1813 年 10 月 14 日，作者在另一封致卡桑德拉的信里说她准备把一条蓝色裙子染成其他颜色。

resentfully: 愤恨地

37 ▸ "We are not in a way to know what Mr. Bingley likes," said her mother resentfully, "since we are not to visit."

38 ▸ "But you forget, mama," said Elizabeth, "that we shall meet him at the assemblies[18], and that Mrs. Long has promised to introduce him."

hypocritical: 虚伪的

39 ▸ "I do not believe Mrs. Long will do any such thing. She has two nieces of her own. She is a selfish, hypocritical woman, and I have no opinion of her."

40 ▸ "No more have I," said Mr. Bennet; "and I am glad to find that you do not depend on her serving you."

deign: 屈尊，垂顾
contain: 克制
scold: 责备

41 ▸ Mrs. Bennet deigned not to make any reply; but unable to contain herself, began scolding one of her daughters.

42 ▸ "Don't keep coughing so, Kitty, for heaven's sake! Have a little compassion on my nerves. You tear them to pieces."

discretion: 自行决定权

43 ▸ "Kitty has no discretion in her coughs," said her father; "she times them ill."

amusement: 娱乐
fretfully: 烦躁地

44 ▸ "I do not cough for my own amusement," replied Kitty fretfully.

45 ▸ "When is your next ball to be, Lizzy?"

46 ▸ "Tomorrow fortnight."

47 ▸ "Aye, so it is," cried her mother, "and Mrs. Long does not come back till the day before; so, it will be impossible for her to introduce him, for she will not know him herself."

48 ▸ "Then, my dear, you may have the advantage of your friend, and introduce Mr. Bingley to her."

teasing: 取笑人的

49 ▸ "Impossible, Mr. Bennet, impossible, when I am not acquainted with him myself; how can you be so teasing?"

circumspection: 慎重

50 ▸ "I honour your circumspection. A fortnight's acquaintance is certainly very little. One cannot know what a man really is by the end of a fortnight.

18　*assembly*: 公共聚会，是18世纪英国城镇生活主要的娱乐活动，也是未婚青年男女相互结识了解的重要场所，通常在酒馆或者公共会堂举行。公共聚会无须请帖，任何人只要买票即可入场，所以与会人员往往各个阶级的都有。

But if we do not venture, somebody else will; and after all, Mrs. Long and her nieces must stand their chance[19]; and therefore, as she will think it an act of kindness, if you decline the office, I will take it on myself."

office: 职责，公务

51 ▸ The girls stared at their father. Mrs. Bennet said only, "Nonsense, nonsense!"

52 ▸ "What can be the meaning of that emphatic exclamation?" cried he. "Do you consider the forms of introduction, and the stress that is laid on them, as nonsense? I cannot quite agree with you there. What say you, Mary? For you are a young lady of deep reflection I know, and read great books, and make extracts."

emphatic: 着重的

exclamation: 感叹

reflection: 深思熟虑

extract: 摘录

53 ▸ Mary wished to say something very sensible, but knew not how.

54 ▸ "While Mary is adjusting her ideas," he continued, "let us return to Mr. Bingley."

55 ▸ "I am sick of Mr. Bingley," cried his wife.

56 ▸ "I am sorry to hear that; but why did not you tell me so before? If I had known as much this morning, I certainly would not have called on him. It is very unlucky; but as I have actually paid the visit, we cannot escape the acquaintance now."

57 ▸ The astonishment of the ladies was just what he wished; that of Mrs. Bennet perhaps surpassing the rest; though when the first tumult of joy was over, she began to declare that it was what she had expected all the while.[20]

58 ▸ "How good it was in you, my dear Mr. Bennet! But I knew I should persuade you at last. I was sure you loved your girls too well to neglect such an acquaintance. Well, how pleased I am! And it is such a good joke, too, that you should have gone this morning, and never said a word about it till now."

59 ▸ "Now, Kitty, you may cough as much as you chuse," said Mr. Bennet; and, as he spoke, he left the room, fatigued with the raptures of his wife.

rapture: 欣喜

---

19 *stand a chance*: 有……的希望；有……的机会。e.g. You stand a very good chance of passing the exam if you work hard. 如果你努力学习，就很有希望通过考试。

20 *The astonishment... all the while*: 该句中的标点已将整个句子分成了几个短句。第一个 that 指代的是 astonishment，最后一个从句中的 it 指的是本尼特先生拜访宾格利先生的事。可译为："母女几人非常吃惊，这正是他想要的效果；本尼特太太更是感到喜出望外；但在一阵欢乐的吵闹过后，她宣称这早在她的意料当中。"

60▶ "What an excellent father you have, girls," said she, when the door was shut. "I do not know how you will ever make him amends for his kindness; or me either, for that matter. At our time of life, it is not so pleasant, I can tell you, to be making new acquaintance every day; but for your sakes, we would do any thing. Lydia, my love, though you are the youngest, I dare say Mr. Bingley will dance with you at the next ball."

stoutly: 坚决地

61▶ "Oh!" said Lydia stoutly, "I am not afraid; for though I am the youngest, I'm the tallest."

62▶ The rest of the evening was spent in conjecturing how soon he would return Mr. Bennet's visit, and determining when they should ask him to dinner.[21]

Chapter III

63▶ Not all that Mrs. Bennet, however, with the assistance of her five daughters, could ask on the subject was sufficient to draw from her husband any satisfactory description of Mr. Bingley.[22] They attacked him in various ways; with barefaced questions, ingenious suppositions, and distant surmises; but he eluded the skill of them all; and they were at last obliged to accept the second-hand intelligence of their neighbour Lady Lucas.[23] Her report was highly favourable. Sir William had been delighted with him. He was quite young, wonderfully handsome, extremely agreeable, and to crown the

ingenious: 机灵的，独特的

supposition: 推测

surmise: 猜度

elude: 回避

oblige: 不得不，迫使

---

21 在简·奥斯汀的时代，由于生活节奏缓慢，加上物质匮乏，英国人每天只吃两顿饭，就是早餐（breakfast）和正餐（dinner）。午餐（lunch）极其罕见，夜宵（supper）相对较为频繁，尤其是在上层阶级，但也只在夜间有亲友聚会时才提供。像本尼特先生这种乡绅家庭，早餐通常在9点吃，正餐则在下午3点——这主要是为了节省柴火，因为英国地处高纬度，冬天太阳很早下山，如果太晚吃饭，那么准备饭菜时厨房需要电灯，这意味着额外的开支。至于更为有钱的贵族和商人，比如达希和宾格利，他们并不在乎这些钱，日常活动也较为丰富，吃正餐的时间比本尼特家要晚三四个小时。

22 *Not all... description of Mr. Bingley*: 该句的主体结构是 Not all... was sufficient...，all 后面是 that 引导的定语从句 that Mrs. Bennet... on the subject。可译为："尽管有五个女儿帮忙询问宾格利先生的情况，本尼特太太却无法从她丈夫那里套出满意的答案。"

23 *They attacked him... of their neighbour Lady Lucas*: 该句的主体结构是 They attacked... with barefaced questions..., but he eluded..., and they were at last obliged to...。可译为："她们用各种办法盘问他，包括直截了当的提问、旁敲侧击的推断、毫无来由的猜测，但始终问不出个所以然来，最后只好接受邻居卢卡斯夫人的二道信息。"

whole[24], he meant to be at the next assembly with a large party. Nothing could be more delightful! To be fond of dancing was a certain step towards falling in love; and very lively hopes of Mr. Bingley's heart were entertained.

64▸ "If I can but see one of my daughters happily settled at Netherfield," said Mrs. Bennet to her husband, "and all the others equally well married, I shall have nothing to wish for."

65▸ In a few days Mr. Bingley returned Mr. Bennet's visit, and sat about ten minutes with him in his library[25]. He had entertained hopes of being admitted to a sight of the young ladies, of whose beauty he had heard much; but he saw only the father. The ladies were somewhat more fortunate, for they had the advantage of ascertaining from an upper window, that he wore a blue coat[26] and rode a black horse.

ascertain: 弄清

66▸ An invitation to dinner was soon afterwards dispatched; and already had Mrs. Bennet planned the courses that were to do credit to[27] her housekeeping, when an answer arrived which deferred it all.[28] Mr. Bingley was obliged to be in town the following day, and consequently unable to accept the honour of their invitation. Mrs. Bennet was quite disconcerted. She could not imagine what business he could have in town so soon after his arrival in Hertfordshire; and she began to fear that he might be always flying about from one place to another, and never settled at Netherfield as he ought to be. Lady Lucas quieted her fears a little by starting the idea of his being gone to London only to get a large party for the ball; and a report soon followed that Mr. Bingley was to

defer: 推迟

disconcerted: 惊慌的

quiet: 安慰

---

24 *to crown the whole*: 更重要的是。e.g. He has a pleasant countenance, of great knowledge and humor, and to crown the whole, he has easy, unaffected manners. 他仪表堂堂，学识丰富，人又很幽默；最重要的一点是，他和颜悦色，没有拘泥做作的习气。

25 *library*: 书房，是英国乡绅阶层住宅的标准房间，它不仅是一个藏书的地方，也是男主人接待男宾的场所。像本尼特太太这样的女主人，通常在休息室（drawing-room）接待来访的女宾。

26 在18世纪的欧洲，限于技术和原料来源，蓝色布匹的生产成本比其他颜色的布匹高，因而蓝色衣服在当时是高贵的象征。

27 *do credit to*: 为某人争光，证明某人有某种才能。e.g. This pupil does credit to your teaching. 这位学生的成绩足以给你的教学增色。

28 *An invitation to dinner... deferred it all*: 该句中有一个倒装句，already 被提前，表示强调；that 引导一个定语从句限定 courses；when 引导的时间状语从句，表示就在这个时候。可译为："宴席的请帖很快发了出去，本尼特太太安排了数道美味佳肴展现自己持家有方，可惜却接到了延期的答复。"

bring twelve ladies and seven gentlemen with him to the assembly. The girls grieved over such a number of ladies; but were comforted the day before the ball by hearing, that instead of twelve, he had brought only six with him from London, his five sisters and a cousin. And when the party entered the assembly room, it consisted of only five altogether; Mr. Bingley, his two sisters, the husband of the eldest, and another young man.

67 ▶ Mr. Bingley was good looking and gentlemanlike; he had a pleasant countenance, and easy, unaffected manners. His sisters were fine women, with an air of decided fashion. His brother-in-law, Mr. Hurst, merely looked the gentleman; but his friend Mr. Darcy soon drew the attention of the room by his fine, tall person, handsome features, noble mien; and the report which was in general circulation within five minutes after his entrance, of his having ten thousand a year[29],[30]. The gentlemen pronounced him to be a fine figure of a man, the ladies declared he was much handsomer than Mr. Bingley, and he was looked at with great admiration for about half the evening, till his manners gave a disgust which turned the tide[31] of his popularity; for he was discovered to be proud, to be above his company, and above being pleased; and not all his large estate in Derbyshire[32] could then save him from having a most forbidding, disagreeable countenance, and being unworthy to be compared with his friend.

68 ▶ Mr. Bingley had soon made himself acquainted with all the principal people in the room; he was lively and unreserved, danced every dance, was angry that the ball closed so early, and talked of giving one himself at

countenance: 面容

unaffected: 真挚的

mien: 风度，仪表

forbidding: 令人生畏的；冷峻的

disagreeable: 难以相处的

---

29 *ten thousand a year*: 这在当时是一笔非常惊人的财富。根据英国历史学家明盖伊估计，18 世纪末全英国大约只有 400 个家庭年收入在 10000 英镑以上。假如这笔收入全部来自地租，那么达希拥有的田园最多将达 20000 英亩（约 81 平方公里），而达希家所在的德比郡总面积不过 2625 平方公里。

30 *but his friend... having ten thousand a year*: 该句前半部分中 by 引导的短语表示吸引人（drew）的方式，后半句中 report 后面有两个修饰成分，一个是 which 引导的定语从句，一个是 of 引出的介词短语。可译为："然而他的朋友达希先生却是高大伟岸，外表俊朗，身上贵气逼人，走进舞厅不久便吸引了众人的注意；他到场还没五分钟，大家已经勾头接耳地传说他年收入多达一万镑。"

31 *turn the tide*: 转变形势，扭转局势。e.g. What turned the tide in the battle was the arrival of fresh reinforcements. 战争形势得以转变是由于有了新的援军赶到。

32 *Derbyshire*: 德比郡，位于英格兰中部，境内有许多俊秀的山脉，历来是著名的旅游胜地。达希在德比郡拥有大片田园，这意味着他和靠做生意挣钱的宾格利不同，属于更受尊敬的传统贵族。

Netherfield. Such amiable qualities must speak for themselves. What a contrast between him and his friend! Mr. Darcy danced only once with Mrs. Hurst and once with Miss Bingley, declined being introduced to any other lady,[33] and spent the rest of the evening in walking about the room, speaking occasionally to one of his own party. His character was decided. He was the proudest, most disagreeable man in the world, and everybody hoped that he would never come there again. Amongst the most violent against him was Mrs. Bennet, whose dislike of his general behaviour was sharpened into particular resentment, by his having slighted one of her daughters.[34]

amiable: 和善的

slight: 怠慢

69 ▸ Elizabeth Bennet had been obliged, by the scarcity of gentlemen, to sit down for two dances;[35] and during part of that time, Mr. Darcy had been standing near enough for her to overhear a conversation between him and Mr. Bingley, who came from the dance for a few minutes, to press his friend to join it.

scarcity: 缺乏

overhear: 偷听

70 ▸ "Come, Darcy," said he, "I must have you dance. I hate to see you standing about by yourself in this stupid manner. You had much better dance."

71 ▸ "I certainly shall not. You know how I detest it, unless I am particularly acquainted with my partner. At such an assembly as this, it would be insupportable. Your sisters are engaged, and there is not another woman in the room, whom it would not be a punishment to me to stand up with."

insupportable: 难以忍受的

72 ▸ "I would not be so fastidious as you are," cried Bingley, "for a kingdom! Upon my honour, I never met with so many pleasant girls in my life, as I have this evening; and there are several of them you see uncommonly pretty."

fastidious: 挑剔的

uncommonly: 罕见地

---

33 按照当时的礼仪，无论在私人舞会还是公共聚会上，男宾都不能邀请陌生女宾跳舞。达希先生拒绝认识其他女宾，就是为了名正言顺地不和她们跳舞。

34 *Amongst the most violent... one of her daughters*：该句的主句是倒装句，whose 引导的定语从句限定 Mrs. Bennet，该从句中，by 引导的短语表示原因。可译为："最讨厌他的要数本尼特太太；除了看不惯其为人，本尼特太太的憎恨还有一个具体的原因：达希先生竟然看不上她的女儿。"

35 为了保证每个到场的人都有跳舞的机会，当时舞会的规矩是：每当跳完一场舞之后，双方必须更换舞伴，只有已经结婚的青年男女除外，但他们也只能一起跳两场。如果征得舞会组织者的同意，同性间也可以结伴跳舞。伊丽莎白干坐了两场，意味着到场女宾比男宾多出至少一倍，从侧面反映了当地想要结识宾格利的女性特别多。

73 ▶ "You are dancing with the only handsome girl in the room," said Mr. Darcy, looking at the eldest Miss Bennet.

74 ▶ "Oh! she is the most beautiful creature I ever beheld! But there is one of her sisters sitting down just behind you, who is very pretty, and I dare say, very agreeable. Do let me ask my partner to introduce you."

75 ▶ "Which do you mean?" and turning round, he looked for a moment at Elizabeth, till catching her eye, he withdrew his own and coldly said, "She is tolerable; but not handsome enough to tempt me; and I am in no humour at present to give consequence to young ladies who are slighted by other men. You had better return to your partner and enjoy her smiles, for you are wasting your time with me."

tolerable: 过得去的

76 ▶ Mr. Bingley followed his advice. Mr. Darcy walked off; and Elizabeth remained with no very cordial feelings towards him. She told the story however with great spirit among her friends; for she had a lively, playful disposition, which delighted in any thing ridiculous.

ridiculous: 滑稽的

77 ▶ The evening altogether passed off pleasantly to the whole family. Mrs. Bennet had seen her eldest daughter much admired by the Netherfield party. Mr. Bingley had danced with her twice, and she had been distinguished by his sisters. Jane was as much gratified by this, as her mother could be, though in a quieter way. Elizabeth felt Jane's pleasure. Mary had heard herself mentioned to Miss Bingley as the most accomplished girl in the neighbourhood; and Catherine and Lydia had been fortunate enough to be never without partners, which was all that they had yet learnt to care for at a ball. They returned therefore in good spirits to Longbourn, the village where they lived, and of which they were the principal inhabitants. They found Mr. Bennet still up. With a book he was regardless of time; and on the present occasion he had a good deal of curiosity as to the event of an evening which had raised such splendid expectations. He had rather hoped that all his wife's views on the stranger would be disappointed; but he soon found that he had a very different story to hear.

gratify: 使高兴

splendid: 绝妙的

78 ▶ "Oh! my dear Mr. Bennet," as she entered the room, "we have had a most delightful evening, a most excellent ball. I wish you had been there. Jane was so admired, nothing could be like it. Everybody said how well she looked; and Mr. Bingley thought her quite beautiful, and danced with her twice. Only think of that my dear; he actually danced with her twice; and she was

the only creature in the room that he asked for a second time.³⁶ First of all, he asked Miss Lucas. I was so vexed to see him stand up with her; but, however, he did not admire her at all: indeed, nobody can, you know; and he seemed quite struck with Jane as she was going down the dance. So, he enquired who she was, and got introduced, and asked her for the two next³⁷. Then, the two third he danced with Miss King, and the two fourth with Maria Lucas, and the two fifth with Jane again, and the two sixth with Lizzy, and the Boulanger³⁸."

79 ▸ "If he had had any compassion for me," cried her husband impatiently, "he would not have danced half so much! For God's sake, say no more of his partners. Oh! that he had sprained his ankle in the first dance!"

sprain: 扭伤

80 ▸ "Oh! my dear," continued Mrs. Bennet, "I am quite delighted with him. He is so excessively handsome! And his sisters are charming women. I never in my life saw any thing more elegant than their dresses. I dare say the lace upon Mrs. Hurst's grown."

excessively: 极度地

81 ▸ Here she was interrupted again. Mr. Bennet protested against any description of finery. She was therefore obliged to seek another branch of the subject, and related, with much bitterness of spirit and some exaggeration, the shocking rudeness of Mr. Darcy.³⁹

finery: 雅致

82 ▸ "But I can assure you," she added, "that Lizzy does not lose much by not suiting his fancy; for he is a most disagreeable, horrid man, not at all worth pleasing. So high and so conceited that there was no enduring him! He walked here, and he walked there, fancying himself so very great! Not handsome enough to dance with! I wish you had been there, my dear, to have given him one of your set downs. I quite detest the man."

horrid: 可怕的

conceited: 自负的

36　正如前面注释指出的，只有已经订婚的青年男女，才可以在公共舞会上跳两场舞。宾格利的行为按照当时的风俗，几乎等于公开示爱，所以本尼特太太才会这么激动。

37　*the two next*: 下一曲双人舞。

38　*Boulanger*: 布罗杰舞，起源于法国，也称面包师舞，是终场舞的一种。这种舞蹈的跳法是所有舞者男女相间，手拉手围成一圈转动，转足一圈后站定，所有女宾和自己对面女宾互换位置，反方向转一圈，然后所有男宾和自己对面的男宾互换位置，接着再反方向转一圈，跳完舞会便结束。

39　*She was therefore... the shocking rudeness of Mr. Darcy*: 该句较长，包含插入成分 with much bitterness of spirit and some exaggeration 用作状态的描述。可译为："无奈之中，她只好换了一个相关的话题，以尖酸刻薄略带夸张的话语，谈起了达希先生那惊人的无礼。"

PART 4

EXERCISES

I. Answer the following questions according to the reading text.

1. Why does Mrs. Bennet insist that her husband visit the newcomer—Mr. Bingley?

2. What are Mrs. and Mr. Bennet's opinions of their daughters?

3. Has Mr. Bennet visited Mr. Bingley? And does Mrs. Bennet know beforehand?

4. Mrs. Bennet keeps talking about Mr. Bingley, but why does she say she is sick of Mr. Bingley in Para. 55?

5. What are the mother's and daughters' reaction when they hear that the father has already paid the visit to Mr. Bingley?

6. What is people's first impression upon Mr. Bingley?

7. What is people's first impression upon Mr. Darcy?

8. How does Mr. Darcy think of Elizabeth? And how does Elizabeth think of Mr. Darcy?

9. What does Mrs. Bennet think of the ball? And what is Mr. Bennet's response to that?

II. Paraphrase the following sentences with your own words, and then translate them into Chinese.

1. "Oh! single, my dear, to be sure! A single man of large fortune; four or five thousand a year. What a fine thing for our girls!" (Para. 14)

2. I certainly have had my share of beauty, but I do not pretend to be any thing extraordinary now. (Para. 20)

3. But I hope you will get over it, and live to see many young men of four thousand a year come into the neighbourhood. (Para. 31)

4. The rest of the evening was spent in conjecturing how soon he would return Mr. Bennet's visit, and determining when they should ask him to dinner. (Para. 62)

5. He had entertained hopes of being admitted to a sight of the young ladies, of whose beauty he had heard much; but he saw only the father. (Para. 65)

6. She could not imagine what business he could have in town so soon after his arrival in Hertfordshire; and she began to fear that he might be always flying about from one

place to another, and never settled at Netherfield as he ought to be. (Para. 66)

7. And not all his large estate in Derbyshire could then save him from having a most forbidding, disagreeable countenance, and being unworthy to be compared with his friend. (Para. 67)

8. With a book he was regardless of time; and on the present occasion he had a good deal of curiosity as to the event of an evening which had raised such splendid expectations. (Para. 77)

III. Figure out the meanings of the phrases in bold, and then make another sentence with each of the phrases.

1. It is a truth universally acknowledged, that a single man in possession of a good fortune, must be **in want of** a wife. (Para. 1)
2. Sir William and Lady Lucas are determined to go, merely **on that account**, for in general you know they visit no new comers. (Para. 24)
3. But you are always **giving her the preference**. (Para. 26)
4. **Depend upon it**, my dear, that when there are twenty, I will visit them all. (Para. 33)
5. If I had known as much this morning, I certainly would not have **called on** him. (Para. 56)
6. Mr. Bingley **was obliged to** be in town the following day, and consequently unable to accept the honour of their invitation. Mrs. Bennet was quite disconcerted. (Para. 66)
7. Such amiable qualities must **speak for** themselves. (Para. 68)
8. Your sisters are engaged, and there is not another woman in the room, whom it would not be a punishment to me to **stand up with**. (Para. 71)

IV. Because of their long history and cultural influence of the West, some words and expressions carry on different meanings. Now try to find out the implications of the following words and expressions.

1. a chaise and four
2. Michaelmas
3. assembly

V. There are several vivid depictions of characters in this reading text. Choose one and make your comments upon him or her with no less than 200 words.

UNIT 10

The Idea of a University
A Discourse

Oral tasks

1. How much do you know about the origin and development of universities in China?
2. How much do you know about Newman and his ideas on university education?

Introduction

Discourse is a conceptual generalization of conversation within each modality and context of communication.

The present era is characterized by multicultural globalization, as enriching and conflictive as any civilization has ever been. Newman directs us towards dialogue with the great authors in order to continue our humanizing intellectual endeavours. This ecumenical spirit, appropriate to every university, pervades Newman's *The Idea of a University*. Newman's vision and treatment of it is of universal scope, and he seeks "to give a normal idea of a university", as historical civilization has handed it down to us. It includes two parts: University Teaching and University Subjects.

John Henry Newman (1801–1890), was a theologian and poet, first an Anglican priest and later a Catholic priest and cardinal. He was an important and controversial figure in the religious history of England in the 19th century. Newman became known as a leader of, and an able polemicist for the Oxford Movement. He was also a literary figure of note, but he saw himself primarily as an educationalist.

The selected part, "Knowledge Its Own End", is mainly concerned with liberal education, in contrast to professional education and commercial education in a university. It is instructive to our current division of subjects.

The Idea of a University: A Discourse UNIT 10

PART 3

TEXTUAL READING[1]

Discourse 5. Knowledge its Own End

1▶ A university may be considered with reference either to its Students or to its Studies; and the principle, that all Knowledge is a whole and the separate Sciences parts of one, which I have hitherto been using in behalf of its studies, is equally important when we direct our attention to its students.[2] Now then I turn to the students, and shall consider the education which, by virtue of this principle, a University will give them; and thus I shall be introduced, Gentlemen, to the second question, which I proposed to discuss, viz., whether and in what sense its teaching, viewed relatively to the taught, carries the attribute of Utility along with it.

reference: 参照

behalf: 代表

propose: 提议

utility: 实用

1.

2▶ I have said that all branches of knowledge are connected together, because the subject-matter of knowledge is intimately united in itself, as being the acts and the work of the Creator. Hence it is that the Sciences, into which our knowledge may be said to be cast, have multiplied bearings one on another, and an internal sympathy, and admit, or rather demand, comparison and adjustment.[3] They complete, correct, balance each other. This consideration, if

intimately: 紧密地

multiply: 增加
bearing: 影响
sympathy: 和谐一致

---

1 本篇出自：John Henry Newman, *The Idea of a University*, Teresa Iglesias, ed. Dublin: Ashifield Press, 2009。

2 *and the principle... to its students*: 该句的主体结构是 the principle... is equally important...，其余部分是分别由 that，which 和 when 引导的从句。that 引导的是同位语从句来说明 principle 的内容，其中，由于 the separate Sciences (are) parts of one 的结构与前面的 all Knowledge is a whole 相同，所以省略了 are；which 引导的定语从句来限定 the principle，在从句中作 using 的宾语；when 引导的是状语从句。可译为："所有的知识都是一个整体，不同的科学都是这个整体的组成部分。这是我迄今为止在从事知识的各项研究时一直使用的原则。这个原则在我们将注意力转向学生时同样重要。"（注：本篇译文参考了高师宁等翻译的《大学的理念》，贵阳：贵州教育出版社，2003。下同。）

3 *Hence it is that the Sciences... and adjustment*: 该句的主体结构是 it is that the Sciences have multiplied...，and admit or rather demand...，其中，into which 引导的定语从句修饰主语 the Sciences。可译为："因此，我们的知识可以说是靠其形成的各门学科之间多种多样的关系，而且还有一种内在的和谐，它们允许，更不如说是要求进行相互比较和相互调节。"

well-founded, must be taken into account, not only as regards the attainment of truth, which is their common end, but as regards the influence which they exercise upon those whose education consists in the study of them.[4] I have said already, that to give undue prominence to one is to be unjust to another; to neglect or supersede these is to divert those from their proper object. It is to unsettle the boundary lines between science and science, to disturb their action, to destroy the harmony which binds them together. Such a proceeding will have a corresponding effect when introduced into a place of education. There is no science but tells a different tale, when viewed as a portion of a whole, from what it is likely to suggest when taken by itself, without the safeguard, as I may call it, of others.[5]

3 ▶ Let me make use of an illustration. In the combination of colours, very different effects are produced by a difference in their selection and juxtaposition; red, green, and white, change their shades, according to the contrast to which they are submitted. And, in like manner, the drift and meaning of a branch of knowledge varies with the company in which it is introduced to the student. If his reading is confined simply to one subject, however such division of labour may favour the advancement of a particular pursuit, a point into which I do not here enter, certainly it has a tendency to contract his mind. If it is incorporated with others, it depends on those others as to the kind of influence which it exerts upon him. Thus the Classics[6], which in England are the means of refining the taste, have in France subserved the

---

4　*This consideration, ... the study of them*：该句的主体结构是 This consideration... must be taken into account, not only as regards... but as regards...。该句中的第一个 which 引导的定语从句，限定 the attainment of truth；第二个 which 引导的定语从句限定 influence，做 exercise 的宾语；whose 引导的定语从句限定 those。可译为："这个因素如果有足够的依据，就必须考虑进来，因为它不仅涉及获取真理——获取真理是这些学科的共同目标——的问题，而且还关乎它们对于受教育者的影响。这些人的教育就是由它们的研究所构成。"

5　*There is no science... as I may call it, of others*：该句主体结构是 there is no science but tells a different tale... from what...，其中 no... but 指 "所有……都……"，实为肯定，所以可改写成 Every science tells a different tale...；两个 when 引导的时间状语短语，其中的 viewed 和 taken 的逻辑主语都是前面的 science。可译为："一门科学被视作整体的一部分时所产生的意义，与其在失去其他科学的支持（如果我可以称其为支持的话）而孤立存在的情况下所产生的意义是不可同日而语的。"

6　*the Classics*：古典文学或古典研究。主要指对古希腊和古罗马语言、文学、哲学以及考古学的研究，被认为是人文研究的基石，典型精英教育的重要组成部分。

spread of revolutionary and deistical doctrines[7]. In Metaphysics, again, Butler's[8] Analogy of Religion, which has had so much to do with the conversion to the Catholic faith of members of the University of Oxford, appeared to Pitt[9] and others, who had received a different training, to operate only in the direction of infidelity. And so again, Watson[10], Bishop of Llandaff, as I think he tells us in the narrative of his life, felt the science of Mathematics to indispose the mind to religious belief, while others see in its investigations the best parallel, and thereby defence, of the Christian Mysteries.[11] In like manner, I suppose, Arcesilaus[12] would not have handled logic as Aristotle, nor Aristotle have criticized poets as Plato; yet reasoning and poetry are subject to scientific rules.

deistical: 自然神论的
Metaphysics: 形而上学
analogy: 类比
infidelity: 无信仰
narrative: 故事
indispose: 使不适当
parallel: 相似

4 ▸ It is a great point then to enlarge the range of studies which a University professes, even for the sake of the students; and, though they cannot pursue every subject which is open to them, they will be the gainers by living among those and under those who represent the whole circle. This I conceive to be the advantage of a seat of universal learning, considered as a place of education. An assemblage of learned men, zealous for their own sciences, and rivals of each other, are brought, by familiar intercourse and for the sake of intellectual peace, to adjust together the claims and relations of their respective subjects of investigation. They learn to respect, to consult, to aid each other. Thus is created a pure and clear atmosphere of thought, which the student also breathes, though in his own case he only pursues a few

profess: 公开表示；宣称
assemblage: 聚集
zealous: 热情的
rival: 对手

---

7   *deistical doctrines*: 自然神论学说。该学说认为上帝创作万物，但不干预万物的运行。它主张理性，反对神启。该学说在启蒙时期获得广泛的认可。

8   *Butler*: 约瑟夫·巴特勒（Joseph Bulter），英国主教、神学家和哲学家。他批判霍布斯和洛克等人的哲学，并影响了包括大卫·休谟和亨利·纽曼等许多哲学家、宗教思想家。

9   *Pitt*: 小威廉·皮特（William Pitt the Younger）。1783 年，他获任首相时年仅 24 岁，是英国历史上最年轻的首相。人们为了将他和他的父亲，老威廉·皮特（William Pitt the Elder）首相区分开来，通常会在他的名字后面加上"小"（the Younger）。

10 *Watson*: 理查德·华特生（Richard Watson），1782 年至 1816 年间担任安立甘教的兰道主教。

11 *And so again, ... the Christian Mysteries*: 该句的主体结构是 Watson... felt..., while others see...，其中 while 连接的是一个对比的结构。可译为："还有，兰达夫主教瓦特生在他关于自己生平的叙述中，曾告诉我们说，他发现数学科学会使心智讨厌宗教信念，而另一些人却在对数学的研究中，发现了同基督教的神秘最相似的东西，因此也发现了为基督教神秘所做的辩护。"

12 *Arcesilaus*: 阿尔克西拉乌斯，柏拉图学派成员，后来成为该学派的带头人。他开启了该学派的怀疑主义时期，是斯多葛认知论重要的批评者。

sciences out of the multitude. He profits by an intellectual tradition, which is independent of particular teachers, which guides him in his choice of subjects, and duly interprets for him those which he chooses. He apprehends the great outlines of knowledge, the principles on which it rests, the scale of its parts, its lights and its shades, its great points and its little, as he otherwise cannot apprehend them. Hence it is that his education is called "Liberal". A habit of mind is formed which lasts through life, of which the attributes are, freedom, equitableness, calmness, moderation, and wisdom; or what in a former Discourse I have ventured to call a philosophical habit.[13] This then I would assign as the special fruit of the education furnished at a University, as contrasted with other places of teaching or modes of teaching. This is the main purpose of a University in its treatment of its students.

5► And now the question is asked me, What is the use of it? and my answer will constitute the main subject of the Discourses which are to follow.

2.

6► Cautious and practical thinkers, I say, will ask of me, what, after all, is the gain of this Philosophy, of which I make such account, and from which I promise so much. Even supposing it to enable us to exercise the degree of trust exactly due to every science respectively, and to estimate precisely the value of every truth which is anywhere to be found, how are we better for this master view of things, which I have been extolling?[14] Does it not reverse the principle of the division of labour? will practical objects be obtained better or worse by its cultivation? to what then does it lead? where does it end? what does it do? how does it profit? what does it promise? Particular sciences are respectively the basis of definite arts, which carry on to results tangible and beneficial the truths which are the subjects of the knowledge

---

13 *A habit of mind... call a philosophical habit*: 该句中，主语是 a habit of mind，后面的两个 which 引导的是限定它的定语从句；what 引导的短语成分用来说明解释 a habit of mind。可译为："这就可以形成一种终生受益的心智习惯，这种习惯的特点有自由、公平、冷静、温和与智慧，或者像我在前面某一讲中冒昧地称呼的那样，是一种哲学的习惯。"

14 *Even supposing it to enable... have been extolling*: 该句的主体结构是 even supposing it to enable us to exercise...，and to estimate...，how are we better for this master view of things...，which 引导的定语从句限定前面的 master view。可译为："即使设想它能使我们建立确切的相应于每一门学科的不同程度的信仰，又能使我们精确地评价在任何地方所发现的每一种真理的价值，你一直在大力赞扬的这种了解事物的观点如何能够使我们变得比以前更好呢？"

attained; what is the Art of this science of sciences? what is the fruit of such a Philosophy? what are we proposing to effect, what inducements do we hold out to the Catholic community, when we set about the enterprise of founding a University?

7 ▸ I am asked what is the end of University Education, and of the Liberal or Philosophical Knowledge which I conceive it to impart: I answer, that what I have already said has been sufficient to show that it has a very tangible, real, and sufficient end, though the end cannot be divided from that knowledge itself. Knowledge is capable of being its own end. Such is the constitution of the human mind, that any kind of knowledge, if it be really such, is its own reward. And if this is true of all knowledge, it is true also of that special Philosophy, which I have made to consist in a comprehensive view of truth in all its branches, of the relations of science to science, of their mutual bearings, and their respective values. What the worth of such an acquirement is, compared with other objects which we seek, —wealth or power or honour or the conveniences and comforts of life, I do not profess here to discuss; but I would maintain, and mean to show, that it is an object, in its own nature so really and undeniably good, as to be the compensation of a great deal of thought in the compassing, and a great deal of trouble in the attaining.[15]

impart: 传授

comprehensive: 全面的

undeniably: 不可否认地

8 ▸ Now, when I say that Knowledge is, not merely a means to something beyond it, or the preliminary of certain arts into which it naturally resolves, but an end sufficient to rest in and to pursue for its own sake, surely I am uttering no paradox, for I am stating what is both intelligible in itself, and has ever been the common judgment of philosophers and the ordinary feeling of mankind.[16] I am saying what at least the public opinion of this day ought to be slow to deny, considering how much we have heard of late years, in opposition

---

15　*it is an object, ... in the attaining*：该句的主体结构是 it is an object... good, as to be...，在此，as to 指的是相对……而言。可译为："该目的就其自身的性质而言，是如此真实又不可否认的美好，足以补偿在追求它的时候所做的大量思考，足以补偿在到达它的途中所付出的大量辛苦。"

16　*Now, when I say that Knowledge is, ... feeling of mankind*：该句的主体结构是 when...，surely I am uttering no paradox, for...，除了中间的主句之外，前面是 when 引导的时间状语从句，后面是 for 引导的原因状语从句。可译为："在此，当我对大家说，知识不仅仅是达到它后面的某种东西的手段，或者它自然融入某些技术的准备，知识就是一种目的，是足以安身立命，或者足以为其自身的缘故而继续追求的目的。我这样说绝没有什么自相矛盾，因为我所说的这些，一方面就其自身是可以理解的，另一方面也一直是哲学家们的共同判断和人类的普遍感受。"

to Religion, of entertaining, curious, and various knowledge. I am but saying what whole volumes have been written to illustrate, viz., by a "selection from the records of Philosophy, Literature, and Art, in all ages and countries, of a body of examples, to show how the most unpropitious circumstances have been unable to conquer an ardent desire for the acquisition of knowledge." That further advantages accrue to us and redound to others by its possession, over and above what it is in itself, I am very far indeed from denying; but, independent of these, we are satisfying a direct need of our nature in its very acquisition; and, whereas our nature, unlike that of the inferior creation, does not at once reach its perfection, but depends, in order to it, on a number of external aids and appliances, Knowledge, as one of the principal of these, is valuable for what its very presence in us does for us after the manner of a habit, even though it be turned to no further account, nor subserve any direct end.[17]

3.

9 ▸ Hence it is that Cicero[18], in enumerating the various heads of mental excellence, lays down the pursuit of Knowledge for its own sake, as the first of them. "This pertains most of all to human nature," he says, "for we are all of us drawn to the pursuit of Knowledge; in which to excel we consider excellent, whereas to mistake, to err, to be ignorant, to be deceived, is both an evil and a disgrace." And he considers Knowledge the very first object to which we are attracted, after the supply of our physical wants. After the calls and duties of our animal existence, as they may be termed, as regards ourselves, our family, and our neighbours, follows, he tells us, "the search after truth. Accordingly, as soon as we escape from the pressure of necessary cares, forthwith we desire to see, to hear, and to learn; and consider the knowledge of what is hidden or is wonderful a condition of our happiness."

10 ▸ This passage, though it is but one of many similar passages in a multitude of authors, I take for the very reason that it is so familiarly known to us; and

---

17 *whereas our nature, ... any direct end*: 该句可以在 Knowledge 前分为两个并列的部分；后半部分的主体结构是 Knowledge... is valuable for..., even though...。可译为："一方面我们的天性不像低级动物的那样一次性地就达到自身的完善，而是要依靠大量的外在帮助和手段以求达到那个目标，而知识就是这些帮助和手段中最主要的。对于它在我们心中的存在本身就像某种习惯那样造成的效果来说，它是极有价值的，即使没有任何进一步的理由，即使无助于任何直接的目的，也是这样。"

18 *Cicero*: 西塞罗，古罗马政治家、雄辩家、著作家。

I wish you to observe, Gentlemen, how distinctly it separates the pursuit of Knowledge from those ulterior objects to which certainly it can be made to conduce, and which are, I suppose, solely contemplated by the persons who would ask of me the use of a University or Liberal Education. So far from dreaming of the cultivation of Knowledge directly and mainly in order to our physical comfort and enjoyment, for the sake of life and person, of health, of the conjugal and family union, of the social tie and civil security, the great Orator implies, that it is only after our physical and political needs are supplied, and when we are "free from necessary duties and cares", that we are in a condition for "desiring to see, to hear, and to learn".[19] Nor does he contemplate in the least degree the reflex or subsequent action of Knowledge, when acquired, upon those material goods which we set out by securing before we seek it; on the contrary, he expressly denies its bearing upon social life altogether, strange as such a procedure is to those who live after the rise of the Baconian philosophy, and he cautions us against such a cultivation of it as will interfere with our duties to our fellow-creatures.[20] "All these methods," he says, "are engaged in the investigation of truth; by the pursuit of which to be carried off from public occupations is a transgression of duty. For the praise of virtue lies altogether in action; yet intermissions often occur, and then we recur to such pursuits; not to say that the incessant activity of the mind is vigorous enough to carry us on in the pursuit of knowledge, even without any exertion of our own." The idea of benefiting society by means of "the pursuit of science and knowledge" did not enter at all into the motives which he would assign for their cultivation.

distinctly: 明确地

ulterior: 外部的

conduce: 有益于

contemplate: 深思熟虑；思索

conjugal: 婚姻的

reflex: 回报

expressly: 明确地

procedure: 程序

Baconian: 培根式的

caution: 告诫

transgression: 越轨；违背

intermission: 间歇

incessant: 不断的

---

19 *So far from dreaming of... and to learn*: 该句的主体结构是 the great Orator implies，它的前面是一个状语结构，后面是一个宾语从句，其中有一个强调句型，即 it is only after... that...。可译为："远不是梦想将知识教养设想为直接或主要是为着物质上的舒适和享受的，是为着生活和个人，为着健康，为着夫妻与家庭关系，为着社会纽带和公民安全等等。他指出，只有在物质的和政治的需要得到满足之后，只有当我们'摆脱了必要的职责和关切之时'，我们才处于这样一种状况，可以'去看，去听，去了解'。"

20 *Nor does he contemplate... our fellow-creatures*: 该句中，when acquired 是限定前面的 Knowledge，securing 的宾语和 it 都是 Knowledge；on the contrary 后面是并列成分，he... denies..., and he cautions... 并列，其中 strange as such... 是一个转折状语从句。可译为："他也根本不考虑在我们获得知识以后，它对于我们在寻求它以前就已着手追求的那些物质利益有什么影响或作用。正相反，他直截了当地否定知识对于社会什么关系，尽管这在生活在培根哲学兴起之后的人们看来是十分奇怪的，而且他还警告我们要提防这种教养，因为它将妨碍我们对于我们周围的所有造物的责任。"

countryman: 国民
embassy: 大使馆
eloquent: 雄辩的
exposition: 阐述
refinement: 文雅

11 ▸ This was the ground of the opposition which the elder Cato[21] made to the introduction of Greek Philosophy among his countrymen, when Carneades[22] and his companions, on occasion of their embassy, were charming the Roman youth with their eloquent expositions of it. The fit representative of a practical people, Cato estimated everything by what it produced; whereas the Pursuit of Knowledge promised nothing beyond Knowledge itself. He despised that refinement or enlargement of mind of which he had no experience.

4.

persist: 存留
issue: 产生

12 ▸ Things, which can bear to be cut off from everything else and yet persist in living, must have life in themselves; pursuits, which issue in nothing, and still maintain their ground for ages, which are regarded as admirable, though they have not as yet proved themselves to be useful, must have their sufficient end in themselves, whatever it turns out to be.[23] And we are brought to the same conclusion by considering the force of the epithet, by which the knowledge under consideration is popularly designated. It is common to speak of "liberal knowledge", of the "liberal arts and studies", and of a "liberal education", as the especial characteristic or property of a University and of a gentleman; what is really meant by the word? Now, first, in its grammatical sense it is opposed to servile; and by "servile work" is understood, as our catechisms inform us, bodily labour, mechanical employment, and the like, in which the mind has little or no part. Parallel to such servile works are those arts, if they deserve the name, of which the poet speaks which owe their origin and their method to hazard, not to skill; as, for instance, the practice and operations

epithet: 名称
designate: 命名

servile: 奴役的
catechism: 问答教学法

hazard: 冒险

21　*the elder Cato*: 老加图（Cato the Elder），罗马共和国时期的政治家、国务活动家、演说家。

22　*Carneades*: 卡涅阿德斯，希腊的怀疑派哲学家，柏拉图学园的首脑之一。

23　*Things, ... turns out to be*: 该句的主体结构是 Things... must have life in themselves; pursuit... must have their sufficient end in themselves...。第一个 which 引导的定语从句限定的是 things；第二个和第三个 which 引导的定语从句限定的是 pursuits；though 引导的转折状语从句用来说明第三个 which 引导的从句。可译为："倘若一种事物能够经受得起同每一种别的事物分离而仍然能够在生活中持续下去，那么，它必定在自身之中就有着一种生命力。这样一些追求并不产生任何东西而又在不同时代都能维持自己的地位，尽管它们并未证明自身有用，却被认为是可取的，这样，它们必然在自身之中有着充分的目的，而不论这种目的到头来是些什么。"

of an empiric.²⁴ As far as this contrast may be considered as a guide into the meaning of the word, liberal education and liberal pursuits are exercises of mind, of reason, of reflection.

13 ▸ But we want something more for its explanation, for there are bodily exercises which are liberal, and mental exercises which are not so. For instance, in ancient times the practitioners in medicine were commonly slaves; yet it was an art as intellectual in its nature, in spite of the pretence, fraud, and quackery with which it might then, as now, be debased, as it was heavenly in its aim.²⁵ And so in like manner, we contrast a liberal education with a commercial education or a professional; yet no one can deny that commerce and the professions afford scope for the highest and most diversified powers of mind. There is then a great variety of intellectual exercises, which are not technically called "liberal"; on the other hand, I say, there are exercises of the body which do receive that appellation. Such, for instance, was the palaestra, in ancient times; such the Olympic games, in which strength and dexterity of body as well as of mind gained the prize. In Xenophon²⁶ we read of the young Persian nobility being taught to ride on horseback and to speak the truth; both being among the accomplishments of a gentleman. War, too, however rough a profession, has ever been accounted liberal, unless in cases when it becomes heroic, which would introduce us to another subject.

14 ▸ Now comparing these instances together, we shall have no difficulty in determining the principle of this apparent variation in the application of the term which I am examining. Manly games, or games of skill, or military prowess, though bodily, are, it seems, accounted liberal; on the other hand,

empiric: 经验主义者

practitioner: 从业者

pretence: 冒牌货

fraud: 欺骗

quackery: 骗子医术

debase: 贬值

diversified: 多元化的

appellation: 称呼

instance: 例子

palaestra: 体育

apparent: 明显的

military: 军事的

prowess: 技艺

---

24 *Parallel to... operations of an empiric*: 该句的主体结构是 Parallel such servile works are those arts... which owe their origin and their method to hazard, not to skill, if... of... 是插入成分，后面的 as 引导的是补充说明成分。the poet 指的是古希腊历史学家和将军色诺芬（Xenophon）。可译为："与这类奴隶式的工作相适应的是那样一些技艺（如果他们配得上技艺这个名称的话），正如一位诗人所说，其起源及其方法都出于某种危险的事情而不是出于技艺。"

25 *For instance, in ancient times... in its aim*: 该句的难点在于理解 in spite of... be debased 是插入成分，另外还有两个并列成分，即 as intellectual in its nature... 和 as it was heavenly in its aim。可译为："例如，在上古时代，医务方面的从业人员通常都是奴隶。然而这一职业就其性质而言却是心智的技艺，尽管它那时正如在今天一样，会由于冒充、欺骗和诈术而堕落，另一方面就其目的而言却是高尚的。"

26 *Xenophon*: 色诺芬，雅典人，历史学家，苏格拉底的弟子，以记录当时的希腊历史和苏格拉底语录而著称。

intellectual: 知识的

mercantile: 商业的

sequel: 后果

contemplation: 思考

absurd: 荒谬的

treatise: 论文

fracture: 骨折

exigency: 紧急情况

theology: 神学

pulpit: 神职人员

meritoriousness: 价值；功德

charitable: 慈善的

condescension: 屈尊

what is merely professional, though highly intellectual, nay, though liberal in comparison of trade and manual labour, is not simply called liberal, and mercantile occupations are not liberal at all. Why this distinction? because that alone is liberal knowledge, which stands on its own pretensions, which is independent of sequel, expects no complement, refuses to be informed (as it is called) by any end, or absorbed into any art, in order duly to present itself to our contemplation. The most ordinary pursuits have this specific character, if they are self-sufficient and complete; the highest lose it, when they minister to something beyond them. It is absurd to balance, in point of worth and importance, a treatise on reducing fractures with a game of cricket or a fox-chase; yet of the two the bodily exercise has that quality which we call "liberal", and the intellectual has it not.[27] And so of the learned professions altogether, considered merely as professions; although one of them be the most popularly beneficial, and another the most politically important, and the third the most intimately divine of all human pursuits, yet the very greatness of their end, the health of the body, or of the commonwealth, or of the soul, diminishes, not increases, their claim to the appellation "liberal", and that still more, if they are cut down to the strict exigencies of that end.[28] If, for instance, Theology, instead of being cultivated as a contemplation, be limited to the purposes of the pulpit or be represented by the catechism, it loses, —not its usefulness, not its divine character, not its meritoriousness (rather it gains a claim upon these titles by such charitable condescension), — but it does lose the particular attribute which I am illustrating; just as a face worn by tears and fasting loses its beauty, or a labourer's hand loses its

---

27　It is absurd... the intellectual has it not：该句的难点在于理解 to balance... a treatise... with a game...，即将论文与游戏相比较。可译为："就价值和意义而言，用板球游戏或狩猎狐狸去与一篇关于减少骨折的论文相比较，那是极其荒谬的。然而，在这两者之中，属于身体操练的游戏，倒是具有我们所谓"博雅"的性质，而属于心智操练的那一项却并不具有这种性质。"

28　And so of the learned professions... of that end：该句的主体结构是 their very greatness... diminishes... their claim to the appellation，their 指的是前面谈到的三种性质的职业及其特征；appellation 指的是 "liberal" 这个称呼；if 引导的条件状语从句，其主句与前面并列，主语为 that，谓语 diminishes 被省略，完整的句子应该是 that (diminishes) still more。可译为："而且如果仅仅从职业来看，那些很有学问的职业也完全如此。尽管这些职业当中，一个可能是广有裨益的，另一个可能是政治上十分重要的，第三个可能在人类的事业中是最为神圣的。然而，这些职业目的的伟大之处，例如为了身体或社会的健康，或灵魂的健康之类，却只是使它们更无权，而不是更有权要求得到博雅这一称呼。而且，如果它们被削减得只剩下对那一目标的纯粹追求的话，那就更配不上这个名称了。"

delicateness; —for Theology thus exercised is not simple knowledge, but rather is an art or a business making use of Theology.²⁹ And thus it appears that even what is supernatural need not be liberal, nor need a hero be a gentleman, for the plain reason that one idea is not another idea. And in like manner the Baconian Philosophy, by using its physical sciences in the service of man, does thereby transfer them from the order of Liberal Pursuits to, I do not say the inferior, but the distinct class of the Useful. And, to take a different instance, hence again, as is evident, whenever personal gain is the motive, still more distinctive an effect has it upon the character of a given pursuit; thus racing, which was a liberal exercise in Greece, forfeits its rank in times like these, so far as it is made the occasion of gambling.³⁰

delicateness: 精致

supernatural: 超自然的

forfeit: 丧失
gamble: 赌博

15▸ All that I have been now saying is summed up in a few characteristic words of the great Philosopher. "Of possessions," he says, "those rather are useful, which bear fruit; those liberal, which tend to enjoyment. By fruitful, I mean, which yield revenue; by enjoyable, where nothing accrues of consequence beyond the using."

revenue: 税收

---

29 *If, for instance, Theology, ... a business making use of Theology*：该句的主体结构是 If... Theology... be limited... or be represented by..., it loses... but it does lose the particular attribute...，其中 attribute 指的是 liberal education 的特征。可译为："例如，假如神学不是作为一种思考来研究，而是被局限于为了教堂里的讲道，或为了在教义问答课上教授的目的，那么，它也就丧失了——不是丧失了它的有用性，不是丧失了它的神圣性，不是丧失了它的美与长处（由于这种仁爱的自我降格，它反而更有权具有这些性质）——确是丧失了我一直为之做出解释的那种特有的属性。正如一张脸由于眼泪和禁食的缘故而丧失了其美丽，或一个工人由于劳作而丧失了其细腻——因为这样来运作的神学就不再是单纯的知识，而是一种技艺或利用神学的事务了。"

30 *And, to take a different instance, ... the occasion of gambling*：该句中 a given pursuit 指的是 liberal education 中的 pursuit。可译为："而且，换一个说法（这样说还是十分清楚的），只要动机在于个人的利益，它就会对任何给定的这类追求之性质带来更加明显的这类效果。例如，在古希腊曾经是一种博雅操练的赛跑，随着时间的推移，当它像别的运动一样被弄成了赌博的手段时，它就丧失了它在博雅等级中的地位。"

PART 4

EXERCISES

I. Answer the following questions according to the reading text.

1. Why does Newman say that all branches of knowledge are connected together?
2. Why does Newman say that it is harmful to give undue prominence to one branch of sciences?
3. What is the advantage of a seat of universal learning?
4. In Newman's opinion, what kind of education can be called "Liberal"?
5. Why does Newman say that knowledge is capable of being its own end?
6. What is really meant by "liberal education"?
7. What is the distinction between liberal education and professional education?

II. Paraphrase the following sentences with your own words, and then translate them into Chinese.

1. Thus I shall be introduced, Gentlemen, to the second question, which I proposed to discuss, viz, whether and in what sense its teaching, viewed relatively to the taught, carries the attribute of Utility along with it. (Para. 1)
2. Hence it is that the Sciences, into which our knowledge may be said to be cast, have multiplied bearings one on another, and an internal sympathy, and admit, or rather demand, comparison and adjustment. (Para. 2)
3. This then I would assign as the special fruit of the education furnished at a University, as contrasted with other places of teaching or modes of teaching. (Para. 4)
4. Selection from the records of Philosophy, Literature, and Art, in all ages and countries, of a body of examples, to show how the most unpropitious circumstances have been unable to conquer an ardent desire for the acquisition of knowledge. (Para. 8)
5. "This pertains most of all to human nature," he says, "for we are all of us drawn to the pursuit of Knowledge; in which to excel we consider excellent, whereas to mistake, to err, to be ignorant, to be deceived, is both an evil and a disgrace." (Para. 9)
6. War, too, however rough a profession, has ever been accounted liberal, unless in cases when it becomes heroic, which would introduce us to another subject. (Para. 13)

7. "Of possessions," he says, "those rather are useful, which bear fruit; those liberal, which tend to enjoyment. (Para. 15)

III. Figure out the meanings of the phrases in bold, and then make another sentence with each of the phrases.

1. Now then I turn to the students, and shall consider the education which, **by virtue of** this principle, a University will give them. (Para. 1)

2. And, **in like manner**, the drift and meaning of a branch of knowledge varies with the company in which it is introduced to the student. (Para. 3)

3. It is a great point then to enlarge the range of studies which a University professes, even **for the sake of** the students. (Para. 4)

4. What are we proposing to effect, what inducements do we hold out to the Catholic community, when we **set about** the enterprise of founding a University? (Para. 6)

5. That further advantages accrue to us and redound to others by its possession, **over and above** what it is in itself, I am very far indeed from denying. (Para. 8)

6. After the calls and duties of our animal existence, as they may be termed, **as regards** ourselves, our family, and our neighbours, follows, he tells us, "the search after truth. (Para. 9)

7. The idea of benefiting society **by means of** "the pursuit of science and knowledge" did not enter at all into the motives which he would assign for their cultivation. (Para. 10)

IV. Find out the cultural meanings of the following words and expressions.

1. Christian Mysteries
2. Catholic community
3. Liberal Education
4. Baconian Philosophy

V. What is your understanding of university education as regards the division of knowledge? Write an essay to illustrate your idea with no less than 200 words.

UNIT 11

I Wandered Lonely as a Cloud
Poems

ORAL TASKS

1. Do you know any poets of English-speaking countries?
2. Have you ever read any particular English poems that left a deep impression on you? What is it?

INTRODUCTION

Poetry is a form of literature that uses aesthetic and rhythmic qualities of language to evoke emotive responses which might suggest different interpretations.

"I Wandered Lonely as a Cloud", also commonly known as "Daffodils", is William Wordsworth's most famous work. The poem was inspired by an event on 15 April 1802, in which Wordsworth and his sister Dorothy came across a "long belt" of daffodils. Written some time between 1804 and 1807, and a revised version was published in 1815. In a poll conducted in 1995 by the BBC Radio 4, *Bookworm* programme to determine the nation's favourite poems, "I Wandered Lonely as a Cloud" came fifth. The poem is commonly seen as a classic of English romantic poetry.

"The Road Not Taken" is a poem by Robert Frost, published in 1916. In 1912, Frost sailed with his family to Great Britain, and he made some important acquaintances, including Ezra Pound and Edward Thomas, who was Frost's inspiration for "The Road Not Taken". Later this poem is a household poem for Americans.

"In a Station of the Metro" is an imagist poem by Ezra Pound published in 1913. It is commonly known as the best imagist poem. Pound got the inspiration from a moment in the underground metro station in Paris in 1912. He "equates" the faces of the individuals in the metro with petals, which is way of the poem's own visuality and it is considered a quintessential imagist text.

PART 3

TEXTUAL READING

I Wandered Lonely as a Cloud

William Wordsworth

    I wandered lonely as a cloud
    That floats on high o'er vales and hills,
    When all at once I saw a crowd,
    A host, of golden daffodils;
5   Beside the lake, beneath the trees,
    Fluttering and dancing in the breeze.[1]
    Continuous as the stars that shine
    And twinkle on the milky way,
    They stretched in never-ending line
10 Along the margin of a bay:
    Ten thousand saw I at a glance,
    Tossing their heads in sprightly dance.[2]
    The waves beside them danced; but they
    Out-did the sparkling waves in glee:
15 A poet could not but be gay,
    In such a jocund company:
    I gazed—and gazed—but little thought
    What wealth the show to me had brought:
    For oft, when on my couch I lie
20 In vacant or in pensive mood,
    They flash upon that inward eye

float: 飘荡
vale: 山谷
host: 许多

flutter: 摇曳

stretch: 延伸
margin: 边沿
glance: 一瞥

sprightly: 活泼地

out-do: 超过；胜过
glee: 欢乐
gay: 快乐的
jocund: 快乐的
gaze: 凝视
vacant: 空虚的
pensive: 沉思的
flash: 闪现

---

1 *I wandered lonely as a cloud /... / Fluttering and dancing in the breeze* (Lines 1–6): 在语法上，第一诗节为一个句子，主语为 I，when 引导时间状语从句；that 引导的定语从句限定 a cloud；fluttering and dancing 表示水仙花的状态。

2 *Continuous as the stars that shine /... / Tossing their heads in sprightly dance* (Lines 7–12): 从语法上讲，这一节是一个完整的句子。主语是 they，指的是水仙花，谓语为 stretched，continuous as the stars... 修饰说明 they，that 引导的定语从句限定 the stars，也指水仙花。Ten thousand saw I... sprightly dance. 进一步解释主句描述的场景，ten thousand 提前，所以主谓倒装成 saw I, tossing... 为伴随状语。

bliss: 极乐
solitude: 独处

Which is the bliss of solitude;
And then my heart with pleasure fills,
And dances with the daffodils.

The Road Not Taken

Robert Frost

diverge: 分叉

Two roads diverged in a yellow wood,
And sorry I could not travel both
And be one traveler, long I stood
And looked down one as far as I could

bent: 蜿蜒
undergrowth: 灌木丛

5   To where it bent in the undergrowth;
Then took the other, as just as fair,
And having perhaps the better claim,³

wear: 踩踏

Because it was grassy and wanted wear;
Though as for that the passing⁴ there
10 Had worn them really about the same,
And both that morning equally lay

tread: 踩踏

In leaves no step had trodden black.
Oh, I kept the first for another day!
Yet knowing how way leads on to way⁵,
15 I doubted if I should ever come back.
I shall be telling this with a sigh
Somewhere ages and ages hence:
Two roads diverged in a wood, and I?
I took the one less traveled by,
20 And that has made all the difference.

In a Station of the Metro

Ezra Pound

apparition: 幽灵
petal: 花瓣

The apparition of these faces in the crowd;
Petals on a wet, black bough.

---

3 *having the better claim*: 具有更好的理由。e.g. Whoever had had the courage to reject that proposal would have had the better claim to be our leader. 无论是谁有勇气拒绝那份提案都将更有理由成为我们的领导。

4 *passing*: 形状造成的踩踏情况。这里是指前面提到的 wear，和后面的 trodden 的情况。

5 *way leads on to way*: 意思为 one way leads on to another way，即"一条路引向另一条路"，指"前路延绵无尽头"。

EXERCISES

I. Recite these poems, and appreciate the beauty in them.

II. Translate the three poems into Chinese, and then compare your translation with those of your classmates and other famous translators.

III. Modeling upon one of the three poems, write an English poem of your own.

UNIT 12

A Scandal in Bohemia
A Detective Fiction

ORAL TASKS

1. Have you ever heard of Sherlock Holmes? What's your impression upon him?
2. Do you know some other detective writings? What are they?

INTRODUCTION

Detective fiction is a subgenre of fiction, or novel, in which an investigator or a detective, who might be official, private, professional, amateur or retired, investigates a crime, or tricky affairs.

Sir Arthur Ignatius Conan Doyle (1859–1930), better known as Conan Doyle, was a Scottish writer best known for his detective fiction featuring the character Sherlock Holmes. Originally a physician, in 1887 Doyle published *A Study in Scarlet*, the first of four novels about Holmes and Dr. Watson. In addition, Doyle wrote over fifty short stories featuring the famous detective.

A Scandal in Bohemia is the first short story, featuring the fictional detective Sherlock Holmes. The story is notable for introducing the character of Irene Adler, who is one of the most notable female characters in the Sherlock Holmes series, despite appearing in only one story. Doyle ranked *A Scandal in Bohemia* fifth in his list of twelve favourite Holmes stories. It was first published on 25 June 1891 in the July issue of *The Strand Magazine*, and was the first of the stories collected in *The Adventures of Sherlock Holmes* in 1892.

A Scandal in Bohemia: A Detective Fiction UNIT 12

PART 3

TEXTUAL READING[1]

I.

...

1 ▸ One night—it was on the twentieth of March, 1888—I was returning from a journey to a patient (for I had now returned to civil practice), when my way led me through Baker Street. ... I rang the bell and was shown up to the chamber which had formerly been in part my own.

...

2 ▸ He threw over a sheet of thick, pink-tinted note-paper which had been lying open upon the table. "It came by the last post," said he. "Read it aloud."

pink-tinted: 带粉色的

3 ▸ The note was undated, and without either signature or address.

undated: 没有注明日期的

signature: 签名

4 ▸ "There will call upon you to-night, at a quarter to eight o'clock," it said, "a gentleman who desires to consult you upon a matter of the very deepest moment. Your recent services to one of the royal houses of Europe have shown that you are one who may safely be trusted with matters which are of an importance which can hardly be exaggerated.[2] This account of you we have from all quarters received. Be in your chamber then at that hour, and do not take it amiss[3] if your visitor wear a mask."

exaggerate: 夸张

amiss: 出差错的

mask: 面具

5 ▸ "This is indeed a mystery," I remarked. "What do you imagine that it means?"

---

1 本篇出自：Arthur Conan Doyle, *A Scandal in Bohemia*, Harlow: Pearson Education, 2008。

2 *Your recent services... hardly be exaggerated*：该句的主体结构是 Your recent services... have shown that... who... which... which..., 主句是 Your recent... have shown..., that 引导的是宾语从句，其中有三个定语从句，分别限定各自前面的先行词。可译为："您最近为一个欧洲皇室提供的服务表明，您是值得托付极其重要事务的人。"（注：本篇译文由编者自译。下同。）

3 *take... amiss*: 对……因某事见怪。e.g. He will take it amiss if you refuse his invitation. 如果你拒绝他的邀请，他会生气的。

capital: 致命的
theorize: 理论化
insensibly: 不自觉地
twist: 曲解
deduce: 推论
presumably: 大概
well to do: 富裕的
endeavour: 致力于
crown: 五先令的硬币
peculiarly: 尤其地；特别地
stiff: 坚挺的
weave: 交织
texture: 纹理
monogram: 字母组合
customary: 习惯的
contraction: 缩写
continental: 大陆的
Gazetteer: 地名辞典
Carlsbad: 卡尔斯巴德
remarkable: 著名的
Wallenstein: 华伦斯坦（捷克贵族）
paper-mill: 纸厂
triumphant: 得胜的
precisely: 的确
uncourteous: 无礼的
hoof: 蹄

6 ▸ "I have no data yet. It is a capital mistake to theorize before one has data. Insensibly one begins to twist facts to suit theories, instead of theories to suit facts. But the note itself. What do you deduce from it?"

7 ▸ I carefully examined the writing, and the paper upon which it was written.

8 ▸ "The man who wrote it was presumably well to do," I remarked, endeavouring to imitate my companion's processes. "Such paper could not be bought under half a crown a packet. It is peculiarly strong and stiff."

9 ▸ "Peculiar—that is the very word," said Holmes. "It is not an English paper at all. Hold it up to the light."

10 ▸ I did so, and saw a large "E" with a small "g", a "P", and a large "G" with a small "t" woven into the texture of the paper.

11 ▸ "What do you make of that?" asked Holmes.

12 ▸ "The name of the maker, no doubt; or his monogram, rather."

13 ▸ "Not at all. The 'G' with the small 't' stands for 'Gesellschaft', which is the German for 'Company'. It is a customary contraction like our 'Co'. 'P', of course, stands for 'Papier'. Now for the 'Eg'. Let us glance at our Continental Gazetteer." He took down a heavy brown volume from his shelves. "Eglow, Eglonitz—here we are, Egria. It is in a German-speaking country—in Bohemia, not far from Carlsbad. 'Remarkable as being the scene of the death of Wallenstein, and for its numerous glass-factories and paper-mills.' Ha, ha, my boy, what do you make of that?" His eyes sparkled, and he sent up a great blue triumphant cloud from his cigarette.

14 ▸ "The paper was made in Bohemia," I said.

15 ▸ "Precisely. And the man who wrote the note is a German. Do you note the peculiar construction of the sentence—'This account of you we have from all quarters received.' A Frenchman or Russian could not have written that. It is the German who is so uncourteous to his verbs. It only remains, therefore, to discover what is wanted by this German who writes upon Bohemian paper and prefers wearing a mask to showing his face. And here he comes, if I am not mistaken, to resolve all our doubts."

16 ▸ As he spoke there was the sharp sound of horses' hoofs and grating wheels

against the curb, followed by a sharp pull at the bell. Holmes whistled.

…

17 ▸ A slow and heavy step, which had been heard upon the stairs and in the passage, paused immediately outside the door. Then there was a loud and authoritative tap.

18 ▸ "Come in!" said Holmes.

19 ▸ A man entered.

…

20 ▸ "You had my note?" he asked with a deep harsh voice and a strongly marked German accent. "I told you that I would call." He looked from one to the other of us, as if uncertain which to address.

21 ▸ "Pray take a seat," said Holmes. "This is my friend and colleague, Dr. Watson, who is occasionally good enough to help me in my cases. Whom have I the honour to address?"

22 ▸ "You may address me as the Count Von Kramm, a Bohemian nobleman. I understand that this gentleman, your friend, is a man of honour and discretion, whom I may trust with a matter of the most extreme importance. If not, I should much prefer to communicate with you alone."

23 ▸ I rose to go, but Holmes caught me by the wrist and pushed me back into my chair. "It is both, or none," said he. "You may say before this gentleman anything which you may say to me."

24 ▸ The Count shrugged his broad shoulders.

…

25 ▸ "The facts are briefly these: Some five years ago, during a lengthy visit to Warsaw, I made the acquaintance of the well-known adventuress, Irene Adler. The name is no doubt familiar to you."

…

26 ▸ "Let me see!" said Holmes. "Hum! Born in New Jersey in the year 1858. Contralto-hum! La Scala, hum! Prima donna Imperial Opera of Warsaw—yes! Retired from operatic stage—ha! Living in London—quite so! Your Majesty, as I understand, became entangled with this young person, wrote

curb: 路沿
whistle: 吹口哨

authoritative: 威严的
tap: 叩击

Count: 伯爵

wrist: 手腕

shrug: 耸肩

lengthy: 漫长的
Warsaw: 华沙
adventuress: 女冒险家

New Jersey: 新泽西
imperial: 帝国的
opera: 剧院
entangle: 纠缠

her some compromising letters, and is now desirous of getting those letters back."

27 ▸ "Precisely so. But how—"

28 ▸ "Was there a secret marriage?"

29 ▸ "None."

30 ▸ "No legal papers or certificates?"

31 ▸ "None."

32 ▸ "Then I fail to follow your Majesty. If this young person should produce her letters for blackmailing or other purposes, how is she to prove their authenticity?"

blackmail: 讹诈，勒索
authenticity: 可信性

33 ▸ "There is the writing."

34 ▸ "Pooh, pooh! Forgery."

forgery: 伪造

35 ▸ "My private note-paper."

36 ▸ "Stolen."

seal: 印章

37 ▸ "My own seal."

38 ▸ "Imitated."

39 ▸ "My photograph."

40 ▸ "Bought."

41 ▸ "We were both in the photograph."

42 ▸ "Oh, dear! That is very bad! Your Majesty has indeed committed an indiscretion."

indiscretion: 草率
insane: 不理智

43 ▸ "I was mad—insane."

44 ▸ "You have compromised yourself seriously."

45 ▸ "I was only Crown Prince then. I was young. I am but thirty now."

recover: 找回

46 ▸ "It must be recovered."

47 ▸ "We have tried and failed."

48 ▸ "Your Majesty must pay. It must be bought."

49 ▸ "She will not sell."

50 ▸ "Stolen, then."

51 ▸ "Five attempts have been made. Twice burglars in my pay ransacked her house. Once we diverted her luggage when she travelled. Twice she has been waylaid. There has been no result."

burglar: 入室行窃

ransack: 搜遍；洗劫

waylay: 伏击

52 ▸ "No sign of it?"

53 ▸ "Absolutely none."

54 ▸ Holmes laughed. "It is quite a pretty little problem," said he.

55 ▸ "But a very serious one to me," returned the King reproachfully.

reproachfully: 责备地

56 ▸ "Very, indeed. And what does she propose to do with the photograph?"

57 ▸ "To ruin me."

58 ▸ "But how?"

59 ▸ "I am about to be married."

60 ▸ "So I have heard."

61 ▸ "To Clotilde Lothman von Saxe-Meningen, second daughter of the King of Scandinavia. You may know the strict principles of her family. She is herself the very soul of delicacy. A shadow of a doubt as to my conduct would bring the matter to an end."

Scandinavia: 斯堪的纳维亚（现在的北欧地区）

62 ▸ "And Irene Adler?"

63 ▸ "Threatens to send them the photograph. And she will do it. I know that she will do it. You do not know her, but she has a soul of steel. She has the face of the most beautiful of women, and the mind of the most resolute of men. Rather than I should marry another woman, there are no lengths to which she would not go—none."

resolute: 坚决的

64 ▸ "You are sure that she has not sent it yet?"

65 ▸ "I am sure."

66 ▸ "And why?"

betrothal: 婚约	67 ▸ "Because she has said that she would send it on the day when the betrothal was publicly proclaimed. That will be next Monday."
yawn: 哈欠	68 ▸ "Oh, then we have three days yet," said Holmes with a yawn. "That is very fortunate, as I have one or two matters of importance to look into just at present. Your Majesty will, of course, stay in London for the present?"
	69 ▸ "Certainly. You will find me at the Langham under the name of the Count Von Kramm."
	70 ▸ "Then I shall drop you a line to let you know how we progress."
	71 ▸ "Pray do so. I shall be all anxiety."
	72 ▸ "Then, as to money?"
carte blanche: 自由行使权	73 ▸ "You have carte blanche."
	74 ▸ "Absolutely?"
study: 书房	75 ▸ The King of Bohemia talking to Holmes and Watson in their study.
	76 ▸ "I tell you that I would give one of the provinces of my kingdom to have that photograph."
	77 ▸ "And for present expenses?"
chamois: 羚羊皮	78 ▸ The King took a heavy chamois leather bag from under his cloak and laid it on the table.
	79 ▸ "There are three hundred pounds in gold and seven hundred in notes," he said.
scribble: 潦草地写 receipt: 收条	80 ▸ Holmes scribbled a receipt upon a sheet of his note-book and handed it to him.
Mademoiselle: 小姐	81 ▸ "And Mademoiselle's address?" he asked.
Serpentine: 蛇纹石（这里取其读音） avenue: 大道 cabinet: 相框	82 ▸ "Is Briony Lodge, Serpentine Avenue, St. John's Wood."
	83 ▸ Holmes took a note of it. "One other question," said he. "Was the photograph a cabinet?"
	84 ▸ "It was."
	85 ▸ "Then, good-night, your Majesty, and I trust that we shall soon have

some good news for you. And good-night, Watson," he added, as the wheels of the royal brougham rolled down the street. "If you will be good enough to call to-morrow afternoon at three o'clock I should like to chat this little matter over with you."

II.

...

86 ▸ It was close upon four before the door opened, and a drunken-looking groom, ill-kempt and side-whiskered, with an inflamed face and disreputable clothes, walked into the room. Accustomed as I was to my friend's amazing powers in the use of disguises, I had to look three times before I was certain that it was indeed he.[4] With a nod he vanished into the bedroom, whence he emerged in five minutes tweed-suited and respectable, as of old. Putting his hands into his pockets, he stretched out his legs in front of the fire and laughed heartily for some minutes.

87 ▸ "Well, really!" he cried, and then he choked and laughed again until he was obliged to lie back, limp and helpless, in the chair.

88 ▸ "What is it?"

89 ▸ "It's quite too funny. I am sure you could never guess how I employed my morning, or what I ended by doing."

90 ▸ "I can't imagine. I suppose that you have been watching the habits, and perhaps the house, of Miss Irene Adler."

91 ▸ "Quite so; but the sequel was rather unusual. I will tell you, however. I left the house a little after eight o'clock this morning in the character of a groom out of work. There is a wonderful sympathy and freemasonry among horsey men. Be one of them, and you will know all that there is to know. I soon found Briony Lodge. It is a bijou villa, with a garden at the back, but built out in front right up to the road, two stories. Chubb lock to the door. Large sitting-room on the right side, well furnished, with long windows almost to the floor, and those preposterous English window fasteners which a child

brougham: 四轮有篷马车

groom: 马夫
ill-kempt: 不整洁的
side-whiskered: 络腮胡子的
inflamed: 红肿的
disreputable: 不体面的
tweed-suited: 花呢西装
heartily: 热烈地
choke: 呛
limp: 疲倦的

freemasonry: 惺惺相惜
horsey: 养马的
villa: 小巧精致的别墅
Chubb lock: 丘伯保险锁
preposterous: 荒谬的
fastener: 扣件

---

4 *Accustomed as I was... it was indeed he*：该句是将 accustomed 提前的倒装句，表示强调和转折，即"尽管我已经习惯了……，但还是……"。可译为："尽管我早已习惯了我朋友的惊人化装术，但我还是再三细看之后才确定这的确是他。"

could open. Behind there was nothing remarkable, save that the passage window could be reached from the top of the coach-house. I walked round it and examined it closely from every point of view, but without noting anything else of interest.

92 ▸ "I then lounged down the street and found, as I expected, that there was a mews in a lane which runs down by one wall of the garden. I lent the ostlers a hand in rubbing down their horses, and received in exchange two pence, a glass of half and half, two fills of shag tobacco, and as much information as I could desire about Miss Adler, to say nothing of half a dozen other people in the neighbourhood in whom I was not in the least interested, but whose biographies I was compelled to listen to."⁵

93 ▸ "And what of Irene Adler?" I asked.

94 ▸ "Oh, she has turned all the men's heads down in that part. She is the daintiest thing under a bonnet⁶ on this planet. So say the Serpentine-mews, to a man. She lives quietly, sings at concerts, drives out at five every day, and returns at seven sharp for dinner. Seldom goes out at other times, except when she sings. Has only one male visitor, but a good deal of him. He is dark, handsome, and dashing, never calls less than once a day, and often twice. He is a Mr. Godfrey Norton, of the Inner Temple. See the advantages of a cabman as a confidant. They had driven him home a dozen times from Serpentine-mews, and knew all about him. When I had listened to all they had to tell, I began to walk up and down near Briony Lodge once more, and to think over my plan of campaign."

95 ▸ "This Godfrey Norton was evidently an important factor in the matter. He was a lawyer. That sounded ominous. What was the relation between them, and what the object of his repeated visits? Was she his client, his

---

mew: 马厩
lane: 巷子
ostler: 马夫
rub: 擦洗
half: 混搭咖啡
shag: 粗毛
biography: 传记

dainty: 讲究的
bonnet: 女帽
sharp: 准时的

dashing: 时髦的
cabman: 车夫

ominous: 不吉利的

5　*I lent the ostlers... to listen to*: 该句的主体结构是 I lent..., and received..., received 后面可以全部看作是它的宾语成分，as much information... 和 to say nothing of... 与前面的 two pence 等并列。可译为: "我帮马车夫擦洗马匹，作为回报，我得到了两便士，一杯混配的咖啡，两根蓬松烟卷，以及我想了解的艾德勒小姐的信息，至于那些我没有半点兴趣，却又不得不听的左邻右舍的八卦消息，就不值一提了。"

6　*under a bonnet*: 女子。bonnet 指旧时女性戴的用丝带固定于下巴的帽子，这里使用借代手法，用女性的佩戴之物来借指女性本身。e.g. He said he would never see such a creature under a bonnet again. 他说他再也不会见到像她这样的女子了。

friend, or his mistress? If the former, she had probably transferred the photograph to his keeping. If the latter, it was less likely. On the issue of this question depended whether I should continue my work at Briony Lodge, or turn my attention to the gentleman's chambers in the Temple.⁷ It was a delicate point, and it widened the field of my inquiry. I fear that I bore you with these details, but I have to let you see my little difficulties, if you are to understand the situation."

96 ▶ "I am following you closely," I answered.

97 ▶ "I was still balancing the matter in my mind when a hansom cab drove up to Briony Lodge, and a gentleman sprang out. He was a remarkably handsome man, dark, aquiline, and moustached—evidently the man of whom I had heard. He appeared to be in a great hurry, shouted to the cabman to wait, and brushed past the maid who opened the door with the air of a man who was thoroughly at home."

98 ▶ "He was in the house about half an hour, and I could catch glimpses of him in the windows of the sitting-room, pacing up and down, talking excitedly, and waving his arms. Of her I could see nothing. Presently he emerged, looking even more flurried than before. As he stepped up to the cab, he pulled a gold watch from his pocket and looked at it earnestly, 'Drive like the devil,'⁸ he shouted, 'first to Gross & Hankey's in Regent Street, and then to the Church of St. Monica in the Edgeware Road. Half a guinea if you do it in twenty minutes!'"

99 ▶ "Away they went, and I was just wondering whether I should not do well to follow them when up the lane came a neat little landau, the coachman with his coat only half-buttoned, and his tie under his ear, while all the tags of his harness were sticking out of the buckles.⁹ It hadn't pulled up before

---

mistress: 情妇

inquiry: 询问

hansom: 一马二轮有盖双座小马车

spring out: 跳出来

aquiline: 鹰钩状的

moustached: 留着胡子的

brush: 擦过

air: 气势

wave: 挥舞

presently: 不久；马上

flurried: 慌张的

Regent: 摄政（这里取其读音）

guinea: 几尼，大约相当于一镑

landau: 四轮马车

half-buttoned: 扣了一半

tag: 挂件

buckle: 搭扣

---

7 *On the issue of... in the Temple*: 这是一个倒装句，正常语序为 whether... depended on the issue of this question，whether 引导的从句作主语。可译为："我该在布里奥尼·洛奇继续工作，还是转向这位绅士在坦普尔的房间取决于这个问题。"

8 *Drive like the devil*: "像魔鬼一样奔驰"，即要求马车夫以最快的速度前进。

9 *Away they went, ... out of the buckles*: 该句中，Away they went, and I was just wondering... 并列作主句，whether 引导的是 wondering 的宾语从句，when 引导的是全句的状语从句，while 引导的伴随状语从句说明马车夫的状态。可译为："他们离开了，我正在想是否应跟上他们，正在这时，一辆干净的四轮马车沿着小巷过来，马车夫一半的衣扣已经解开了，领带绕到了脖子上，马具上所有箍头都凸出了带扣。"

she shot out of the hall door and into it. I only caught a glimpse of her at the moment, but she was a lovely woman, with a face that a man might die for."

sovereign: 金镑

100 ▸ "'The Church of St. Monica, John,' she cried, 'and half a sovereign if you reach it in twenty minutes.'"

perch: 蹲坐
shabby: 寒碜的
fare: 乘客

101 ▸ "This was quite too good to lose, Watson. I was just balancing whether I should run for it, or whether I should perch behind her landau when a cab came through the street. The driver looked twice at such a shabby fare, but I jumped in before he could object. 'The Church of St. Monica,' said I, 'and half a sovereign if you reach it in twenty minutes.' It was twenty-five minutes to twelve, and of course it was clear enough what was in the wind[10]."

cabby: 马夫
steaming: 冒热气的
soul: 人
save: 除了
surpliced: 穿白色法袍的
expostulate: 劝诫
knot: 婚姻的结合状态
aisle: 过道
idler: 无所事事的人

102 ▸ "My cabby drove fast. I don't think I ever drove faster, but the others were there before us. The cab and the landau with their steaming horses were in front of the door when I arrived. I paid the man and hurried into the church. There was not a soul there save the two whom I had followed and a surpliced clergyman, who seemed to be expostulating with them. They were all three standing in a knot in front of the altar. I lounged up the side aisle like any other idler who has dropped into a church. Suddenly, to my surprise, the three at the altar faced round to me, and Godfrey Norton came running as hard as he could towards me.

103 ▸ "'he cried. 'You'll do. Come! Come!'

104 ▸ "'What then?' I asked.

105 ▸ "'Come, man, come, only three minutes, or it won't be legal.'

half-drag: 半拉
mumble: 喃喃自语
whisper: 低语
vouch: 保证

106 ▸ "I was half-dragged up to the altar, and before I knew where I was I found myself mumbling responses which were whispered in my ear, and vouching for things of which I knew nothing, and generally assisting in the

---

10 *in the wind*: (尤指秘密的事)正在进行，将要发生。e.g. By the mid-1980s, change was in the wind again. 20 世纪 80 年代中期，变革又呈山雨欲来之势。

secure tying up of Irene Adler, spinster, to Godfrey Norton, bachelor.¹¹ It was all done in an instant, and there was the gentleman thanking me on the one side and the lady on the other, while the clergyman beamed on me in front. It was the most preposterous position in which I ever found myself in my life, and it was the thought of it that started me laughing just now. It seems that there had been some informality about their license, that the clergyman absolutely refused to marry them without a witness of some sort, and that my lucky appearance saved the bridegroom from having to sally out into the streets in search of a best man.¹² The bride gave me a sovereign, and I mean to wear it on my watch-chain in memory of the occasion."

spinster: 老处女

beam: 满脸堆笑

informality: 不正式
license: 许可证
sally: 外出
best man: 伴郎

107 ▶ "This is a very unexpected turn of affairs," said I; "and what then?"

108 ▶ "Well, I found my plans very seriously menaced. It looked as if the pair might take an immediate departure, and so necessitate very prompt and energetic measures on my part. At the church door, however, they separated, he driving back to the Temple, and she to her own house. 'I shall drive out in the park at five as usual,' she said as she left him. I heard no more. They drove away in different directions, and I went off to make my own arrangements."

menace: 威胁
departure: 离开
necessitate: 使……成为必需
prompt: 迅速的

109 ▶ "Which are?"

110 ▶ "Some cold beef and a glass of beer," he answered, ringing the bell. "I have been too busy to think of food, and I am likely to be busier still this evening. By the way, Doctor, I shall want your co-operation."

111 ▶ "I shall be delighted."

112 ▶ "You don't mind breaking the law?"

113 ▶ "Not in the least."

---

11 *I was half-dragged... to Godfrey Norton, bachelor*: 该句中 I was half-dragged... 和 I found myself mumbling responses... 并列，其余都是附属从句或结构，其中 mumbling... and vouching..., and generally assisting... 三个结构并列作 found myself 的补充说明。可译为："我被连拖带拉到了圣坛前，我还不知道这到底是什么地方，就发现自己在喃喃地回应着我耳边的低语，对我一无所知的事情作出保证，并且为艾琳·艾德勒女士和戈德弗瑞·诺顿先生的结合提供支持。"

12 *It seems that there had been... in search of a best man*: 该句的主体结构是 It seems that..., that... and that...，其中的三个 that 引导的成分并列。可译为："似乎他们的结合不合程序，牧师坚决拒绝在没有见证人的情况下将他们两人结合，而我机缘巧合的出现就免得新郎到大街上去找一个男傧相了。"

arrest: 逮捕

114 ▸ "Nor running a chance of arrest?"

115 ▸ "Not in a good cause."

116 ▸ "Oh, the cause is excellent!"

117 ▸ "Then I am your man."

118 ▸ "I was sure that I might rely on you."

119 ▸ "But what is it you wish?"

120 ▸ "When Mrs. Turner has brought in the tray I will make it clear to you. Now," he said as he turned hungrily on the simple fare that our landlady had provided, "I must discuss it while I eat, for I have not much time. It is nearly five now. In two hours we must be on the scene of action. Miss Irene, or Madame, rather, returns from her drive at seven. We must be at Briony Lodge to meet her."

landlady: 房东太太

121 ▸ "And what then?"

122 ▸ "You must leave that to me. I have already arranged what is to occur. There is only one point on which I must insist. You must not interfere, come what may[13]. You understand?"

interfere: 干扰

neutral: 中性的；不采取行动的

123 ▸ "I am to be neutral?"

124 ▸ "To do nothing whatever. There will probably be some small unpleasantness. Do not join in it. It will end in my being conveyed into the house. Four or five minutes afterwards the sitting-room window will open. You are to station yourself close to that open window."

125 ▸ "Yes."

126 ▸ "You are to watch me, for I will be visible to you."

127 ▸ "Yes."

128 ▸ "And when I raise my hand—so—you will throw into the room what I give you to throw, and will, at the same time, raise the cry of fire. You quite follow me?"

13　*come what may*: 不论发生什么事情，不管怎样。e.g. Come what may, we must finish this work today. 不管怎么样，反正我们今天必须完成这项工作。

129 ▶ "Entirely."

130 ▶ "It is nothing very formidable," he said, taking a long cigar-shaped roll from his pocket. "It is an ordinary plumber's smoke-rocket, fitted with a cap at either end to make it self-lighting. Your task is confined to that. When you raise your cry of fire, it will be taken up by quite a number of people. You may then walk to the end of the street, and I will rejoin you in ten minutes. I hope that I have made myself clear?"

131 ▶ "I am to remain neutral, to get near the window, to watch you, and at the signal to throw in this object, then to raise the cry of fire, and to wait you at the corner of the street."

132 ▶ "Precisely."

133 ▶ "Then you may entirely rely on me."

134 ▶ "That is excellent. I think, perhaps, it is almost time that I prepare for the new role I have to play."

135 ▶ He disappeared into his bedroom and returned in a few minutes in the character of an amiable and simple-minded Nonconformist clergyman... It was a quarter past six when we left Baker Street, and it still wanted ten minutes to the hour when we found ourselves in Serpentine Avenue...

136 ▶ "You see," remarked Holmes, as we paced to and fro in front of the house, "this marriage rather simplifies matters. The photograph becomes a double-edged weapon now. The chances are that she would be as averse to its being seen by Mr. Godfrey Norton, as our client is to its coming to the eyes of his princess.[14] Now the question is, where are we to find the photograph?"

---

14 *The chances are... the eyes of his princess*：该句的句型结构是 The chances are..., 表示"有可能……"。e.g. The chances are that you have either played it, or seen someone else playing it or been invited to play it. 很有可能你要么玩过，要么看别人玩过，再不然就是有人叫你一起玩过。该句的从句句型是 sb1. is as... to..., as sb2. is to...。可译为："很有可能，她并不希望照片被诺顿先生看到，就像我们的委托人不愿意让他的公主看到照片一样。"

---

entirely: 完全地

formidable: 可怕的

roll: 卷筒

plumber: 水管工

smoke-rocket: 管子

nonconformist: 不信奉国教的

clergyman: 牧师

137 ▸ "Where, indeed?"

138 ▸ "It is most unlikely that she carries it about with her. It is cabinet size. Too large for easy concealment about a woman's dress. She knows that the King is capable of having her waylaid and searched. Two attempts of the sort have already been made. We may take it, then, that she does not carry it about with her."

concealment: 隐藏

139 ▸ "Where, then?"

140 ▸ "Her banker or her lawyer. There is that double possibility. But I am inclined to think neither. Women are naturally secretive, and they like to do their own secreting. Why should she hand it over to anyone else? She could trust her own guardianship, but she could not tell what indirect or political influence might be brought to bear upon a business man. Besides, remember that she had resolved to use it within a few days. It must be where she can lay her hands upon it. It must be in her own house."

secretive: 遮掩的

guardianship: 监护人的职责

141 ▸ "But it has twice been burgled."

burgle: 抢劫

142 ▸ "Pshaw! They did not know how to look."

143 ▸ "But how will you look?"

144 ▸ "I will not look."

145 ▸ "What then?"

146 ▸ "I will get her to show me."

147 ▸ "But she will refuse."

148 ▸ "She will not be able to. But I hear the rumble of wheels. It is her carriage. Now carry out my orders to the letter."

rumble: 隆隆声

149 ▸ As he spoke the gleam of the side-lights of a carriage came round the curve of the avenue. It was a smart little landau which rattled up to the door of Briony Lodge... Holmes dashed into the crowd to protect the lady; but just as he reached her he gave a cry and dropped to the ground, with the blood running freely down his face...

rattle: 发出咯吱声

dash: 冲出去

150 ▸ "Is the poor gentleman much hurt?" she [Irene Adler] asked.

151 ▸ "He is dead," cried several voices.

152 ▶ "No, no, there's life in him!" shouted another. "But he'll be gone before you can get him to hospital."

153 ▶ "He's a brave fellow," said a woman. "They would have had the lady's purse and watch if it hadn't been for him. They were a gang, and a rough one, too. Ah, he's breathing now."

gang: 团伙

154 ▶ "He can't lie in the street. May we bring him in, marm?"

155 ▶ "Surely. Bring him into the sitting-room. There is a comfortable sofa. This way, please!"

156 ▶ Slowly and solemnly he was borne into Briony Lodge and laid out in the principal room, while I still observed the proceedings from my post by the window...

157 ▶ Holmes had sat up upon the couch, and I saw him motion like a man who is in need of air. A maid rushed across and threw open the window. At the same instant I saw him raise his hand and at the signal I tossed my rocket into the room with a cry of "Fire!" The word was no sooner out of my mouth than the whole crowd of spectators, well dressed and ill—gentlemen, ostlers, and servant-maids—joined in a general shriek of "Fire!" Thick clouds of smoke curled through the room and out at the open window. I caught a glimpse of rushing figures, and a moment later the voice of Holmes from within assuring them that it was a false alarm. Slipping through the shouting crowd I made my way to the corner of the street, and in ten minutes was rejoiced to find my friend's arm in mine, and to get away from the scene of uproar.[15] He walked swiftly and in silence for some few minutes until we had turned down one of the quiet streets which lead towards the Edgeware Road.

rocket: 烟花

shriek: 尖叫

curl: 围绕

rejoice: 高兴; 欣喜

swiftly: 飞快地

158 ▶ "You did it very nicely, Doctor," he remarked. "Nothing could have been better. It is all right."

159 ▶ "You have the photograph?"

160 ▶ "I know where it is."

---

15 *Slipping through... from the scene of uproar*: 该句的主语是 I，made 和 was rejoiced 是并列谓语。可译为："穿过喧闹的人群，我来到了街角，十分钟后就与我的朋友手挽着手，离开了骚动的场景。"

161 ▸ "And how did you find out?"

162 ▸ "She showed me, as I told you she would."

163 ▸ "I am still in the dark[16]."

164 ▸ "I do not wish to make a mystery," said he, laughing. "The matter was perfectly simple. You, of course, saw that everyone in the street was an accomplice. They were all engaged for the evening."

165 ▸ "I guessed as much."

166 ▸ "Then, when the row broke out, I had a little moist red paint in the palm of my hand. I rushed forward, fell down, clapped my hand to my face, and became a piteous spectacle. It is an old trick."

167 ▸ "That also I could fathom."

168 ▸ "Then they carried me in. She was bound to have me in. What else could she do? And into her sitting-room, which was the very room which I suspected. It lay between that and her bedroom, and I was determined to see which. They laid me on a couch, I motioned for air, they were compelled to open the window, and you had your chance."

169 ▸ "How did that help you?"

170 ▸ "It was all-important. When a woman thinks that her house is on fire, her instinct is at once to rush to the thing which she values most. It is a perfectly overpowering impulse, and I have more than once taken advantage of it. In the case of the Darlington substitution scandal it was of use to me, and also in the Arnsworth Castle business. A married woman grabs at her baby; an unmarried one reaches for her jewel-box. Now it was clear to me that our lady of to-day had nothing in the house more precious to her than what we are in quest of. She would rush to secure it. The alarm of fire was admirably done. The smoke and shouting were enough to shake nerves of steel. She responded beautifully. The photograph is in a recess behind a sliding panel just above the right bell-pull. She was there in an instant, and I caught a glimpse of it as she half-drew it out. When I cried out that it was a false

accomplice: 共谋

moist: 湿润的

piteous: 可怜的
spectacle: 景象

motion: 摆手

instinct: 本能
overpowering: 无法抵抗的
impulse: 冲动
substitution: 替换
scandal: 丑闻
admirably: 值得敬佩地
recess: 壁龛
sliding: 滑动的
panel: 嵌板
bell-pull: 拉铃带

---

16 *in the dark*: 不知道，不清楚。e.g. Even my mother is in the dark about it, to say nothing of me! 这事连我妈都不知道，别说我了！

alarm, she replaced it, glanced at the rocket, rushed from the room, and I have not seen her since. I rose, and, making my excuses, escaped from the house. I hesitated whether to attempt to secure the photograph at once; but the coachman had come in, and as he was watching me narrowly it seemed safer to wait. A little over-precipitance may ruin all."

precipitance: 仓促

171 ▸ "And now?" I asked.

172 ▸ "Our quest is practically finished. I shall call with the King to-morrow, and with you, if you care to come with us. We will be shown into the sitting-room to wait for the lady, but it is probable that when she comes she may find neither us nor the photograph. It might be a satisfaction to his Majesty to regain it with his own hands."

173 ▸ "And when will you call?"

174 ▸ "At eight in the morning. She will not be up, so that we shall have a clear field. Besides, we must be prompt, for this marriage may mean a complete change in her life and habits. I must wire to the King without delay."

wire: 发电报

175 ▸ We had reached Baker Street and had stopped at the door. He was searching his pockets for the key when someone passing said:

176 ▸ "Good-night, Mister Sherlock Holmes."

177 ▸ There were several people on the pavement at the time, but the greeting appeared to come from a slim youth in an ulster who had hurried by.

pavement: 人行道

slim: 瘦削的

ulster: 阿尔斯特大衣

dimly: 模糊地

178 ▸ "I've heard that voice before," said Holmes, staring down the dimly lit street. "Now, I wonder who the deuce[17] that could have been."

III.

179 ▸ I slept at Baker Street that night, and we were engaged upon our toast and coffee in the morning when the King of Bohemia rushed into the room.

180 ▸ "You have really got it!" he cried, grasping Sherlock Holmes by either shoulder and looking eagerly into his face.

---

17 *the deuce*: 究竟。e.g. Who the deuce is that? 那究竟是谁?

181 ▶ "Not yet."

182 ▶ "But you have hopes?"

183 ▶ "I have hopes."

184 ▶ "Then, come. I am all impatience to be gone."

185 ▶ "We must have a cab."

186 ▶ "No, my brougham is waiting."

187 ▶ "Then that will simplify matters." We descended and started off once more for Briony Lodge.

188 ▶ "Irene Adler is married," remarked Holmes.

189 ▶ "Married! When?"

190 ▶ "Yesterday."

191 ▶ "But to whom?"

192 ▶ "To an English lawyer named Norton."

193 ▶ "But she could not love him."

194 ▶ "I am in hopes that she does."

195 ▶ "And why in hopes?"

annoyance: 烦扰

196 ▶ "Because it would spare your Majesty all fear of future annoyance. If the lady loves her husband, she does not love your Majesty. If she does not love your Majesty, there is no reason why she should interfere with your Majesty's plan."

station: 身份
relapse: 重新陷入
moody: 情绪化的
sardonic: 讽刺的

197 ▶ "It is true. And yet—Well! I wish she had been of my own station! What a queen she would have made!" He relapsed into a moody silence, which was not broken until we drew up in Serpentine Avenue.

198 ▶ The door of Briony Lodge was open, and an elderly woman stood upon the steps. She watched us with a sardonic eye as we stepped from the brougham.

199 ▶ "Mr. Sherlock Holmes, I believe?" said she.

A Scandal in Bohemia: A Detective Fiction UNIT 12

200 ▸ "I am Mr. Holmes," answered my companion, looking at her with a questioning and rather startled gaze.

startled: 惊诧的

201 ▸ "Indeed! My mistress told me that you were likely to call. She left this morning with her husband by the 5: 15 train from Charing Cross for the Continent."

202 ▸ "What!" Sherlock Holmes staggered back, white with chagrin and surprise. "Do you mean that she has left England?"

stagger: 摇摇晃晃

203 ▸ "Never to return."

204 ▸ "And the papers?" asked the King hoarsely. "All is lost."

205 ▸ "We shall see." He pushed past the servant and rushed into the drawing-room, followed by the King and myself. The furniture was scattered about in every direction, with dismantled shelves and open drawers, as if the lady had hurriedly ransacked them before her flight. Holmes rushed at the bell-pull, tore back a small sliding shutter, and, plunging in his hand, pulled out a photograph and a letter. The photograph was of Irene Adler herself in evening dress, the letter was superscribed to "Sherlock Holmes, Esq. To be left till called for." My friend tore it open and we all three read it together. It was dated at midnight of the preceding night and ran in this way:

dismantle: 拆除
drawer: 抽屉
flight: 逃离
shutter: 遮板
plunge: 插入
superscribe: 上面写着

206 ▸ "MY DEAR MR. SHERLOCK HOLMES, —You really did it very well. You took me in completely. Until after the alarm of fire, I had not a suspicion. But then, when I found how I had betrayed myself, I began to think. I had been warned against you months ago. I had been told that if the King employed an agent it would certainly be you. And your address had been given me. Yet, with all this, you made me reveal what you wanted to know. Even after I became suspicious, I found it hard to think evil of such a dear, kind old clergyman. But, you know, I have been trained as an actress myself. Male costume is nothing new to me. I often take advantage of the freedom which it gives. I sent John, the coachman, to watch you, ran up stairs, got into my walking-clothes, as I call them, and came down just as you departed.

suspicion: 怀疑

costume: 服饰

207 ▸ "Well, I followed you to your door, and so made sure that I was really an object of interest to the celebrated Mr. Sherlock Holmes. Then I, rather imprudently, wished you good-night, and started for the Temple to see my husband.

celebrated: 杰出的
imprudently: 鲁莽地

208 ▸ "We both thought the best resource was flight, when pursued by so formidable an antagonist; so you will find the nest empty when you call to-morrow. As to the photograph, your client may rest in peace. I love and am loved by a better man than he. The King may do what he will without hindrance from one whom he has cruelly wronged. I keep it only to safeguard myself, and to preserve a weapon which will always secure me from any steps which he might take in the future.[18] I leave a photograph which he might care to possess; and I remain, dear Mr. Sherlock Holmes,

209 ▸ "Very truly yours,

210 ▸ "IRENE NORTON, née ADLER."

211 ▸ "What a woman—oh, what a woman!" cried the King of Bohemia, when we had all three read this epistle. "Did I not tell you how quick and resolute she was? Would she not have made an admirable queen? Is it not a pity that she was not on my level?"

212 ▸ "From what I have seen of the lady she seems indeed to be on a very different level to your Majesty," said Holmes coldly. "I am sorry that I have not been able to bring your Majesty's business to a more successful conclusion."

213 ▸ "On the contrary, my dear sir," cried the King; "nothing could be more successful. I know that her word is inviolate. The photograph is now as safe as if it were in the fire."

214 ▸ "I am glad to hear your Majesty say so."

215 ▸ "I am immensely indebted to you. Pray tell me in what way I can reward you. This ring—" He slipped an emerald snake ring from his finger and held it out upon the palm of his hand.

216 ▸ "Your Majesty has something which I should value even more highly," said Holmes.

217 ▸ "You have but to name it."

18　*I keep it only... in the future*: 该句的主体结构是 I keep it only to safeguard..., and to preserve...，该句中前一个 which 引导的定语从句限定 weapon，后一个 which 引导的定语从句限定 steps。可译为："我保留它只是为了保护我自己，保留一个武器，使我以后免遭他任何进一步的行动。"

218 ▸ "This photograph!"

219 ▸ The King stared at him in amazement.

amazement: 惊讶

220 ▸ "Irene's photograph!" he cried. "Certainly, if you wish it."

221 ▸ "I thank your Majesty. Then there is no more to be done in the matter. I have the honour to wish you a very good-morning." He bowed, and, turning away without observing the hand which the King had stretched out to him, he set off in my company for his chambers.

…

PART 4

EXERCISES

I. Answer the following questions according to the reading text.

1. What information have Holmes and Dr. Watson got from the letter paper?
2. Who is the man looking for Holmes's help? And what did he want Holmes to do?
3. To get his photograph back, what had the man done? Why is the photograph so important to him?
4. How did Holmes manage to know anything about Miss Irene Adler? And what was it?
5. What happened to Holmes on that night when he followed the couple to the church?
6. What was Dr. Watson supposed to do after Holmes decided to take actions at Miss Irene Adler's house?
7. How did Lady Irene Idler find out that she had been deceived by Holmes?
8. Was the King satisfied with the result? Why?
9. Guess, most likely, who greeted "Good-night, Mister Sherlock Holmes" in para. 176?

II. Paraphrase the following sentences with your own words, and then translate them into Chinese.

1. It is a capital mistake to theorize before one has data. Insensibly one begins to twist facts to suit theories, instead of theories to suit facts. (Para. 6)

2. It only remains, therefore, to discover what is wanted by this German who writes upon Bohemian paper and prefers wearing a mask to showing his face. (Para. 15)

3. She has the face of the most beautiful of women, and the mind of the most resolute of men. (Para. 63)

4. It was close upon four before the door opened, and a drunken-looking groom, ill-kempt and side-whiskered, with an inflamed face and disreputable clothes, walked into the room. (Para. 86)

5. I only caught a glimpse of her at the moment, but she was a lovely woman, with a face that a man might die for. (Para. 99)

6. It looked as if the pair might take an immediate departure, and so necessitate very prompt and energetic measures on my part. (Para. 108)

7. I am to remain neutral, to get near the window, to watch you, and at the signal to throw in this object, then to raise the cry of fire, and to wait you at the corner of the street. (Para. 131)

8. Holmes dashed into the crowd to protect the lady; but just as he reached her he gave a cry and dropped to the ground, with the blood running freely down his face. (Para. 149)

9. The photograph was of Irene Adler herself in evening dress, the letter was superscribed to "Sherlock Holmes, Esq. To be left till called for." (Para. 205)

III. Figure out the meanings of the phrases in bold, and then make another sentence with each of the phrases.

1. I rang the bell and **was shown up** to the chamber which had formerly been in part my own. (Para. 1)

2. The man who wrote it was presumably **well to do**. (Para. 8)

3. When I had listened to all they had to tell, I began to walk up and down near Briony Lodge once more, and to **think over** my plan of campaign. (Para. 94)

4. He was in the house about half an hour, and I could **catch glimpses of** him in the windows of the sitting-room, pacing up and down, talking excitedly, and waving his arms. (Para. 98)

5. I lounged up the side aisle like any other idler who has **dropped into** a church. (Para. 102)

6. You will **throw into** the room what I give you to throw. (Para. 128)

7. Now it was clear to me that our lady of to-day had nothing in the house more precious to her than what we are **in quest of**. (Para. 170)

8. We will be **shown into** the sitting-room to wait for the lady, but it is probable that when she comes she may find neither us nor the photograph. (Para. 172)

9. He relapsed into a moody silence, which was not broken until we **drew up** in Serpentine Avenue. (Para. 197)

IV. Find out the cultural meanings of the following words.

1. Freemasonry
2. Nonconformist

V. Summarize the whole story in your own words with no less than 200 words.